Monuments

and Museums

The Past in the Present

edited by

Marilyn Lake

MELBOURNE
UNIVERSITY
PRESS

The Australian
Academy of
the Humanities

MELBOURNE UNIVERSITY PRESS
An imprint of Melbourne University Publishing Ltd
187 Grattan Street, Carlton, Victoria 3053, Australia
mup-info@unimelb.edu.au
www.mup.com.au

Published in association with the Australian Academy of the Humanities
(Academy Editor: Bruce Bennett)

First published 2006
Text © The Australian Academy of the Humanities, 2006
Design and typography © Melbourne University Publishing Ltd, 2006

Typeset in Bembo by Syarikat Seng Teik Sdn. Bhd., Malaysia
Printed in Australia by Griffin Press, Netley, South Australia

National Library of Australia Cataloguing-in-Publication entry

Memory, monuments and museums: the past in the present.

Bibliography.
Includes index.
ISBN 978 0 522 85250 9
ISBN 0 522 85250 5.

1. Historiography – Australia. 2. History – Psychological aspects. 3. Memory
(Philosophy). I. Lake, Marilyn.

907.20994

CONTENTS

CONTRIBUTORS

Ien Ang is Professor of Cultural Studies and was founding director of the Centre for Cultural Research at the University of Western Sydney, where she currently is an ARC Professorial Fellow. Her influential books include: *On Not Speaking Chinese: Living between Asia and the West* (2001), *Living Room Wars: Rethinking Media Audiences for a Postmodern World* (1996), and *Watching Dallas* (1985). She also co-authored (with Elizabeth Cassity) the AAH report *Attraction of Strangers: Partnerships in Humanities Research* (2004).

Michael Bennett is Professor of History at the University of Tasmania. He is a specialist in late Medieval and early Tudor English History and the author of *Richard II and the Revolution of 1399* (1999), *Lambert Simnel and the Battle of Stoke* (1987) and *The Battle of Bosworth* (1985).

Dawn Casey is Chief Executive Officer of the Western Australian Museum. Prior to her appointment as director of the National Museum of Australia in 1999, she was chief general manager of the Acton Peninsula Project Task Force, the body responsible for the construction of the new National Museum. Ms Casey has wide-ranging experience in the management of Indigenous and cultural heritage policy issues. She has received honorary doctorates from the University of Queensland and Charles Sturt University.

Peter Conrad is an internationally acclaimed expatriate Australian writer and cultural critic. He currently teaches English at Christ Church College, Oxford. He is best known for his many books, including works on the history of English literature and opera, and his regular contributions to the *Observer*, London. He delivered the 2004 Boyer Lectures on ABC Radio National.

Graeme Davison is Professor of History at Monash University. He is the author of *The Rise and Fall of Marvellous Melbourne* (2004), *Car Wars: How the Car Won Our Hearts and Conquered Our Cities* (2004) and co-editor of *Yesterday's Tomorrows: The Powerhouse Museum and Its Precursors 1880–2005* (2005). He has been active as an advisor to heritage bodies, and was an historical advisor to the National Museum of Australia.

Jim Everett is an Aboriginal poet and playwright. He is a respected member of the Tasmanian Aboriginal community who has been active in Aboriginal issues for the past three decades. He is from the Clan Plangermairreenner of the Ben Lomond people, Clan of the Cape Portland nation in northeast Tasmania. He began writing poetry at an early age. His written works now include plays, political papers and short stories, and he has been published in eight major anthologies. His other work includes television documentary, educational video and theatre production.

John Frow is Professor of English at the University of Melbourne. He is the author of *Marxism and Literary History* (1986), *Cultural Studies and Cultural Value* (1995), *Time and Commodity Culture* (1997), (with Tony Bennett and Mike

Emmison) *Accounting for Tastes: Australian Everyday Cultures* (1999) and *Geure* (2005).

Bill Gammage is Adjunct Professor of History at the Humanities Research Centre, Australian National University, researching in Aboriginal land management at the time of contact. His books include *Sky Travellers: Journeys in New Guinea 1938–39* (1998), *The Broken Years: Australian Soldiers in the Great War* (1974) and *Narrandera Shire* (1986).

Roslynn Haynes is Adjunct Associate Professor in English at the University of New South Wales and an Honorary Fellow of the University of Tasmania. Her research interests are nineteenth and twentieth century Australian literature, science and literature, and landscapes in literature and art. She is currently completing a book on Tasmanian landscapes in literature, art and photography.

Katie Holmes is a Senior Lecturer in the History Program at La Trobe University. Her book *Spaces in Her Day* (1995) on women's diary writing was shortlisted for the NSW and Victorian Premier's awards and she has co-edited a number of anthologies including *Freedom Bound II* (1995) and *Green Pens* (2004). Her co-authored book on the cultural history of gardens and gardening in Australia will be published by MUP in 2006.

Marilyn Lake holds an Australian Professorial Fellowship based at La Trobe University and the Humanities Research Centre at the Australian National University. Her most recent book is the award-winning *FAITH: Faith Bandler, Gentle Activist* (2002). A new work, *Connected Worlds: History in Trans-National Perspective*, co-edited with Ann Curthoys, will be published by ANU Press in 2006.

Iain McCalman is a Federation Fellow jointly at the Humanities Research Centre and the Centre for Cross Cultural

Research at the Australian National University. His books include *Radical Underworld: Prophets, Revolutionaries, and Pornographers in London, 1795–1840* (1988), *The Oxford Companion to the Romantic Age: British Culture, 1776–1832* (1999) and *The Seven Ordeals of Count Cagliostro* (2003).

Susan K. Martin is a Senior Lecturer in English at La Trobe University. Her research interests include nineteenth and twentieth century Australian writing and culture, writing dealing with space and place, and Victorian literature and culture. She has published on Australian literature, Australian culture, and gardens. Forthcoming books include the co-authored *Gardening Place* with MUP.

Henry Reynolds is Honorary Research Professor in the Department of History and Classics at the University of Tasmania. He is also the recipient of an Australia Council Senior Writers Fellowship. His most recent books are *North of Capricorn* (2004) and *Nowhere People* (2005).

Michael Roe is Emeritus Professor in the School of History and Classics at the University of Tasmania. Recently he has published *The State of Tasmania: Identity at Federation Time* (2001), *Life over Death: Tasmanians and Tuberculosis* (1999) and *Australia, Britain, and Migration, 1915–1940: A Study of Desperate Hopes* (1995). His current project is 'The Wreck of *George III*, D'Entrecasteaux Channel, April 1835'.

Nicholas Shakespeare's novels include *The Vision of Elena Silves* (1989), winner of the Somerset Maugham Award, *The High Flyer* (1993), for which he was nominated one of Granta's Best of Young British Novelists, *The Dancer Upstairs*, which was selected by the American Libraries Association as the best novel of 1997 and *In Tasmania* (2004). He is a Fellow of the Royal Society of Literature. He lives half the year in Tasmania.

ACKNOWLEDGEMENTS

This book is based on papers delivered to the annual symposium of the Australian Academy of the Humanities, held in Tasmania's bicentennial year of 2004, at the University of Tasmania School of Art on the Hobart waterfront. My co-conveners, who did much of the on-ground co-ordination, were Michael Bennett and Henry Reynolds. The symposium received generous financial and logistical support from the University of Tasmania, and in particular from Vice-Chancellor Professor Daryl Le Grew, the School of History and Classics and the Faculty of Arts. The transformation of a collection of stimulating conference papers into this handsome and accessible book has been made possible by the financial support of the Australian Academy of the Humanities and the commitment of its staff. I would especially like to thank John Byron and Kate Fullagar for all their work on this project over the past twelve months. At Melbourne University Publishing, I would like to thank Louise Adler and Cinzia Cavallaro for their creative imagination and professional support. And finally, I pay tribute to the authors of the wonderful essays presented here and thank them for their prompt and courteous response to editorial queries and submission deadlines. It is their book.

INTRODUCTION: THE PAST IN THE PRESENT

Marilyn Lake

What can we know of the past and how can we best represent it? Must the discipline of history make good the fallibility of memory or does the imaginative work of fiction do a better job of enlivening past experience than the stern empiricism of the historian? In their recollection of experience do the creative arts of poetry and painting—like history and religion—represent a triumph over death, a different kind of second coming? Certainly a sonnet or a painting can immortalise a loved one as memorably as a gravestone or monument.

Public memorials and monuments were erected with increasing frequency in the late nineteenth century as an insurance against the failure of collective memory: 'Lest We Forget'. In his essay on Civil War monuments in the United States, Kirk Savage has observed that 'public monuments' worked to perpetuate 'memory in external deposits, located not within people, but within shared public space'. He wondered whether the increasing tendency in the nineteenth century 'to construct memory in physical monuments'—to inscribe it on the landscape itself—was symptomatic of 'an increasing anxiety about memory left to its own unseen devices'.[1] Indeed, an anxiety about mortality itself.

'Monuments', Savage notes, served to 'anchor collective remembering—a process dispersed, ever changing and ultimately intangible—in highly condensed, fixed and tangible sites'. Furthermore, public monuments embodied and legitimated the idea of 'a common memory' and by extension the idea of a people who possessed and rallied around such a memory.[2] Monuments constructed communities—as pioneers, as settlers, as subjects of the empire—even as they were constructed by them.[3] Yet monuments and memorials could also contest established power structures and historical narratives, turning some public spaces into 'representational battlegrounds'.[4]

Libraries, archives and museums were also built to 'perpetuate memory in external deposits', marking the transition —in Pierre Nora's terms—from the *milieu de mémoire* of premodern times to *lieux de mémoire* instituted by nation-states.[5] Established to conserve documents, books, personal papers, paintings, engravings and other material objects as evidence of a past that might otherwise be forgotten, these repositories of public memory are now called on to meet new challenges and even threats to their institutional existence.

In addressing some of these issues, the contributors to this collection—leading scholars, writers and activists—offer illuminating reflections on the fraught relationship between the past and the present. At a time when we are continually urged to move on, to put the past behind us, the perverse persistence of the past is everywhere evident—in monuments and memorials, in claims for land rights and heritage listings, in debates over the content of museums and the legacy of White Australia, in commemorations of Anzac Day and Sorry Day.[6] As many contributors demonstrate, the past retains the power to haunt and seduce us, to shame us and make us proud.

And the past continues to challenge us. In 2004, in the official year of Tasmania's bicentenary, the Academy of the

Humanities held its annual symposium, organised around the theme of 'Memory, Monuments and Museums', on the historic Hobart waterfront. The fact that European settlement had actually first occurred two hundred and one years earlier —in 1803—raised questions about the politics of bicentennial commemoration and focused attention on the late Premier Jim Bacon's apparent determination to ignore the first British settlement at Risdon Cove, on the east bank of the Derwent, because of its association with the first Aboriginal massacre in Tasmania. This collection of essays is based on the papers presented to the Academy symposium in November 2004. The debate over the choice of date for the bicentenary is discussed by Michael Roe and Henry Reynolds.

While the construction of historical memory continues to excite controversy, it is important that we understand the reasons for people's investment in the past and the relationship between collective memory and contemporary identity. One of the more potent forms of attachment to the past in current times, explored by historian Iain McCalman in his study of his family's experience of the British-African Raj, is nostalgia; another, as Tasmanian Aboriginal elder Jim Everett suggests in his chapter on 'Dispossession', is grief—born of the recognition that lost lands, culture and freedom are in a profound sense irretrievable. Despite exhortations that we must learn to live with, but not in, the past, grief and nostalgia, pride and shame can exert a powerful hold.[7]

In his lead essay on the Greek deity Mnemosyne, Peter Conrad invokes the mother of the muses to suggest that the creative arts most fundamentally perform a regenerative act: 'in the man-made religion of art, experience has a second coming'. But whereas classical understandings of memory emphasised the discipline of devotional and methodical practice to enhance the power of memory, romantic memory delighted in its involuntariness and inventiveness. It is the skittishness of memory that inspires literary creation as well as psychoanalytic insight. Patriarchal history—adjudicating and regulating knowledge about the past—admonishes memory for being unreliable. 'Literature', Conrad suggests, 'is more tolerant of memory's fictionality, and treats its lapses as creative leaps'.

Nicholas Shakespeare similarly argues for the creative potential of memory lapses and gaps in the historical record. The creation of an imaginative landscape is thus freed to concentrate on forging a sense of common humanity. By 'dramatising the particular, the idiosyncratic and the personal', fiction 'invites our empathy and therefore holds out the promise of being less cruel'. The 'more public, general and detached business of history', on the other hand, is constrained by its empiricist method and analytical objectives. Memory attests to the emotional power of past experience. To grasp the truth about that experience, to gain real insight, Shakespeare suggests, 'history needs to forget just as much as fiction needs to remember'.

It was the emotional dimension of his family's attachment to the British-African Raj, symbolised in the family's *bon bon* dishes that were actually the toenails of the first bull elephant shot by ex-President Theodore Roosevelt on his famous Kenyan safari, that inspired historian Iain McCalman's intellectual enquiry into the nature of their African experience and the power of their subsequent nostalgia. His essay raises the question of whether we should regard nostalgia—a condition of wistful yearning for a past purged of pain—as a sickness in need of a cure or as a productive energy that might be channelled into projects such as heritage conservation and constructive social policy.

In writing about the more baneful effects of 'trauma', Dominick LaCapra commends history as 'a mode of critical thought and practice' that in drawing a distinction between past and present offers necessary narrative closure.[8] McCalman also stresses history's role as a critical intellectual practice. Confronted with 'socially pervasive' nostalgia, historians can do more than wallow in longing. They can analyse, interrogate and explain. In his analysis of the 'lure of the white man's country' of Kenya, McCalman identifies the power of masculine nostalgia for the lost 'values of the Wild West'. United States adventurers such as Theodore Roosevelt, thrilled by the 'rough masculine camaraderie of the hard-bit set' he found in Africa, were 'keen on testing their frontier manhood'. Dead wild animals became trophies of masculine triumph.

In my study of 'Monuments of Manhood' in the Australian context—their absence as well as their presence—I suggest we look at the compensatory work of war memorials in a country that failed to achieve a manly independence in the political realm, when political leaders eschewed the model of manly American republicanism in favour of continuing colonial dependency. The American model of political independence inspired the author of the first draft of the Australian constitution, Tasmanian Attorney-General and Supreme Court judge, Andrew Inglis Clark, but no monuments were erected to his memory and his example of republican nationalism is for the most part lost to historical memory. Indeed, no monuments were erected to commemorate the achievement of Federation, an absence that surely raises interesting questions about the limits of that achievement.

In Australia, national memory has been powerfully influenced by the militarisation of history through the construction of war memorials and the annual commemoration of Anzac and Remembrance days. The richly endowed Australian War Memorial in Canberra has been described as our most important historical museum. Recent controversy centred on the National Museum of Australia and its depiction of frontier warfare—significantly absent from the Australian War Memorial—reminds us of the importance of cultural institutions in shaping historical memory. Many more thousands of people visit museums, archives and libraries than read history books and testify in surveys that they place much greater trust in the information gained from museums than from history teachers. The representations of the national past encountered in museums often have direct political implications for the present, which is one reason they excite such fierce debate.

By looking at a range of museums in different countries, Graeme Davison charts the changing purpose and expectations of museums from the nineteenth into the twentieth century. Once their primary purpose was to 'collect, study and display' specimens of the natural world and human heritage. He notes the difficulties that arose once museums were asked to tell the national story and represent a national identity, but also points to recent examples of museum exhibits—in Germany and South Africa, for example—that subvert or interrogate that expectation.

In Johannesburg, the Museum Afrika has an exhibition on the Treason Trials in the 1950s and 1960s that enables visitors, including relatives of the accused, to write their personal responses, which in some instances 'tap a reservoir of unrelieved bitterness'. The Apartheid Museum hands visitors cards, randomly assigning them a racial identity as black or white as they enter and requiring them to walk down separate corridors past the signs that routinely structured everyday life in South Africa along racial lines. Optimistically, the separate paths converge in a promise of future racial harmony, despite the persistence of the gross inequalities of apartheid into the present.

In Germany, a nation also obliged to wrestle with issues of national guilt and trauma, Daniel Libeskind's Jewish Museum is constructed around three intersecting underground pathways, suggesting a past in which the contradictions do not lend themselves to a resolution, while the Deutsches Historisches Museum stages an exhibition *Myths of the Nations: the Arena of Memories* that foregrounds the problem of historical memory and the ever-changing uses made of the past. Davison suggests that this sophisticated attempt to explore the ways in which national communities are constituted through the mobilisation of collective memories might be emulated at the troubled National Museum of Australia.

Dawn Casey recounts her experience as director of the National Museum of Australia, between 2001 and 2003, when she found herself the target of political campaigns that attacked her professionalism, as well as the content and captions of museum exhibits. She tells of the difficulties, not just of addressing the current imperative of presenting 'multiple points of view', but also of attempting to meet the varying demands of governing boards, governments, curators, commercial investors and diverse visitor groups—locals, tourists and schoolchildren. Contemporary national museums are expected to be interactive and entertaining, as well as informative and instructive, providing an acceptable account of the national experience. This, she concludes, cannot revive a 'simple narrative of national progress', but rather must present 'the interplay of many stories and points of view' in keeping with the approach of contemporary museology.

In her chapter, Ien Ang discusses the constraints on presenting many stories and points of view in an art museum, such as the Art Gallery of New South Wales, traditionally the upholder of 'tradition and privilege' and 'the imperious status of the art work'. Despite the desire of director Edmund Capon to attract more diverse audiences, especially people from Asian backgrounds, he also suggests that the very idea of the art museum, in which objects are valued for their artistic rather than their historic or civilisational significance, is foreign to most Asian cultures.

The Art Gallery of New South Wales has addressed the challenge of diversity by surrounding exhibitions of Asian art—for example, *India: Dancing to the Flute* and *Masks of Mystery*—with relevant cultural events and performances. This approach stands in contrasts to that adopted for European art. There has been no suggestion that *Renoir to Picasso* should be accompanied by performances of the can-can, for instance.

Should this difference be interpreted as a case of 'abject Euro-centrism' or, rather, as an 'unsettling of the aesthetic codes of Western art'? Ang discusses the reception of *Buddha: Radiant Awakening*, with its 'Wisdom Room' inviting innovative community participation. In the end, she concludes, the challenge of pluralism was effectively contained. The status of the 'work of art' remained paramount, so that the art museum could continue to operate as itself a monument to Western art.

Perhaps the major task of museums, libraries and archives, as repositories of public memory, is to conserve art objects, written works, material artefacts and other vestiges of the past for posterity. In his chapter on 'The Archive under Threat', John Frow examines the implications of the conversion of the traditional 'commons in information' into privately owned holdings facilitated by the technology of digitisation: 'libraries are increasingly purchasing or leasing digitised materials that are based on collections held in other libraries: it is the intermediaries that are profiting from this exploitation of the value of special collections'. Libraries are also being charged massive fees for access to new databases and meta-databases, while at the same time large populations are unable to afford 'the entry fee at the doors of the digital archive'. Increasingly, 'the archives that have been bequeathed to us, and that we ourselves have in part helped to construct, are removed from our control'.

The archive is one important site of public memory. Landscape is another. When space is inscribed with memory and thus made meaningful in new ways, it becomes place—or in Aboriginal terms, country. In his meticulous charting of Tasmanian burning regimes over a period of several thousand years prior to European settlement, Bill Gammage shows the ways in which local custodians of country shaped a landscape that was fruitful and meaningful, but ever-changing. Through burning strategies that produced adjacent areas of rainforest, grass and eucalyptus, Tasmanians continually transformed the landscape. They did so purposefully, skilfully and systematically, according to the Law, encoded in memory, passed down through countless generations. When you go into the bush, writes Gammage, the memory and monuments of Indigenous Tasmanians will be all around you.

When Europeans took up residence in the Australian colonies in the late eighteenth and early nineteenth centuries, they set about transforming that landscape, driven by memories of homes left behind. Michael Bennett suggests that it was homesickness and a sense of exile that generated an idea of 'the heritage of Old England' in the colonies before such a sense of national heritage had emerged in England itself. This sense of heritage was often nurtured through the institution of the church and was important in shaping a sense of English identity in the new world. Pyrs Gruffud suggests that a sense of exile or loss was probably a necessary context for the construction of 'heritage'.[9] More generally, Paul Shakel observes that an interest in 'heritage' was fuelled by the massive migrations of the last two hundred years which left people cut off from their past.[10]

In her study of the making of Australian colonial gardens, Katie Holmes points to the gendered dimensions of this process, with women playing a central role as 'bearers of culture and transmitters of memories'—in the creation of domestic gardens and in writing letters about them, thus forging a sense of belonging in the new country. The gardens were not just exercises in nostalgia, however, but rather encoded a double vision, representing an investment in a different future as well as a yearning for a remembered past. Women incorporated native plants into their gardens as part of the process of accommodating themselves to their new homes, while unfamiliar landscapes generated new memories and thus a new attachment to place.

Susan Martin, in her chapter on 'Remembering the Self', points out that the practice of gardening was important in producing a sense of self as well as a sense of place. Nineteenth century gardening can thus be understood as 'one aspect of the performance of a colonial subjectivity'. For those who undertook the adventure, the process of 'settlement' could in fact be profoundly 'unsettling'. In this context, gardening—for commercial profit or for pleasure—could reaffirm colonists' sense of self, whether as productive agriculturalists and orchardists or as beneficent ladies, dispensing produce to the poor.

Inevitably, colonists made sense of the new land in terms of established discursive frameworks, whether musing on the tenantless wilderness, the Romantic Sublime or historic horrors. Roslynn Haynes' chapter on 'Tasmanian Landscapes in Painting, Poetry and Print' points to the ways in which writers rhapsodising over the 'untouched landscape'—the land without history—contributed powerfully to the popular fantasy of *terra nullius*. The painter John Glover, on the other hand, often depicted groups of Aboriginal Tasmanians in his landscapes, inspired by their sense of attachment to their country and what he described as their 'gaiety'.

When writers ranging from nineteenth century historian John West to his twentieth century successor Robert Hughes depicted the horrors of convictism in Van Diemen's Land, 'nature' with its decayed undergrowth, dreary beaches and desolation seemed complicit in the evil system. Nature had bestowed its own 'kiss of death' on the place. Even the Hobart Rivulet was inherently malign, whether in the writing of Hal Porter ('maggots and putrescence') or later Christopher Koch ('Hobart Town's cloaca'). However, in more recent writing, the convict system, for so long a source of personal and social shame in Tasmania, as Michael Roe points out in his chapter on 'Commemoration', has been reconceptualised to signify British oppression and local resistance to it.

The past seems to weigh especially heavily on Tasmania. Jim Everett and Michael Roe discuss the shame experienced, respectively, by Aborigines and convicts and their many descendants. Yet both writers refuse a pessimistic determinism.

Despite the devastation of colonisation for Aboriginal peoples and continuing problems such as unemployment, loss of culture and debilitating health conditions, Everett believes that local Aboriginal leaders can contribute to community planning and development and 'bring life into Aboriginal people as a people'. But it is also necessary, he believes, for acknowledgement to be made of what happened in the past and that Aboriginal children be able to learn about their heroes and the part they played in defending their country from the invaders. Henry Reynolds describes the controversy surrounding the Labor government's choice of 2004 as the official bicentenary year and the perception that the government was intent on rewriting history. In the event, and largely left to their own devices, Tasmanians chose to record local histories and commemorate local heroes.

Coming to terms with the past is necessary, Michael Roe believes, to present-day self-respect. His chapter suggests that it is with humility and tolerance, rather than pride or vituperation, that we should commemorate the past. Together this collection reminds us of the presumption of those who would speak on behalf of the dead, but also the unavoidable necessity of doing so. For as memory, monuments and museums all testify, the paradox of the past lies in its perverse persistence.

PART I

Memory
as Muse

I A HISTORY
OF MEMORY

Peter Conrad

A mortal man who presumes to present a history of memory in a mere 6000 words needs some supernatural help. So I begin with an invocation, an address to the goddess who hovers in the air above us, whether we recognise her or not: Mnemosyne, the deity who was the mother of the muses and thus the begetter of all the arts. The Greeks personified and thus invented her, but she has made at least one local landfall. My invocation comes from a poem in which Mnemosyne, enthroned on the Organ Pipes at the summit of Mount Wellington, is sighted in Tasmania. It is by Gwen Harwood, and it begins:

> Sing, memory, sing those seasons in the freezing
> suburb of Fern Tree, a rock-shaded place
> with tree ferns, gullies, snowfalls and eye-pleasing
> prospects from paths along the mountain-face.

The memories—of early marriage and child rearing—are the poet's own, but she needs the help of a deity to infuse them with lyrical energy and eloquence. Together the goddess and her female acolyte succeed in turning Mount Wellington from a stern male overseer into a soft, wet, nurturing Magna Mater. At the end of the poem Harwood and a woman friend climb towards the summit, spiritually elated and elevated 'like gods or blessed spirits', and look down from

> *above the leafy dazzle of the streams*
> *to fractured rock, where water had its birth,*
> *and stood in silence, at the roots of dreams,*
> *content to know: our children walk the earth.*[1]

Appeals to a tutelary divinity used to be customary, but they are seldom as bold and proprietorial as this. Although Gwen Harwood claims to be taking dictation from Mnemosyne, in fact she is ventriloquially putting words into her mouth. She asks or perhaps commands the mother of the muses to sing. When Vladimir Nabokov gave his memoirs the title *Speak, Memory*, his request was more modest: Mnemosyne was to talk not sing, and to do so in prose not Harwood's rhapsodic verse. Nabokov explained that he did not dare to address Mnemosyne by her proper name, because his publisher warned that the unpronounceable Greek word would deter little old English ladies from buying the book.

I wonder why writers, who surely want to sing or speak words never heard before, defer to this mnemonic mother and credit her with foreknowing the words they go on to utter? And why did the myth accord Mnemosyne that maternal responsibility for all the arts, through her prolific output of daughters who are the separate, specialised muses of history, poetry, song, dance and so on? Perhaps it is because art is experience preserved, time saved from itself. Art is our personal victory over the past, our abolition of history (since great artists, no matter when they lived, feel like our contemporaries), and our assault on death—for even the obscurest of individuals is not irrevocably dead so long as he or she is remembered: hence the monuments that other contributors to this collection discuss.

A monument can be a slab of sandstone commemorating a short life in a harsh and indigent colony, like the gravestones cemented into a wall in St David's Park in Hobart, but it can also be the fragile papery entablature of a sonnet, as when Shakespeare declares in Sonnet 18 that his words have the power to immortalise the loved one they address—'So long lives this, and this gives life to thee'. The medium of our lives is time, which obliterates everything; hence the need for memory, to make amends for that erasure.

Greek myths tell us most of what we need to know about ourselves. A rebellious Titan endowed us with our mental powers, so, thanks to Prometheus and his uprising against Zeus, consciousness is our means of defying fate and arguing with mortality. If Mnemosyne is the mother of the arts, Prometheus, who taught men how to write, is their father. Unable to see or know what goes on inside our heads, we imagine the chemical, neural and electrical reactions that produce thought, and select images to represent them. For the Greeks, memory was a writer, a sort of recording angel. From the first, this unique human faculty was treated as an inborn literary aptitude. It made possible our authorship of our own identities, the recomposition of existence as a story. Plato, in *Theaetetus*, supposed that our cranium contained a block of wax on which, as he said, 'Mnemosyne, the mother of the muses', imprinted insignia of whatever we needed to remember, as if pressing a signet ring into the malleable surface. If the wax were dirty or hard, it wouldn't receive the impression: could Plato have fancied that our grey matter overflowed into those deposits that harden in our ears? And if the impression were smudged, that particular memory would be effaced.

Because memory was considered to be a mode of notation, it soon became a proud proof of mental regulation and retentiveness. It conferred power on the rememberer, because he had control over the invisible functions of his own brain. Cicero was celebrated for speaking to the Roman Senate for two hours without using notes. He managed the feat by an act of mnemonic construction, taking a leisurely tour of a mansion inside his head whose separate rooms stored the information he needed, as he describes in *On Oratory*. Remembering for him was the work of a builder; his imaginary architecture took control of space, redesigning his mental interior as if it were a strictly catalogued library.

Classical memory advertised an act of volition. Romantic memory, as I will go on to explain, delights in its own involuntariness. We soon enough came to rely on technologies of recollection that looked after the data we needed to safeguard: the book, the Filofax, the computer hard drive. When that happened, memory was allowed out to play, or permitted to concentrate on the private, trivial incidents that somehow in retrospect turn out to be the primal scenes of our lives. Cicero had his classical palace; my drab, lowly, horizontal equivalent was the Main Road from the northern suburbs back into Hobart, which I used to revisit in the twilight of consciousness during my first years away from home, walking along it in order to put myself to sleep. Each of those dingy shopfronts and timber yards and used-car lots, like Cicero's marble apartments, was a depository for some aspect of my early life in Tasmania. Cicero, of course, would not have approved of my memory street. My trips along it were wayward, straggling, unpurposeful, and they always ended in unconsciousness; they hardly mobilised private memories to support a public oration. Cicero disapproved of Themistocles, who refused to learn the systematic, architectonic drill of memory because he could remember things naturally. Memory offered us the chance to re-educate the brain, to change the organ into a proud, lofty artifice like that palace.

The trained, harnessed memories of classical and medieval men vouched for moral discipline, and censured idle thoughts. Abbot Suger, who rebuilt and gloriously redecorated the Abbey of Saint-Denis in Paris during the twelfth century, believed that the architectural fabric he had raised and ornamented with gold and precious stones was a bulwark against eroding time, an attack on 'Oblivion, the jealous rival of Truth'. Memory for Suger was a sanctum, a shrine for protecting and preserving truth. Petrarch's *Rerum memorandum libri* (*Books on Matters to be Remembered*) compiled a digest of moral mementoes: as Frances Yates points out, the list of things to be remembered begins with the virtue of Prudence.[2] The scaffolding that held up those memory palaces and memory theatres stiffened a human consciousness that, being fallen and faulty, needed stricture. In a Christian dispensation, the primary activity of memory was the recollection of our original sin. Thomas Aquinas, who decreed that the faithful man should 'dispose those things which he wishes to remember in a certain order' and 'repeat them with frequent meditation', rationalised the activity of remembering and made it into a devotional practice.

Memory's digressions and discoveries were curtailed; as a result, it possessed no autonomy, no creative independence. A change occurred, as Yates argues, when the hermetic mystics of the Renaissance, such as Giordano Bruno or Pico della Mirandola, claimed a share in the divine power of memory, a magical capacity that enabled them to conjure up new earths and heavens inside their heads and to devise new identities for themselves. Aquinas believed that only God could create, which reduced men to slavish mimicry of that initial feat. Renaissance philosophy implanted the creative capacity within each of us, if only we could remember—by employing memory as sorcery—how to use it.

It is never easy to establish the reality of what Yates vaguely calls an 'inner event', but I find this new art of memory everywhere in Shakespeare. The medieval notion of memory as a dutiful commandment remains, of course: the Ghost's instruction to Hamlet is 'Remember me', and Hamlet calls for his tables so he can set down a moral memento in writing. But he soon forgets the remonstrance, and in any case are we bound to believe the Ghost's account of his own death? Is he remembering his past, or inventing it? Throughout Shakespeare's plays, memory—and its blessed concomitant, forgetfulness—offers characters the chance to re-create themselves.

As You Like It begins with Orlando saying, 'As I remember, Adam …' There's an inaudible comma in the line, which he addresses to an old man called Adam, who is the obliging pretext for some exposition of events in Orlando's family and the terms of his father's will. What we expect, if we elide the comma, is that the play will be a remembrance of Adam, and therefore of Eve and of Eden—which turns out, when the ejected courtiers take refuge in Arden, to be exactly what happens: pastoral is the voluntary reconstitution of paradise. The creative fiat occurs within the imaginations of the characters. In the forest, Rosalind finds amorous tributes to her pinned to the trees, and says she was 'never so berhymed since Pythagoras' time when I was an Irish rat, which I can hardly remember'. It is an astonishing assertion. She is cheekily deploying the Pythagorean doctrine of metempsychosis, which contends that the mind migrates between bodies, escaping from them when they die and pursuing its adventures elsewhere, not bothering whether the organism it inhabits is a rodent or a human being. Rosalind remembers all this, or rather makes it up, and then has the impudence to admit that she hardly remembers it at all. Shakespearean characters enjoy a precious freedom that allows them to remember what they never knew, and also to forget themselves. In *Cymbeline*, Imogen escapes from the court with her comforter Pisanio, who advises her about self-protection: 'Well then, here's the point: You must forget to be a woman'. It is as easily said as done, and the next time we see her she has become a man. If memory inculcates prudence, as Petrarch thought, then amnesia liberates us to be whoever we like.

Such remembering is magical, indistinguishable from dreaming. Miranda in *The Tempest* worries about her confused recollections of her previous life, 'rather like a dream than an assurance / That my remembrance warrants'. Obeying moral tradition, she expects remembrance to be a warranty and an assurance, a legal guarantee that events actually occurred, like the imprimatur of that Platonic signet ring in the wax. But Prospero, in telling her what to remember, breaks away from the classical or Thomistic regime of rote learning, gives her a dizzy glimpse into the gulf of creative chaos inside her head, and encourages her to fantasise:

> ... *how is it*
> *That this lives in thy mind? What seest thou else*
> *In the dark backward and abyss of time?*
> *If thou rememb'rest aught ere thou cam'st here,*
> *How thou cam'st here thou may'st.*

Shakespeare obliquely glances at this magical art of memory in Sonnet 30, which begins with an incantation, a conjurer's spell: 'When to the sessions of sweet silent thought / I summon up remembrance of things past'. The summons is an abracadabra, and the sessions are a séance. The memories enticed out of the abyss are personal, fugitive and grievous—dead friends, lost loves. This is not the 'frequent meditation' advised for the good of the soul by Thomist preachers, and it provokes moaning distress. Memory can be the generator of remorse and misery. The image Shakespeare uses is grimly financial: he likens these resurrected woes to debts that have already been paid but must be paid all over again. We are in danger of surrendering to that old equation between memory and penitence upheld by the Ghost in *Hamlet*, who died unconfessed and is therefore condemned to repine in purgatory. But Shakespeare saves himself from despair in the glibly triumphant final couplet of Sonnet 30, where the rememberer like a magus cancels the past and exempts a loved one from the assault of time: '... if the while I think on thee, dear friend, / All losses are restored, and sorrows end'.

All losses are restored, all sorrows end. It is a brave boast, because it resurrects the dead and immortalises the living. Memory can be a hell, choked with our guilty regrets. But here it creates a heaven, and lodges the secret of eternal life inside the artist's mind: our defunct happiness lives again if we remember it. Falstaff bestows the same grace on Shallow in *Henry IV Part 2* when, reminiscing about youthful misdemeanours, he says, 'We have heard the chimes at midnight ...' Is midnight the end of one day or the beginning of the next? Does it belong to the past or the future? Falstaff says that one of the trollops they used to romp with fifty-five years ago is 'old, old', but Shallow rejuvenates himself in remembering her.

The Enlightenment, examining the mechanisms of what Locke called 'human understanding', upheld Plato's notion of the memory. Locke likened it to a 'waxen tablet', but now it received the imprint of sensations as well as those insignia that for Plato compressed knowledge. Memory, in the age of the encyclopaedists, no longer had to store data; though— as Locke said in *Essay Concerning Human Understanding*—it initially resembled 'white paper, void of all characters', what men wrote on it was the story of their own lives, not the history of the world. Sterne's *Tristram Shandy* begins with Tristram's memory of his own conception: we know who we are because we remember the experiences that have formed us, going back to that first accidental encounter between the tadpole and the egg. Though we call this science of mind enlightened, its imagery emphasises darkness. Cicero's roomy palace, a forum for shared and exchanged information, became during the eighteenth century a more private, reclusive place. In Locke's *Essay*, the understanding resembles 'a closet wholly shut from light, with only some little openings left'. Through those apertures, pictures leak into the dark room; he wished they could be retained there and made to 'lie ... orderly'.

In describing this cranial *camera obscura*, Locke had imagined that great mnemonic tool invented by the next century, the camera. Theology did its best to keep up with evolving technology. The photographer Julia Margaret Cameron made a portrait in 1868 of a lush, languid, introverted young woman called Marie Spartali, and entitled the print *Memory*. It is a photograph of Mnemosyne in person. Her hair is a cataract, and she is crowned and festooned with leaves: memory is seasonal and cyclical, our inborn capacity to regenerate ourselves, like the earth's recovery from its annual death. But looped around her bare wrist and dangling from her arm, she has a mnemonic aid that belongs to the heritage of classical lore not, like the leaves or her waist-length pre-Raphaelite tresses, to romantic nature. It is a string of beads, longer and chunkier than a rosary, but serving the same purpose. Telling beads is a labour of enumeration, a lesson in establishing chronology and hierarchy, since as Locke said it requires the recovered information to be sorted into order: memory takes work, and is more than a natural instinct.

The eighteenth century was forced to admit the faultiness of human understanding, its frisky unreliability. In his *Dictionary*, Samuel Johnson, who nicknamed himself 'the Rambler', defined the essay as a 'loose sally of the mind'. The mind rambled or, in Sterne, digressed, proceeding by association; as an organic capacity, lodged in the body, it delighted in indiscretion, remembering what we should have forgotten or should never have known, as when Tristram Shandy eavesdrops on his parents as they lumber through the business of procreating him. Wordsworth—for whom poetry was a personal memorial, even an epitaph for his own existence—set himself to restore the classical connection between memory and morality. Hence his definition of poetry as 'emotion recollected in

traquillity', with recollection as the tranquillising agent. Wordsworth praised the rote learning practised by dame schools
because it 'practised the memory', and in a letter apologised
for forgetting a message because 'both my body and my
memory were run off my legs'. Here he substitutes memory
for the mind or soul, which are conventionally placed in appo-
sition to the body, and equips mental power with physical
appendages by giving the memory legs: memory is a walk
inside the head.

For Wordsworth, correctness of recall was a legal duty. In
1825 his sister Dorothy asked Walter Scott to settle a dispute
between herself and Wordsworth about an incident sixteen
years earlier. Scott agreed with William who, far from chortling
because he had won a bet, sagely assessed his submission like
evidence proffered in court: 'Your testimony, though negative
only, and inferential, tends to establish the truth of my recollection'. But despite Wordsworth's self-scrutinising conscience,
are recollections ever true? At least Jane Austen retained a sense
of the mind's skittishness, and valued our capacity to free
ourselves from the past by wiping inconvenient memories out,
getting back to the clean slate described by Locke. At the end
of *Pride and Prejudice*, Jane is confused by Elizabeth's change of
heart: she has despised Darcy throughout the novel, but now is
going to marry him. Elizabeth says, 'That is all to be forgot ...
In such cases as these, a good memory is unpardonable'.
Forgiving depends on forgetting, and we are always quick to
forgive ourselves. Wordsworth contrasted our fickle memories
with the encyclopaedic memory of the earth, which consumes
us all and stores our remains. A grave, as he said in his *Essay upon
Epitaphs*, is 'a tranquillising object'—more or less synonymous
with a poem. Wordsworth's characters can be seen constructing
monuments to their own obscure existences, as when Michael
piles rocks to form his sheep-fold. They hope to leave some
token of themselves above ground, but the real remembering
is subterranean: any cross-section of earth is a geological

memory book, going back to the creation of the world. Sometimes that history breaks through the oblivious surface and rears into the sky. Mount Wellington is a reminder of something we have all forgotten—a time when the peak was a beach, and what is now Hobart sat on the ocean floor. Uluru remembers a different creation, when two lizard men butchered an emu and left in the desert a hunk of bleeding meat, which toughened into sandstone.

Stones, because they mark graves, are the most ancient symbols of memory; they are the primal building blocks of Cicero's palaces or of Renaissance memory theatres. Victor Hugo likened the cathedral of Notre Dame to the early Celtic cromlech, and sympathised with the 'overcharged memory of the early races', for whom 'every tradition was sealed beneath a monument'. Locke's closet has become oppressive, retentively bolted or secured. But these architectonic assemblages of memory, as Hugo argued in *Notre Dame de Paris*, grew lighter and lost their monumentality after the invention of the book. A breathtaking metaphor covers the change: thanks to print, the 'mass of stone … turned into a flock of birds, winging its way in all directions', and memory 'passed from durability to immortality'. The process continued with the invention of the camera, which with the help of a chemical emulsion detained fugitive, winged moments and fixed them on paper, and then with that of the computer, which—in theory at least—allows us to avail ourselves of a world's worth of memory without needing to bother about the tedious drill of actually remembering any of it. The rememberers of the Renaissance were magicians, like Rosalind reeling through her previous Pythagorean lives or Shakespeare in the sonnet that summons up memories as if they were spirits. The contemporary equivalent of the necromancer appears in William Gibson's novel *Neuromancer*, about a 'console cowboy' who plugs his brain directly into the Internet, or in the hero of Terry Bisson's *Johnny Mnemonic*.

Yet this electronic gadgetry has not rendered the mind's more imperfect, faltering efforts redundant. Classical memory, the proud advertisement of self-discipline that regulated Cicero's orations, relied on volition. Machines volunteered to take over such tasks; this left memory free to behave involuntarily, exempt from the supervision of the educated, orderly will. Proust—whose great novel takes its English title, *Remembrance of Things Past*, from Shakespeare's sonnet about memory and magic—announced a new vocation for memory in an interview in 1913. He believed, he said, that 'it is almost solely from involuntary memories that the artist ought to take the central substance of his work'. Freud would have agreed: the memories that articulate the desires of his neurotics are involuntary, almost emetic, ventilated in dreams. The Freudian analysis of memory leads to the restoration of rational mental health. Proust's involuntary memories are not threatening, and do not have to be explained away; they are not treacherously sexual but nourishingly sensuous. Their place of storage, rather than the head, is the nose or the taste buds, so that the nostalgic taste of a cake can make present again a whole lost era of the narrator's personal past. The image he uses to describe the process is culinary or perhaps medicinal, but certainly not therapeutic. Involuntary memories 'bring things back to us in an exactly right dosage of recollection and forgetfulness', and by liberating a sensation from circumstance and contingency they 'give us its extra-temporal essence'. That 'extra-temporal essence' evokes immortality, as the art of memory so often does, and reminds us that we can save our souls or at least safeguard them by creating a personal, mental heaven. Remembering of this kind defies the pitiless, irreversible logic of modern physics by demonstrating that time does not travel only in one direction; it can go backwards, or wheel around in circles. If we can re-experience the past with such a shocking physical immediacy, then perhaps after all we can change it.

For Proust, memory is mystical not technological. He inevitably employs the photographic analogy, but with a difference. Discussing pleasure, he says that what we take physically from the beloved is 'merely a negative film'. It becomes a positive when, in reverie later and alone, we literally develop it. The process happens in our 'inner darkroom, the entrance to which is barred to us so long as we are with other people'. The developing intensifies our delight: how much we miss if we send our snaps to the photolab! Dipping the memories in some cerebral fluid and hanging them up to dry, we are fixing them forever. Even a lapse in memory tantalises Proust and gives him extra reason to admire the faculty's power. In a passage on sleeping draughts, he worries about the status of 'a memory which we do not recall'. We possess all our memories, although from time to time we may not be able to recall them; perhaps we can remember back beyond our birth and recollect an 'anterior existence'. The operations of memory inclined Wordsworth, like Rosalind in *As You Like It*, to believe in pre-existence. His intimations of immortality are not previews of future grace in paradise but flashbacks to a happiness we enjoyed before we slumped into our current incarnation.

Proust derived from memory a myth of creation, a map of a cosmos that can fit into the individual brain. Remembering his forgetfulness about Albertine's liaisons, the narrator says that 'Memory, instead of being a duplicate always present before our eyes of the various events of our life, is rather an abyss from which at odd moments a chance resemblance enables us to draw up, restored to life, dead impressions'. The abyss is the gulf, without form and void, into which the creator dips, as the myths describe it, to mould the world; remembering, for Proust, is the same kind of creative miracle, imposing shape on chaos. It recapitulates Genesis but it also anticipates the day of judgement, since it triumphantly raises dead impressions from their graves. These are the depths that memory dredges. There are also heights, from which gods swoop down to perform miracles. Elsewhere in *The Captive*, Proust broods about sleep, dreams, and the oblivion into which we die each night, reviving or resuscitating ourselves (if we're lucky) in the morning. What if we awake feeling stupefied, stricken, hardly existing, unable to recollect—to collect around ourselves again—the paraphernalia of identity? 'Then from the highest heaven the goddess Mnemosyne bends down and holds out to us in the formula "the habit of ringing for coffee" the hope of resurrection.'

Scott-Moncrieff's old translation of *The Captive* Latinises Mnemosyne and calls her Mnemotechnia, which to me makes her sound more like a machine than a goddess; I have therefore given her back her original Greek name—and this reminds me to make good my initial promise: to explain why the myth identified Mnemosyne as the progenitor of poetry, history, music, dance and all the other arts. I think it is because, in the man-made religion of art, experience has a second coming. Memory is innately sad, since it records our losses (going back to that of Eden). Still, the process of remembering is in itself a consolation, as time enables us to overcome grief and convert pain into a kind of pleasure. Virgil, describing a moment of raw anguish in his epic *Aeneid*, looks ahead to the healing, redeeming intercession of art: 'Who knows but some day this too will perhaps be remembered with pleasure?' says the hero Aeneas as his ship is ravaged by a storm. Jean-Luc Godard makes the same point, also with the help of a Greek myth, when he declares that 'only the cinema authorises Orpheus to look back without letting Eurydice die'. His mistake is to assume that only the cinema permits this forbidden glance backwards, with its defiance of time's irreversibility: every art performs such a regenerative act. As André Malraux put it, using an image of sacrificial incineration, 'Art is what is reborn in what has been burnt'. When the Dionysian women slaughtered Orpheus, they tore off his head, which floated down the river. It was still singing.

Nabokov in *Speak, Memory* celebrates the 'supreme achievement of memory', which is that it harmonises and stabilises the detritus of the past and composes an internal narrative which is the story of our lives, the ground of our being. A story, not a history: although I may seem cheeky to say so in a collection that includes so many historians, I suspect that history is about regulating memory, disciplining it as Cicero did, whereas literature encourages memory to wander and to bring back souvenirs that are precious in proportion to their apparent insignificance. Ours is a country that is almost self-tormentingly determined to remember, to understand and to make atonement for its painful past. It may be too much of a burden. Judith Wright remembered a conversation she once had with a visiting American, who was shocked that we were still so mired in ancestral guilt and anxious for expiation. America too 'was once a convict settlement', but has 'vigorously forgotten' it, just as it only vaguely remembers the dispossession of native Americans; the country is officially amnesiac. Historians are the tribunes of the people, although the people they so valiantly defend are long since dead. I do not deny that this is noble and necessary work. Milan Kundera in *The Book of Laughter and Forgetting* describes the doctoring of a Soviet photograph to remove the face of a politician who had become a nonperson. 'The struggle of man against power', Kundera says, 'is the struggle of memory against forgetting'. Much as I revere Kundera, I still wonder whether history has the right to co-opt and monopolise memory. What is the historical status of those involuntary memories that, for Proust, were the genetic substance of human life and the inevitable material of literature? Literary characters might be defined as those who—as George Eliot puts it at the very end of *Middlemarch*—perform 'unhistorical acts', and who accordingly, like Dorothea Brooke, rest in 'unvisited tombs'.

Walter Benjamin paradoxically and puzzlingly suggested that 'History … is an image from involuntary memory, an image that suddenly occurs to the subject of history in the moment of danger'. Yet the sudden occurrence of the image in a moment of danger sounds to me like a recipe for literary re-creation, not historical research. Historians see the past from a distance, whereas literary characters—Richard III calling for a fresh horse at Bosworth, Pierre stumbling through a torched Moscow in *War and Peace*, Jim the Australian bird-watcher entombed in the trenches of Flanders in David Malouf's *Fly Away, Peter*—are still alive in it. For them it is and always will be the present. Art occupies its own charmed realm where, as Octavio Paz says, 'time … reincarnates and re-engenders itself'. There is no need for memory's wispy elegies: music— thanks to one of Mnemosyne's litter of daughters—arrests time and grants us, while we are listening, a surrogate immortality. History is an adjudication about memory, like that in which city fathers engage when they decide to construct a monument; it needs to establish truth, to reach a verdict about what actually happened and who was responsible. Literature is more tolerant of memory's fictionality, and treats its lapses as creative leaps. When Iris Murdoch's grip on who she was and what she had done began to fail, she was taken to a doctor for appraisal. He asked her to tell him who the prime minister was. She didn't know, but was still cunning enough to evade admitting it. 'Does it matter?' she groaned. For the subject of history, it certainly does; for the writer, probably not, so long as he or she can retrieve other unhistorical memories that are private and even secretive, idiosyncratic and not communally pooled. In retrospect, one incidental bonus of Alzheimer's disease may be that it dispenses you from having to remember who Tony Blair and John Howard are.

At the end of *Speak, Memory*, Nabokov mocks the 'fool-made history' that had expelled his family from its homeland. But the speech or song of memory offers compensation for his expatriated state. He migrates around Europe, and the parks of the cities he passes through—tantalising, inexact replicas of the country gardens outside St Petersburg where he grew up—uproot themselves and travel along with him in his mental luggage. He imagines these gravelled walks and radial avenues quitting Prague or Paris to waft through the air, and that fantastical sight begets an image which sees roots elasticising themselves to follow him into exile: 'Roots, roots of remembered greenery, roots of memory and pungent plants, roots, in a word, are enabled to traverse long distances by surmounting some obstacles, penetrating others and insinuating themselves into narrow cracks'. Classical memory was a palace, but romantic memory is the ground beneath the marble floor, a soil knitted together by living filaments.

Those green organic roots implicitly find their way back to Russia, even though Nabokov never did. For me, the roots would have to be transoceanic cables, because they have a much greater distance to get across. Mnemosyne, being a goddess, connects us to heaven, which is why Gwen Harwood positioned her on Mount Wellington. But memory also attaches us to the earth, or embeds us in it; and underground, where the roots entangle and entwine, we are all part of one another. Thomas Mann in his Indian legend *The Transposed Heads* describes memory mounting 'in the mind of man' like a sacrificial vessel slowly filling with blood, and explains those seeping, sanguinary memories as an expression of 'nostalgia for the Mother', offerings at the shrine of 'the great World-Nurse' who is gratified by the severed heads or penises of her devotees. Perhaps Kali is another name for Mnemosyne, and perhaps too the sickly nostalgia that Iain McCalman writes about elsewhere in this volume is a collective death-wish, despite the hope of rebirth with which it teases us.

My conclusion, after a circular journey that has brought me back to where I started from, is another quotation. It's a line of verse you may know, and although it is by a very minor poet it is for many of us synonymous with poetry, not only because we first heard it at school (where we were probably made to learn it, as the saying was, by heart) but also because it catches the urgent emotional pull of poetry and, in its opening repetition, hints at the spell or summons or invocation by which poets call for Mnemosyne's assistance. Writing it down here could be a bit of a risk, one of those 'moments of danger' referred to by Benjamin. The poet is Thomas Hood, and the line that starts with the enchanted repetition, as you may have guessed, is this: 'I remember, I remember, the house where I was born'. Well, I certainly do. But I cannot go on because I don't remember the rest of the poem ...

2 REMEMBERING AND FORGETTING

Nicholas Shakespeare

Through a series of strange circumstances, I had the opportunity as an English schoolboy to read aloud to the blind Argentine writer Jorge Luis Borges. I was sixteen when I first climbed the five floors to his drawing room in Avenida Maipu: a small dark room with a glass-fronted cabinet in which he stored his favourite texts and from which, according to his instructions, I one afternoon picked out the complete works of Shakespeare. He wanted me to check a quote from *Hamlet*. Borges remembered the line as: 'There's nothing good or bad but thinking makes it so'. I discovered that Shakespeare had in fact written: 'There's nothing *either* good or bad but thinking makes it so'. Borges contemplated the extra word and said, 'My version is better. Memory has made it better.'

Memory has made it better. One could also say that a *failure* of memory had made it better. Borges had improved the sentence by forgetting what he believed to be a superfluous, inconvenient, unrhythmical word.

This tendency towards memory lapse, which is anathema to the historian, is sometimes the very tendency that allows the novelist to go wild. 'The thing that allowed me to write', Barry Lopez once remarked, 'is that I can never remember anything'. Whereas a historian has to be concerned with numbers and facts, indeed with remembering everything (as does the protagonist in the marvellous Borges story 'Funes, the Memorious'), fiction tends to concern itself with describing an individual's experience. The American philosopher Richard Rorty famously suggests that another way fiction differs from history is that it forces the reader to experience a subject's pain. 'Cruelty', Rorty says, 'is the worst thing we can do'.[1] By imagining another's suffering, it becomes harder for us to inflict pain. Fiction, in other words, by dramatising the particular, the idiosyncratic and the personal invites our empathy and therefore holds out the promise of making us less cruel.

The more public, general and detached business of history/ philosophy is not so demanding of our empathy: it appeals to our intellect over our emotion. The fact is, if you are too enslaved by fact or theory there is no way you can write good fiction—witness the plotless meanderings that characterise the modern German or French novel. But good fiction, on the other hand, can help us to engage with history. Why else if we wish to experience the authentic flavour of, say, the Napoleonic Wars do we keep returning to Tolstoy? And isn't it significant that after a housemaid accidentally (or not) incinerated his manuscript, Thomas Carlyle prepared himself to rewrite, that is to say remember, his lost history of the French Revolution by spending three weeks reading novels? Likewise, for us to comprehend Leichhardt's journey into the Australian outback—come to that, any journey into Australia's interior —it would be necessary, I would have thought, to read Patrick White's re-creation of it in *Voss*.

Rorty proposes a world in which narrative is privileged over theory; in which truth is composed by human beings in the same way that Borges created his sentences. 'Since truth is a property of sentences, since sentences are dependent for their existence upon vocabularies, and since vocabularies are made by human beings, so are truths.' Rorty would like to see the elimination of cruelty and humiliation through our ability to perceive other human beings and cultures as having more in common with ourselves than not. In his mind, the 'imaginative ability to see strange people as fellow sufferers can cause people to re-evaluate their own capacity for cruelty and thereby redescribe themselves'.[2]

In *The Art of the Novel*, Milan Kundera offers a further reason for taking seriously the novelist's method. 'The novel's wisdom is different from that of philosophy. The novel is born not out of the theoretical spirit but of the spirit of humour ...' Moreover, 'the art inspired by God's laughter does not by nature serve ideological certitudes, it contradicts them. Like Penelope, it undoes each night the tapestry that the theologians, philosophers and learned men have woven the day before'. Novelists, writes Kundera, do not search for the one correct answer; nor do they seek ideological certitudes. 'It is precisely in losing the certainty for truth and the unanimous agreement of others that man [*sic*] becomes an individual. The novel is the imaginary paradise of individuals. It is the territory where no one possesses the truth, neither Anna nor Karenin, but where everyone has the right to be understood, both Anna and Karenin.'[3]

In his autobiography, *Living to Tell the Tale*, possibly the world's greatest living novelist, the Colombian writer Gabriel García Márquez, writes of a so-called 'massacre' that took place in 1928 in the Colombian coastal town of Aracataca when soldiers protecting the American-owned United Fruit Company opened fire on striking workers from the local banana plantation. The episode came to occupy a significant place in the consciousness of his nation and in his fiction. Much later, Márquez tried to piece together the events of that day:

I spoke with survivors and witnesses and searched through newspaper archives and official documents and I realised that the truth did not lie anywhere. Conformists said, in effect, that there had been no deaths. Those at the other extreme affirmed without a quaver in their voices that there had been more than a hundred.

Márquez inflated this in a novel to a figure of 3000 dead, and in the end, he wrote, real life did him justice when the Speaker of the Senate asked for a moment's silence in memory of the 3000 anonymous martyrs 'sacrificed by the forces of law and order'.[4] Aracataca, I feel, has a lot in common with Risdon Cove.

The story of Risdon may be well known to you, a story that has demanded to be retold over and over as an incantation against forgetting. On the east bank of the Derwent, Risdon Cove was the site of the first European settlement in Tasmania. What happened there on an autumn day in May 1804 was, wrote Mark Twain, out of all keeping with the place, 'a sort of bringing of heaven and hell together'. Twenty-six years after the event, a former convict, Edward White, testified that he was hoeing ground near the creek when there suddenly appeared a circle of 300 Aborigines, including women and children, hemming in a mob of kangaroos. 'They looked at me with all their eyes', White remembered memorably, suggesting that the sight of him turning the soil was the first indication that they had had of any English settlement on the island. White was positive, he said, 'they did not know there was a white man in the country when they came down to Risdon'. The Aborigines did not threaten him and he claimed not to be afraid of them. Even so, White reported their presence to some soldiers and resumed his hoeing. Then, at about eleven in the morning, he heard gunfire. The great difficulty is to imagine what happened in the next three hours until, at about two in the afternoon, troops under the nervous command of Lieutenant Moore apparently fired grapeshot into the crowd, who had, Moore claimed, turned hostile. According to White, 'there were a great many of the Natives slaughtered and wounded; I don't know how many'.[5] Nor can anyone else know how many. The true figure floats in a porous region between the written record of the occupiers—which reports that the bodies of three Aborigines were recovered—and the oral record of the occupied, which claims that up to one hundred Aborigines died. But the incident stuck in the historical memory and, likened frequently to Eve's bite of the apple, came to be understood as the original transgression.

Whatever happened in the trees beside the Derwent, in some important way Risdon departed the world of history and entered our imaginative landscape as representing the pain of the Indigenous displacement. To know the exact numbers who died on that day, what is this going to give us? To accept the documentary figure of, say, three dead is to imply that the incident was not too serious—that it is almost trivial compared to the numbers of Aborigines reportedly killed afterwards at, say, Toombs Lake or Campbell Town—and some of us recoil from that number because we know instinctively that it does not measure up to our sense of the suffering that was inflicted. Anyone who sticks at three risks being understood as refusing, somehow, to validate the great injustice experienced by the Aboriginal people; and yet the voice of the empiricist whispers ... *Be accurate. What are the numbers? What, actually, constitutes a massacre?*

In the end, after sifting the available material, I find myself siding with another North American philosopher, Charles Taylor, who warns that there is no single framework of experience one can cleave to exclusively without, he says, 'disaster or impoverishment'.[6] I would argue that to understand properly what went on at Risdon, as at Aracataca, one has to both remember and forget. In other words, borrow from the complementary arsenals of both historian and novelist to look at the past with 'all our eyes', which is what good and great writers have done since Day One, and indeed what Dickens did when he drew on Carlyle's at-long-last-published history of the French Revolution to write his novel *A Tale of Two Cities*.

My thoughts on this subject have been wonderfully concentrated by the antics of a 31-year-old British officer named Anthony Fenn Kemp who 200 years ago claimed the northern half of Van Diemen's Land for Britain. An enamel portrait of the period shows the strong profile of a determined sensualist. Details of his life are sketchier. Kemp's bald entry in his regiment's official history reads: 'Renowned bully'. One of the three lieutenant-governors whom he managed to get recalled described him as 'a turbulent, sordid and mischievous man with a slanderous tongue and a black heart'. A vigorous entrepreneur and a tremendous rumour-monger, he was to become known in fits and starts as 'the Father of Tasmania'.

In September 1830, at a time of maximum tension in the colony, Kemp chaired an urgent meeting in the Hobart Court House. The hall was packed with the colony's most prominent citizens and Kemp was first to address them. What he said, as reported in the *Hobart Town Courier*, was not quite what anyone expected:

> Mr Kemp commented at some length upon the aggressions committed by the blacks, which he attributed in a great degree to some officers of his own regiment (the late 102nd) who had, as he considered, most improperly fired a four-pounder upon a body of them, which having done much mischief, they had since borne that attack in mind and have retaliated upon the white people whenever opportunity offered.

As Henry Reynolds said to me: 'It's a pretty extraordinary thing to say about your own regiment. A regiment is like a club. Even a cad doesn't badmouth his own regiment.' Kemp went further in his condemnation when speaking to the historian James Bonwick. Although referred to only as 'a settler of

1804', he is the probable source of Bonwick's story that the Aborigines killed at Risdon were the result of 'a half-drunken spree ... from a brutal desire to see the Niggers run'. Kemp repeated what could only be described as a defence of the Aborigines to a commission of inquiry in 1820 as a way to explain their bitter attitude: 'the spirit of hostility and revenge that they still cherish for an act of unjustifiable violence formerly committed upon them'.

Now what puzzled me was why did Kemp, in every other respect an absolute and black-hearted rorter, spring to the defence of these Indigenous people, that is to say those who were understood to jeopardise the continued existence of his colony? Why was Kemp of all people suddenly imbued with Richard Rorty's 'imaginative ability to see strange people as fellow sufferers'?

In the end, the only way into Kemp's head—that is, into the contradictions—was through my own albeit unreliable imagination. Wrongly or rightly, I felt I was able to locate an explanation for his uncharacteristically sympathetic attitude in his original voyage to New South Wales thirty-five years before when, for seven months, he was shipmates on board the *Reliance* with the sick Aborigine, Bennelong.

The man who restored Bennelong to health was the *Reliance*'s surgeon, a six-foot Lincolnshire man named George Bass. Bennelong reciprocated by teaching the young surgeon his language, so that Bass was able to communicate with the Aborigines near Sydney. From his positive remarks about Tasmania's Aborigines, it is possible that Kemp, never willingly excluded from any conversation, also may have gossiped on the poop with Bennelong, or felt drawn to play bridge or cards with him, or to sit beside him carving buttons from a shark's skeleton. Crammed together for 206 days, it is not inconceivable that in conversations with Bennelong the so-called 'Father of Tasmania' learned, in Rorty's words, to re-evaluate his own capacity for cruelty and thereby redescribe himself.

How do we reconcile the disparity between the claim that no one was killed on that day in Colombia and a novelist's claim that 3000 were killed? Between the claim of one historian that three were killed near a rivulet in Tasmania and the oral tradition that 100 were killed? Instead of speculating on the motives of historians and storytellers, is it not more fruitful to imagine the experience of those involved at the scene, to resuscitate individual lives? In other words, history needs to forget just as much as fiction needs to remember, and in that intersection there should be ample space to build an open house—a monument, if you like—of competing narratives.

We know, by now, that the author of the *Hamlet* quote I was trying to check in the feeble light of a Buenos Aires drawing room is not necessarily the author we think he was. The Bard may have been one of any number of people—at the last count, 109—including, in Freud's opinion, a Frenchman called Jacques Pierre and also a nun called Anna Whately from Temple Grafton. As a novelist, I would like to end with an anecdote about one of the leading claimants supposed to have composed *Hamlet*, Francis Bacon. It illustrates, for me, the challenge that faces anyone who battles to reconstruct the past. It is a story the painter Balthus tells, of how Bacon gave up writing a history of mankind after he learnt that his account of a murder he had himself observed from his window deviated from the accounts of every other person who had witnessed it.

PART II

Memories of

Manhood

3 MONUMENTS OF MANHOOD AND COLONIAL DEPENDENCE: THE CULT OF ANZAC AS COMPENSATION

MARILYN LAKE

Every excess causes a defect and every defect an excess
Ralph Waldo Emerson, 'Compensation'

In his wonderful study of the stories about his mother's country in Ireland, *Remembering Ahanagran*, the American historian Richard White wrote:

> I once thought of my mother's stories as history. I thought memory was history. Then I became a historian, and after many years I have come to realize that only careless historians confuse memory and history. History is the enemy of memory. The two stalk each other across the fields of the past, claiming the same terrain.

In this ongoing contestation, history, White asserts, has special weapons in the documents and other materials the past has left behind. 'Few non-historians realize how many scraps a life leaves,' writes White. 'These scraps do not necessarily form a story in and of themselves, but they are always calling stories into doubt, always challenging memories, always trailing off into forgotten places.'[1]

White is not alone among historians in his suspicion of the claims of memory. In Australia, Bain Attwood and John Murphy have also attacked 'memory' in the name of the greater authority and interpretive power of 'history'.[2] As Paula Hamilton has observed, 'history and memory are ... assumed by and large to be in opposition, the battle lines firmly drawn', but prefers herself to emphasise 'an essential interdependence between memory and history'.[3] In thinking about 'Monuments of Manhood' I, too, would question the conceptual opposition drawn between memory and history, not least because it occludes understanding of that powerful compound form, historical memory.[4]

In his history of the federal movement in Australia, *The Sentimental Nation*, John Hirst offers a novel dedication: 'to the 422,788 Yes voters who have no other memorial'.[5] Absences can be illuminating. For we might also note that there are no memorials to the achievements of the political leaders who championed the federal cause: men such as Tasmanian Attorney-General and Supreme Court judge Andrew Inglis Clark, author of the first draft of the Australian constitution and ardent republican; and Victorians Alfred Deakin, the movement's most eloquent intellectual, and H. B. Higgins, a chief theorist of White Australia and the necessity of a living wage for workers.

We have no equivalents of the American monuments to political achievement—the Washington Monument, the Jefferson Memorial and the Lincoln Memorial that grace the US capital—not in Melbourne, our first national capital, nor in

Canberra, our permanent capital. Nor do we have the equivalent of the numerous Cuban memorials that honour that champion of national independence, and heroic contemporary of Alfred Deakin, José Marti. Furthermore there are no national sites in Australia commemorating the conventions and meetings that led to Federation, as the meeting halls and state houses of Boston and Philadelphia proudly mark the declaration of independence. John Hirst's dedication alerts us to an interesting national and emotional absence that is larger, I think, and more significant than he recognises.

What this nation does have, of course, is a superabundance of war memorials—as Ken Inglis has shown in his fine study *Sacred Places*, our landscape has been 'transformed' by war memorials, small and large, local and national, statues of diggers in the hundreds, obelisks, cairns and cenotaphs—he estimated some 5000 in all.[6] And they are expanding and proliferating. The cult of Anzac has been naturalised in Australia, but to a newcomer, or critical observer, the monumental honoring of war service might look excessive. Countries that suffered much higher losses in World War I, such as Britain itself, don't have nearly the number of war memorials.

It seems to me that the absence identified by John Hirst and the omnipresence documented by Ken Inglis are conceptually and historically related, and might be better understood if we recognise that the purpose of monuments was to memorialise heroic manhood in its many and changing guises —men in their capacities as governors, explorers, aviators, churchmen, sportsmen and as soldiers.[7] As C. E. W. Bean first argued with regard to the military defeat that was Gallipoli, the Anzacs' achievement was in proving 'the mettle of the men themselves'. World War I, he declared, was a vindication of Australian manhood.[8] Which prompts the question: why did Australian manhood have to be vindicated?

The clue lies in the absence of monumental honoring of the 'federal fathers', who failed to secure the heroic goal of

Australian independence. Far from achieving a manly political independence and democratic sovereignty, Federation consolidated Australia's colonial dependence on Britain. As Deakin and others were made painfully aware in the decade following 1901, when they discovered the real limits of Australian self-government, they were locked indefinitely into a demeaning and emasculating identity as colonials.

In 1908, for example, the Colonial Office expressed its exasperation with Deakin's failure to acknowledge the impropriety of issuing an invitation to US President Theodore Roosevelt without first seeking British permission. 'I should be disposed to ignore Mr Deakin,' sniffed Francis Hopwood. Lord Elgin could only agree: 'It is useless to explain to Mr Deakin'.[9] The insubordination of the colonials was a continuing source of vexation to their British rulers in the years before World War I, but they had to exercise forbearance in their public response, because the example of the American declaration of independence loomed large in British and Australian historical memory.

In his invitation to the American Naval Fleet to visit Australia, sent via the American Consul-General in Sydney, Deakin had been 'effusive' (as the Colonial Office sourly noted) in his description of the similarities between Australia and the United States: 'No other Federation in the world possesses so many features of likeness to that of the United States as does the Commonwealth of Australia and I doubt whether any two peoples could be found who are in nearer touch with each other, and are likely to benefit more by anything that tends to knit their relations more closely'.[10]

The United States was the first post-colonial nation and its example of republican independence was always before the Australians. Even the Central and South Americans—even Haiti—had followed the United States in establishing republics. Charles Henry Pearson, mentor of Deakin and Higgins and author of an article on Haiti significantly entitled 'The Black Republic', warned his friend, the Liberal politician and historian James Bryce, in 1892 that if the British tried to impose their authority on the Australians in matters that were important to them—such as tariffs, coloured labour and Chinese immigration—'it would result in a declaration of Australian Independence within five years'.[11] Pearson urged Bryce and the British to do everything necessary to avoid this outcome. They should, moreover, give due consideration to the value of Australia in a future European war: 'We have a larger male population in proportion to raw numbers than any European state ... I think we should raise 100,000 in the event of a European war'.[12]

The example of the 'great republic of the west' shaped federal thinking in the 1890s. James Bryce's *The American Commonwealth*, first published in 1888, and in an expanded version in 1893, was especially influential among the federal convention delegates—their 'bible', according to J. A. LaNauze and, following him, John Hirst.[13] Perhaps the greatest champion of the American example was Andrew Inglis Clark, friend of US Supreme Court judge Oliver Wendell Holmes and probably Australia's leading authority on American law, politics and history. At the time of the 1897 federal convention he was away, off on a second visit to the east coast of the United States, armed with a letter of introduction from the American Consul in Sydney, George Bell, which confirmed to all who might meet him that Clark was, indeed, 'a great admirer of the splendid manhood of our dear America'.[14]

Hirst notes in *A Sentimental Nation* that Clark's first trip overseas in 1890 became a pilgrimage to the United States, 'the home of liberty', and to Italy, which had been united by 'dashing and passionate patriots'.[15] Clark wrote poems and essays extolling democracy and popular sovereignty, and ended his essay 'Why I am a Democrat' by calling up the 'long line of heroes before our eyes' and quoting the words of Longfellow regarding America as the symbol of Democracy: 'Sail on, O Union strong and great!'[16]

In 1901, the year of Australian federation and the assassination of US President McKinley, which led to vice-president Theodore Roosevelt assuming presidential office, Clark wrote wistfully to Wendell Holmes, who had recently returned from a trip to England:

> I suppose that you had a good time in England. I often wish that Australia was as near to California as Massachusetts is to England. I should then see Boston every three or four years, and would probably be preparing now for a journey there early next year. But I must bow to the geographical configuration of the earth and all its consequences and wait in patience until my time to cross the Pacific Ocean again arrives.[17]

Within seven years, the American Fleet would be crossing the Pacific Ocean to visit Melbourne and Sydney in response to the very cordial invitation of Prime Minister Deakin.

Roosevelt reciprocated Deakin's warm regard. The great exponent of 'The Strenuous Life', he admired the 'vigour' of the new white Commonwealth of Australia, as he confided in a letter to his friend, the English diplomat Cecil Arthur Spring Rice.[18] For both Deakin and Roosevelt, the manly virtues were essential to personal and national character. In his autobiography, Roosevelt recalled with great pleasure the reception accorded by Australians to the American Fleet:

> It was not originally my intention that the fleet should visit Australia, but the Australian Government sent a most cordial invitation, which I gladly accepted; for I have, as every American ought to have, a hearty admiration for, and fellow feeling with, Australia ... The reception accorded the fleet in Australia was wonderful, and it showed the fundamental continuity of feeling between ourselves and the great commonwealth of the South

Seas. The considerate, generous, and open-handed hospitality with which the entire Australian people treated our officers and men could not have been surpassed had they been our own countrymen.[19]

Deakin followed up the success of the visit with a further invitation to Roosevelt to visit Australia at the end of his term as president in his private capacity—as a man—but the prospect of a safari in Kenya, discussed by Iain McCalman in the next chapter, proved rather more alluring. The British were again furious with Deakin's invitation to Roosevelt. Charles Lucas considered it 'a most objectionable message and I cannot help thinking meant to be unpalatable to us'.[20] In his invitation, Deakin had praised Roosevelt's world leadership, which would bring lasting benefit to his 'fellow citizens of the United States and of all self-governing people especially this new Commonwealth of Australia'.[21] Deakin never wasted an opportunity to remind the British that the Australians enjoyed the manly prerogative of self-government.

Deakin had encountered his first example of American men on their home territory in 1885 in San Francisco, where he had gone to investigate the Californian experiment in irrigation. He was chiefly impressed by their 'quiet assurance'. 'The men dress well & nearly all shave', observed the bearded young Australian. Their 'chief distinguishing feature was brightness of eye & quiet assurance which seem to say American'.[22]

Deakin's mentor at the University of Melbourne, Charles Pearson, had himself been lured to the United States in 1868, drawn in particular to the company of the intellectuals and poets of New England: Emerson, Agissiz, Longfellow, Lowell, Wendell Holmes, Wendell Phillips and Charles Eliot Norton. He travelled first to New York, where he met Godkin, editor of the influential journal *Nation*, who impressed him as 'a solid, sterling man, whom I liked very much'.[23] Many years later, Pearson recalled:

I did not stay long in New York, however, as I was generally advised to go on quickly to Boston. My ten days in Boston will always remain in my memory as among the pleasantest incidents of my life. Acland had told me that the society he met in Boston could not, he thought, be surpassed anywhere in the world and I had listened incredulously; but I am bound to say I came over to his opinion.[24]

That opinion, we can assume, was passed on to his protégés in the University of Melbourne Debating Club, Deakin and Higgins. Pearson met Longfellow ('I only remember his sweet amiable features and patriarchal grace'), Wendell Holmes senior —'a cheery, genial, frank little man, beaming with vivacity, the very picture of his books'—and enigmatic, self-reliant Emerson, who impressed him 'very strongly': 'His manner was quiet and kind, & seemed to cover an infinitude of silent thought under habitual reserve'.[25]

James Russell Lowell, on the other hand, gave Pearson 'the impression of a certain unfriendliness to Englishmen', under-standable, in Pearson's view: 'Any American might well be excused for some disgust towards the mother country after the conduct of our wealthy classes during the Civil War'. They compared notes about national types of manhood: 'He talked to me about the Maine lumbermen, whose delight it was to drift over the rapids seated astride pieces of timber, in constant peril of death, for the mere excitement of a plunge'.[26]

Pearson travelled across the country, sometimes armed with a rifle to ward off wild Indians. Like Roosevelt, who would later write a long, admiring review of his book *National Life and Character*, Pearson admired the manly prowess of rail-way workers. Reporting on his train trip to Cheyenne, he remarked that 'the navvies employed in making this line were the finest set of men I ever saw'.[27] ('Have you ever thought', Roosevelt would later write to Pearson, 'that there are certain modern trades which entail the exercise of the manlier virtues to a degree that hardly any trade ever did formerly? [virtues such as] hardihood, daring, self-reliance ... physical strength and endurance'. Such trades were well represented in railroad work and prepared one well, according to Roosevelt, for military work.[28]

During his American trip, Pearson formed an enduring friendship with Charles Eliot Norton, Professor of Fine Arts at Harvard. 'In Norton,' he recalled, 'as afterwards in Judge Force of Illinois, I found that peculiar refinement & scholarly taste which we are apt to associate in England with the intellectual side of aristocratic society mellowed by centuries and traditions. What made it more charming in Norton was his thorough sympathy with the primitive habits of a New England village, and with the democratic tone of American institutions.' It was that democratic tone that was missing in Britain. 'A well-bred American', Pearson concluded, 'is generally pleasanter than a well-bred Englishman. The American has less stiffness of manner, and, I think, more good-nature.'[29]

When Deakin travelled to the United States in 1885 his task, as a member of the Victorian Legislative Assembly, was to investigate irrigation. He was just thirty years of age and his letters home provide an engaging account of his impressions of foreign places and peoples—in Hawaii, California and Mexico, where, with the aid of water, 'the desert has been made to blossom like the rose'.[30]

Deakin's identification with the manly aspirations of Americans was poignantly evident in his account of this trip, when he could not help but make meaning of what he saw in a comparative frame. He compared San Francisco with Melbourne, Walden Pond with Albert Park Lake, and Broadway with Collins Street. In San Francisco, he was impressed by the extensive use of timber for residential building: 'This is a great city ... Most private residences are of wood at least two storeys & often charming ... richly decorated within & without. We have no idea in Melbourne what wood is capable of ... San

Francisco as a city seems busier & brighter than Melbourne.'
Indians encountered in Arizona were 'rough fellows but of a
fine manly type'.[31]

New York made him realise what a great city truly was: he
realised how 'small a unit' he was and 'with what small ideas of
a great city'. He walked down Broadway, 'every inch of it finer
than the finest part of Collins Street'. Brooklyn Bridge was the
greatest achievement of modern engineering: 'a marvellous &
beautiful bridge & there is nothing in the world like it'. New
York had 'Bigger banks, bigger offices & bigger shops by far
than in Melbourne'.[32] But his real destination, like Pearson's,
was Boston and he hurried there from New York.

Just as today's historically minded young Australians make
their pilgrimage to Gallipoli or the Somme or the Kokoda
Trail—now the pre-eminent sites of Australian historical
memory—so Deakin, like Pearson and Clark, made his 'pilgrimage' to New England, especially to Boston and to Concord,
the country of Emerson and site of the battlegrounds of the
Revolutionary War.

On 4 March 1885, Deakin recorded: 'Woke up at 6am
in Boston hurriedly obtaining direction to Concord the main
end of my visit'. Unfortunately, in his haste, he took the train
to the wrong Concord (ending up in New Hampshire): 'Only
the thought of Emerson enabled me to bear up against this
blow'. The next day, he rose again at 6 a.m. and went out
before breakfast to 'the Bunker Hill Monument, which records
the British Victory that became a defeat by its lessons. Saw the
Harbor into which the tea was thrown, thus precipitating
the Revolution.' After breakfast, he travelled to Lexington, 'the
little town thro' wh. the dispirited British soldiers retired from
their first encounter with the Provincials who harrassed them
in their retreat so that they lost 300 men. Then came Walden
Pond little larger apparently than Albert Park lagoon, a little
deeper, but rendered pretty by hoary hills & cliffs & broken
stones.'[33] There were no hoary hills in South Melbourne.

Deakin found the right train to Concord: 'I was the only passenger to alight from a nearly empty train tho' it seemed to me that there ought to be a daily pilgrimage to the tomb of Emerson'.[34] The American writer was Deakin's intellectual hero: 'his was the most important prose of the century', he had written in his notebooks.[35] Emerson's essay on 'The American Scholar', hailed by his biographer Oliver Wendell Holmes senior as an 'intellectual declaration of independence', was read as the New World's nationalist manifesto: 'Our day of dependence, our long apprenticeship to the learning from other lands, draws to a close'.

In his recent study of Emerson, Lawrence Buell emphasises Emerson's transnational appeal: in Britain, Carlyle hailed his 'man's voice', while George Eliot declared him 'the first man I have ever seen'. In South Africa, Olive Schreiner said that Emerson's works 'were just like a bible to me'. Emerson's doctrine of 'Self-Reliance'—'the best single key to his thought and influence', in Buell's estimation—was read as having spiritual, mental and political implications.[36]

At Sleepy Hollow cemetery, Deakin finally found the great man's grave, in which he had been buried just three years before: 'Between two pines there is only a long green mound & underneath that green mound lies all that was mortal of Emerson—a little to the right along the same ridge lies Hawthorne—a little half moonstone at the head and foot. On the same narrow slope lies Thoreau'. The scene from Emerson's grave was 'a pretty piece of woodland friendly in feature, cold & wild perhaps but with the wildness that has been tamed by man'. The scene was implanted in Deakin's memory: 'I shall see it long'.[37]

Deakin then drove on to Hawthorne's Old Manse and stood 'on the spot where the first shot was fired in the war of Revolution—here by the low fence which surrounds the old Manse about 3 ft high is the grave of the two nameless English soldiers who fell at the first fight'.[38] There was a monument where the British had stood and another of a farmer with Emerson's lines upon it:

> *Here the embattled farmers stood*
> *And fired the shot heard round the world.*

Deakin wandered some more in the cemeteries before taking the train back to Boston.

The next day he 'hurried to Faneuil Hall in which so many great speeches have been made. It is only the size of the Atheneum squared and has some old paintings in it.' Then to the State House, 'where the governor presided in the old colonial days' and he 'saw the windows from which the Declaration of American Independence was read'. Walking his own Freedom Trail, he found Christchurch, the oldest church in the city, from whose steeple Paul Revere hung his warning light the night the soldiers marched to Concord, and then the old Smith Street Chapel, where many popular meetings were held during the struggle and where the English stabled their horses while occupying Boston. Then on to Boston Common to 'the Liberty Tree under whose boughs the revolutionists used to meet'. Boston was 'altogether a very fine and remarkably interesting city', he concluded, 'of many historic memories'.[39]

These were the 'historic memories' that shaped Deakin's political identifications and those of contemporaries such as Clark and Higgins, memories that haunted the 'federal fathers' even as they turned their backs on republican manhood and settled into the stifling imperial embrace. In Deakin's subsequent clashes with the imperial government, he came to lament the limited and demeaning nature of Australian self-government post-Federation. So many aspects of the relationship were unsatisfactory. The Colonial Office didn't consult the federal government. Australia lacked the capacity for self-defence. It wanted its own navy. What was at issue, according to Deakin, was: 'self-respect, self-esteem, self-assertion, whatever name is given to it, a sentiment of the duty of self-defence strong already, is growing stronger'. Whereas Britain was a European power, preoccupied with German manoeuvres in the North Sea, Australia's future was tied up with developments in the Pacific. But when Britain declared war in 1914, as a result of conflict in the Balkans, and a terrible conflagration ensued, Australia also found itself at war in Europe.

Could—would—young Australian men pass the test of manhood? Would Australian manhood be vindicated? In the event, some 60 000 young Australian men would die fighting for Britain, thousands of miles from home, on European battle-fields. Australian sons were doomed to prove their manhood by fighting for British imperial power, not, as the Americans did, in struggle against it. The psychological cost of Australia's continuing condition of colonial dependency was—and remains—high.

Henry Bournes Higgins had strongly opposed Australia's decision to send more troops to fight for Britain in South Africa in 1902: why should Australia join Britain in subjugating two Boer republics, in killing every Boer who refused to submit to British tyranny, he asked in federal parliament. 'The position was the same in regard to the war against the colonies which afterwards became the United States of America. It was the same way with the Opium War against China.' Should Australia blindly submit to imperial power? Higgins continued:

Are we without going into the causes of the wars of Great Britain, to adopt the principle that we should actively side with Great Britain, no matter what is done? The adoption of such a course will commit Australia to the principle that she must aid the Imperial Government in all wars with her young lives—and there are few enough lives to spare in Australia—although she has no voice in the negotiations which precede war and is not to be consulted in regard to its expediency or necessity.[40]

The Prime Minister was setting a terrible precedent, he warned. Twelve years later it would be adhered to when Australia automatically followed Britain into war in Europe, a war that tragically took Higgins' own son's life: 'My grief has condemned me to hard labour for the rest of my life', he wrote in his diary, using an idiom of punishment, as Ken Inglis has noted, that hinted at guilt as well as grief.[41]

Young Australians were exhorted to prove Australian manhood in 1914. The sons were called upon to make good the failure of the fathers. The proliferation of postwar monument building was, one could say, over-determined. The cult of Anzac became a cult of military sacrifice as historical memory recast colonial vassalage as national service. They went to fight for King and Empire, the war memorial in the small Tasmanian town of Cygnet reminds us. But in the revision of historical memory they fought for the nation. The Anzac emerged from the war, declared the nationalist journal *Lone Hand*, looking the 'most virile thing on earth'.[42] 'Every excess causes a defect', wrote Emerson in his essay on 'Compensation', 'every defect an excess'.

In Australia, war commemoration now dominates historical memory. Our history has been militarised and our military heritage grows more weighty by the week. Everywhere and every week, seemingly, we are incited to remembrance. New books relive old battles and reunite disbanded battalions, aged diggers are feted and accorded national burials, new monuments are built, and pilgrimages to war graves are advertised in the daily press. Remembrance Day has gained momentum and now vies with Anzac Day for the attention of broadcasters and schoolchildren.

Historical memory is a powerful force in shaping personal and political identifications. As a critical practice, history is well placed to analyse its production. Using a military metaphor, Richard White has suggested that history can forge weapons from what memory has forgotten or suppressed. It can bring to our attention 'forgotten places'. In *Sacred Places*, Ken Inglis reminds us that there used to be a spirit of critical questioning with regard to war in Australia. In 1959, Alan Seymour caused controversy with his subversive play *The One Day of the Year*. In 1964, University of Sydney students tied a clothesline, hung with women's underwear, between the soldier and sailor on the cenotaph in Martin Place. Inglis comments that there was no political message here, but the Returned Servicemen's League knew better and denounced the 'intolerable desecration'.[43]

On Anzac Day in 1966, some twenty women wearing SOS (Save Our Sons) sashes gathered at the Shrine of Remembrance in Melbourne to lay posies inscribed 'Honour the dead with peace' and resisted male efforts to move them on. In 1968 an Anzac Day anti-war protest in Adelaide carried a placard with the injunction: 'Lest we forget the Vietnamese'.[44] And so on, but no more. Historians have now enrolled in the pilgrimages as guides and interpreters and joined the publishing bonanza that is war commemoration. For the time being at least, it would seem that history—as a critical practice—has been disarmed.

4   TEDDY ROOSEVELT'S TROPHY: HISTORY AND NOSTALGIA

IAIN McCALMAN

At the end of every Christmas dinner during my boyhood in Central Africa my mother used to bring out from the sideboard what she called *bon bon* dishes containing lollies and nuts. These dishes, beautiful in their way, looked to be made of lacquered tortoiseshell with silver rims and silver ball feet. But their special status in the family had nothing to do with aesthetics. Scratched crudely on their honey-coloured sides were the initials 'LJT from TR', and they were actually the toenails of the first bull elephant shot by ex-President Theodore Roosevelt on his famous Kenya safari of 1909–10. He had given them as a commemorative trophy to my Australian great-uncle Leslie Jefferies Tarlton in gratitude for organising and leading the safari.

I like to think that as soon as my sister and I learnt that these delicate *objets d'art* had been hacked from a stately wild elephant they became grotesque in our eyes, but this would be to read back from later adult perspectives. In fact, for some

Figure 4.1: *'LJT from TR': Bull Elephant toenails.*[1]

years after our migration to Australia in the mid-1960s the
dishes were magnets for multiple secret nostalgias—they reminded my father of his Kenyan boyhood, my mother of
being a white *Dona* in the Central African Raj, and my sister
and me of African Christmases past.

I have chosen the dishes for my meditation on history and
nostalgia because they are clearly icons of imperial memory
and commemoration. The toenails, along with several other
relics from Roosevelt—a twelve-bore shotgun and an air-rifle
—were passed on to my father by his maternal uncle Captain
Eliot Tarlton, who was born in Launceston, Tasmania, around
1889. The Australian family patriarch, Robert Tarlton, a successful South Australian banker, politician and grazier, had
moved his large family to Tasmania that year hoping the
climate would improve his eldest son's tuberculosis. In fact,
young Tatham's condition worsened, leading him to try the
famed dry air of the Transvaal Highlands, which was thought
to be conducive to bronchial healing. The migration to South
Africa of Robert Tarlton's two eldest sons, combined with
news of the Rand gold seams, convinced him to shift the
entire family to South Africa in 1894.[2]

Tatham died within the year but the three remaining older sons, who had learnt to ride and shoot on the rugged family property at Emu Plain near the Gawler Ranges, fought in the Boer War with the South Australia Mounted Rifles. Afterwards, Leslie, his brother Henry and an Adelaide friend, Victor Newland, joined a straggling band of Australian and British ex-soldiers who trekked to British and German East Africa in search of fortune. Some of these adventurers purchased tracts of bushland or were allotted soldier-settlements in the British East African Highlands, but the less successful began hiring themselves as professional guides for foreign sportsmen attracted by the abundance and exoticism of East African game.

Small, wiry, red-headed Leslie Tarlton arrived in the village of Nairobi in 1903 when it was hardly more than a few tin shacks, but he quickly sensed the potential of the safari industry. The following year he, brother Henry and their mate Vic pieced together a capital sum of two hundred pounds. They signed up the half-dozen hunters of the district, erected a sign 'Newland and Tarlton Safari Outfitters' over a tin shed, and dispatched a well-connected Englishman to trawl for custom in the club-lands of London's West End. Newland and Tarlton, known as 'N and T', was the first business of its kind in Africa and probably the most successful ever.[3]

Running safaris from remote Nairobi was a complex business: Victor Newland managed the finances and Leslie Tarlton, the logistics. Each client required thirty porters carrying a sixty-pound load of supplies for a safari that could last between three months and a year. They needed tents, guns, ammunition, medicines, mosquito nets, preserving equipment, portable beds, baths and chairs, food, water and, of course, bottles of champagne—which apparently fared better on the swaying heads of bearers than ordinary wine. The safari would march out of Nairobi in a serpentine column of porters and gun-bearers, all wearing blue uniforms embroidered with the red initials 'N and T'. For comfort, most porters carried their boots strung emblematically around their necks. As the small white community applauded through a haze of gin from the *stoep* of the Stanley Hotel, *kudu* horns sounded, the safari clown chanted a marching song and *askaris* shouldered arms to prevent last-minute desertions. Clients, immaculately clothed in bush jackets by a local Asian tailor, mounted their mules or ponies, knowing that their comfort and safety for the next months rested entirely on the vigilance and shooting skill of a professional white hunter.[4]

Leslie Tarlton frequently served in the latter capacity himself. The US photographer Carl Akeley's famous hunting memoir, *In Brightest Africa* (1927), claimed that Leslie was 'one of the best rifle shots of all time'.[5] He was also a fine horseman, able to round up a hundred ostriches careering at speed across the savannah—perhaps growing up on Emu Plain had given him practice. He helped perfect the local hunting speciality known as 'riding lion': this entailed chasing lion through the long grass on horseback until the animal turned at bay, usually at a distance of around thirty-five yards. The horseman then dismounted and shot the beast as it charged at over forty miles per hour.[6] Needless to say it was a hazardous business: Leslie was twice mauled, and several of his stable of white hunters were ultimately killed.

It is difficult to tell from Leslie's matter-of-fact letters how conscious he was of operating a white nostalgia business, but that is what it was. Even the term 'white hunter', with its half-comical overtones of race and the Raj, sounds uncomfortably archaic today, though it actually originated from wordplay on the name of a Scottish-born hunter, Alan Black, who had to be distinguished from a black Somali hunter on the same payroll.[7] There is no doubt, though, that the colony of Kenya was a magnet for wistful white fantasies. Again and again, Theodore Roosevelt in *African Game Trails* describes it as a perfect site to become a 'white man's country'.[8] My father's near neighbour in Thika, Elspeth Huxley, used the same phrase without irony as the title for an influential book of 1935, in which she also called Kenya a literal fulfilment of 'Rider Haggard's dream'.[9]

Being on the equator at more than 5000 feet above sea level, Kenya's high country had a climate and picturesque beauty that made it unusually healthy and congenial for disease-susceptible whites. Rich volcanic soil, abundant water, a large potential workforce and, of course, a plethora of wildlife completed the appeal. Almost from its first European settlement in the 1890s, British East Africa became what today would be called an 'anachronistic enclave'.[10] Two nostalgic fantasies proved especially potent. To a small élite of Britons and Europeans, Kenya became a playground for re-enacting the pleasures of a fading aristocracy; and to a string of wealthy Americans, the savannahs promised a chance to live out the frontier romance of the vanishing Wild West.

Of the aristocrats who came to Kenya some had real blue-blood lineages, including the sporty Lord Cranworth who became a director of 'N and T'. Others were adventure-loving younger sons of minor noble twigs. Most, including the legendary Swede, Baron Blore Blixen-Finecke, and his wife, Karen, were desperately trying to escape the decline and fall of their kind. In Kenya, these aristocratic avatars could still afford large tracts of cheap land on which to run cattle or grow coffee. They could hunt the abundant game, drink the famous cocktails of the Mathaiga Club, and bet on the races at the East African Turf Club (where another Australian uncle, Henry Tarlton, was the only professional jockey). Wilder spirits, such as the novelist Evelyn Waugh on his several visits, could gravitate to the 'Happy Valley' set who lived the life of 'Bright Young Things' in a fever of drink, cocaine and fornication.[11] The lure of the white man's country extended even to British royalty. Leslie organised special safaris during the 1930s for both the philandering Prince of Wales, later Edward VIII, and his quieter brother the Duke of York, later George VI.[12] At its best this aristocratic Eldorado could produce the type of pastoral idyll made famous by Karen Blixen's *Out of Africa*,[13] but it could also be snobbish, philistine and deeply exploitative.

A now nearly forgotten nexus also existed between Kenya and the Wild West. It originated with the burly US millionaire William Northrop Macmillan who, after being shipwrecked exploring the Blue Nile gorge, bought a major landholding north of Nairobi in 1905.[14] His connections and stories soon drew Mid-Western rancher Edgar Beecher Bronson in search of pristine hunting country. Another wealthy family, the Kleins,[15] bought a farm near ours at Eldoret, and Al Klein joined 'N and T' as the first of several American-born white hunters. Even the Commissioner of Guaso Nyero had once been a Wyoming 'cow puncher'.[16] Soon the famous 'lunatic line' from Mombasa to Nairobi was chugging a stream of American adventurers to the doors of 'N and T'. Australian white hunter George Outram led the Ohio banker Kenyon Painter on the first of Painter's forty-one eventual safaris. Carl Akeley's 'Field Museum' safari of 1906 with Leslie Tarlton and R. J. Cunninghame produced a mauling from a leopard in Somaliland and the foundations of Akeley's later hunting memoir. Preacher–author W. S. Rainsford's safari of 1908 generated his influential *The Land of the Lion*, published the following year.[17]

These fervent hunting testimonials, including Wild West novelist Stewart Edward White's *The Land of Footprints* (1913), incited aspirant US adventurers to try ever more risky ways of testing their frontier manhood. In 1925 Leslie took the pioneer US archer and western writer Dr Sexton Pope on safari to hunt lion with his bow and arrow, some from as close as twelve yards. He killed seven, though Leslie forbade him to shoot at buffalo, elephant and rhino for fear of merely wounding the animals. One of Pope's cast-off yew bows, nicknamed 'Shenzi'—Swahili for 'useless'—was for years mounted on the back *stoep* of our family farm.[18] No species restriction was placed on Colonel Charles 'Buffalo' Jones, Zane

Grey's legendary 'Last Plainsman', who brought over a squad of trained Texas horses and lasso experts to round up hippo, lion and rhino, which he then paraded through the streets of Nairobi.[19]

The ideological ground was already well prepared for Theodore Roosevelt when he decided to mount a major Kenyan safari at the completion of his second term of office in 1909. By this time Roosevelt was suffering acute nostalgia for the vanishing landscapes and values of the Wild West. His political and personal identity had been built on a frontier mythos: he was Teddy Roosevelt, buckskin bear-hunter, rancher of the South Dakota badlands, and horseback colonel who had led a band of 'Rough Riders' on dare-devil charges in the Spanish–American War. During the 1890s he had issued scores of works advocating the values of muscular and civilised American manhood, an ideal supposedly forged in the dusty crucible of the West and destined to spread throughout the world at the expense of weak or barbaric peoples.[20]

Roosevelt knew that the raw Wild West had by 1909 become a mirage: railroads and cities had devoured the plains; red-eyed Texas Longhorns had become placid Herefords; Indians had been shunted onto reservations; and Buffalo Bill was a circus entertainer.[21] Roosevelt, typically, had taken action to halt the trend. Memories of his boyhood nature-collecting and excited reading of Mayne Reid's buffalo-hunting romances underlay his adoption of a vigorous conservation program. By 1909 he had started a national forest system, passed a National Monuments Act, established sixteen national parks and monuments including Yellowstone and the Grand Canyon, and created fifty-one bird reservations.[22] Evidently, though, the conservationist-minded Dr Jekyll in him still longed to become the predatory Mr Hyde for one last time.

Roosevelt's dream of hunting in Africa started early in life when he was intoxicated by Rider Haggard's epic stories about the ice-cool white hunter Alan Quartermaine, hero of

Figure 4.2: *Leslie Tarlton with President Teddy Roosevelt, Kenya, 1909.*[23]

King Solomon's Mines. Years later the President invited both Rider Haggard and his real-life inspiration for Quartermaine, Frederick Courtney Selous, to the White House. Selous, a legendary South African explorer and naturalist, became the President's intimate friend, and the Roosevelt children were raised on nightly readings from his *African Nature Notes*. Another White House invitee, Carl Akeley, fed Roosevelt's cowboy fantasies with tales of Leslie Tarlton's galloping hunts, and of Kenya's Dodge City, Nairobi, where drunks and lions shambled up the dusty streets.[24]

Roosevelt prepared for the safari by a painstaking course of reading and consultation. He pored over gun catalogues and supplemented his custom-made Springfield .38 and western classic .405 Winchester with hand-tailored heavy-gauge rifles and shotguns from the British gunsmiths Holland and Holland, each fitted with special telescopic sights to cope with his poor vision. His double-barrelled Holland 450–500 elephant gun could stop a small tank.[25] He also steeped himself in works on East African flora and fauna, using his reputation as a naturalist to persuade the Smithsonian Institution in Washington to fund the safari as a scientific expedition. The remainder of an estimated half-million dollars came from Roosevelt's billionaire friend Andrew Carnegie and from advances on the books and stories that the ex-President agreed to write.[26]

Outfitting the massive year-long expedition turned 'N and T' into one of the largest private businesses in Africa. The safari was an East African microcosm: Goanese cooks, Afghan camel-drivers, Arab guides, Somali gunbearers and *askaris*, Wakamba trackers and skinners, Australian and British-born white hunters, and 500 Wanyumwezi, Luo, Kavirondo, Kikuyu and Swahili *pagazi* or porters.[27] The single-file line extended for a full mile, carrying, among other things, Roosevelt's sixty favourite books and quantities of Boston beans and American gingersnaps. Each evening the 'stars and stripes' fluttered from Roosevelt's tent. 'Bwana King ya Amerik' was in a state of mystical rapture. The native bearers seemed to him to have come, childlike, straight from the bowels of the Pleistocene age.[28] The landscape reminded him of the great plains and the foothills of the Rockies, and he equated the settlers—whether American, English, Afrikaans or Australian—directly with the manly type of the American West. Sometimes he felt himself transported back thirty years to the habitats of his youth, sometimes seventy years to the time of Western buffalo hunters and African explorers armed only with muzzle-loaders.[29] Still more exhilarating was to be taken to the Lado enclave, East Africa's equivalent of the badlands, where freelance hunters gathered to poach ivory across the borders of Somaliland and the Congo. Roosevelt was thrilled by the rough masculine camaraderie of this 'hard-bit set'; they in turn respected his courage, though were bemused by his refusal to drink.[30]

Roosevelt's famous later account, *African Game Trails*, fails, however, to reveal the gap that sometimes yawned between these heroic fantasies and the realities of the safari business. Equating himself with manly predecessors such as the hunters Chapman and Buxton, he omits to mention women such as Mary Kingsley and Agnes and Cecily Herbert, who had undertaken far more dangerous hunts on foot without professional guides.[31] In Roosevelt's case, moreover, the professionals had to ensure that a slow, overweight man with poor eyesight, riding a dumpy little pony, could bag his share of trophies without enduring too much hardship or risk. The task was complicated by Roosevelt's habit of opening fire on game he could scarcely see, at distances of 300 to 600 yards, when most professional hunters regarded 100 yards as excessive. Frequently his bullets fell short or merely wounded game, and he compensated for poor shooting by pouring fusillades of bullets into his targets. Underlying strains of jealousy and melancholy in *African Game Trails* hint at his insecurity about living up to the sporting standards of the men he so admired.[32] He was thrilled when Swahili porters addressed him as 'Bwana Mkubwa', or Great Master, but he omitted to mention their usual nickname for him of 'Bwana Tumbo' or 'Mr Big Belly'. His son, the unfortunately named Kermit, fared no better: he was given the unflattering nickname of 'Bwana Maridari' or 'Mr Fancy-Pants'.[33]

In *African Game Trails* Roosevelt had also to reconcile the primitive urge to gather trophies with his countervailing ethic of conservation. Like most white hunters at the time, he justified his carnage on the grounds of the abundance of wildlife in East Africa and of the nuisance value that animals such as lion posed to the white civilising mission. By the end of the safari he and Kermit had, between them, killed 512 animals from more than eighty species, a tally, which—Roosevelt later claimed in his own defence—was relatively modest compared with some safaris. Maybe so; but at a time when the white rhino was on the verge of extinction and Roosevelt explicitly called for its protection, he and Kermit managed to kill nine, including two pregnant cows. They also wounded a further two calves.[34] Though Roosevelt glossed over this sorry incident, he did admit in later writings that the East African safari business would eventually have to shift from hunting or witness the same decline in wildlife as the United States.

The contradictions of Roosevelt's position were transmitted directly to succeeding generations of white hunters. On the one hand, the safari's vast publicity stimulated a new wave of Western-style hunter-adventurers, including Mississippi coal baron Paul J. Rainey with his lethal pack of lion-hunting dogs, and the colt-toting maverick Charles Cottar, whose safari company survives to this day.[35] Roosevelt's visit also stamped a Western cowboy imprint on the identity of many younger white Kenyan males. Yet, as the game grew scarcer, the Tarlton brothers and others in the business began increasingly to share Roosevelt's concern. When Leslie Tarlton stayed at the Roosevelt ranch in July 1910, he was proudly shown US nature reserves.[36] With his hunting lust satiated, Roosevelt's concern to preserve vanishing places and values grew. He mused that as one prepared to face life's 'rifle-pits', the urge to recapture childhood habitats overrode even the primal need to hunt.[37]

Like those two great imperial pundits Kipling and Rider Haggard, the Tarltons also had their values shaken by the death of relatives in World War I. Leslie's nephew Lionel Tarlton, aged eighteen, was killed at Longido in the opening battle of East Africa against the Germans, and his Tasmanian-born younger brother, Eliot, had his leg shattered in the campaign soon after. Three years later, in 1919, the Tarlton brothers decided to dissolve 'N and T', although they encouraged Vic Newland to reconstitute it as a new company called Safariland Ltd. By the time Arthur Conan Doyle visited Kenya at the end of the 1920s, Henry Tarlton had turned his ranch at Ruaraka into a small game park,[38] and Leslie was campaigning strongly for safari companies to restrict their game quotas.

Of course, my father and many of his generation of Kenyans grew up in a culture in which the muscular frontier ethos of Roosevelt was still rampant. In the Kenya of the 1920s and 1930s, guns were as natural a part of life as shoes. The family farm in Solai still teemed with wild animals, and the McCalman boys were expected to shoot francolin, guinea fowl and reedbok for the pot. Dangerous snakes, such as puff-adders, king cobras and mambas, had often to be dispatched with a shotgun. My grandfather Alex McCalman, though always a reluctant hunter, was several times pressured by his labourers to kill rogue lion and elephant on the farm.[39] Shooting an elephant, as George Orwell argued in his brilliant essay of that title, was part of the warped obligation that accompanied being a white Sahib or Bwana.[40] My father, David McCalman, grew up hearing his uncle's stories and, like most male children of Empire, he read Kipling, Haggard and that bestselling US creation of the early twentieth century, *Tarzan of the Apes* by Edgar Rice Burroughs.

Clarence E. Mulford, former Western cowboy turned pulp fiction writer, also gave new zest to Western nostalgia during the 1920s and 1930s by inventing the grittily realistic sage-brush sagas of Hopalong Cassidy and the Bar 20 ranch. He inspired young males as geographically dispersed as David McCalman in Solai and Robin Wallace-Crabbe in Melbourne.[41] My father's cowboy fantasies were, however, easier to enact than Wallace-Crabbe's, who had to wait until much later in life to become a Braidwood rancher. Young McCalman carved and fitted ivory stocks to his Colt .22 Police Positive revolver, and, as a vet assistant at Kabete, had to lasso cattle from his Harley Davidson and to ride headlong across the veldt shooting at marauding hyenas.[42]

Yet for this generation of Kenyans the nostalgic hunting dream underwent a decisive shift from seeking corporal to photographic trophies. In December 1928 David McCalman's two prizes at Kenton College in Kijabe comprised a book called *Heroes of Modern Adventure* filled with stories of 'Buffalo Bill's days' and *Photographing Wild Life across the World* by the legendary US game photographer Cherry Kearton.[43] In the same year, David saw a screening at Kenya's Natural History Museum of US film-maker Martin Johnson's wildlife documentary *Lake Paradise*, shot at nearby Lake Marsabit.[44] After this, game photography became his passion. During the later 1930s he and a friend, Freddie Pelling—later a celebrated game photographer—would travel each weekend to the rugged bushland around Tsavo and Amboselli to photograph game. Here's a typical extract from his diary for 17 December 1938:

> Left Kabete with Freddie in the Plymouth armed with some of my 50% proof, home made, Green Chartreuse. Still very sore where I fell from Boycey's Norton chasing hyenas on Thursday. At the usual place we hid our tracks … Saw 16 wild dogs chasing a lone Grant's Gazelle; scared them off with a shot from my

Figure 4.3: *Rhinoceros. Photographed by David McCalman, c. 1938.*[45]

Colt. 45 'Frontier'. Walking down to the waterhole two rhinos came out of the scrub unpleasantly close. Stood stock still til 'Auntie Mame' could see I was human (about 6 yards distant) … Freddie and I took pictures.[46]

Those of this generation who did stay in the professional hunting business, such as our cousin Alan Tarlton and David's friends Donald Ker and David Lunan, also turned increasingly to the representation rather than destruction of wildlife. Though there was still a steady trickle of macho clients like Ernest Hemingway who wanted to test themselves in combat against wild animals, Alan Tarlton and his colleagues preferred working with film stars Deborah Kerr, Clark Gable and Ava Gardner to provide wildlife settings for movies such as *King Solomon's Mines*, *The Snows of Kilimanjaro* and *Mogambo*.[47] When this market became satiated, many of the same hunters turned into game wardens, protecting the animals they had been licensed to kill. Alan Tarlton became a snake farmer, providing pythons for Hollywood movies and venom for medical uses.

From 1939, of course, David and his generation also displaced their urges for hunting and adventure into war. Roosevelt's old telescopic sight found its uses for him in the Kings African Rifles, fighting against the Italians in Ethiopia and the Japanese in Burma and Ceylon. And even after the war, the possibilities for manly adventure were not quite exhausted. As a district commissioner working for the British Civil Service from 1947 in the remote bush provinces of Nyasaland, David had to undertake regular safaris on foot to administer British law, collect taxes, dispense medicine, hunt rogue animals, build roads and bridges, and establish the country's first game park at Kasungu.[48] When I was one, he helped to rescue Laurens Van Der Post from Mulanje Mountain during that explorer's ill-fated *Venture into the Interior*;[49] when I was four, he was skirmishing with Mau Mau on the farm in Kenya; and, when I was ten, he came close to killing himself in a light plane crash outside Chileka in Nyasaland.[50]

When the British colonial service was officially wound up in Nyasaland at the beginning of 1964 it was probably a form of nostalgia that influenced David to take his family to Australia rather than to Britain or South Africa with most of his former colleagues. Thanks to Tarlton family legends, he had always thought of himself as part-Australian, and he was undeterred by dire warnings about the yellow peril from his Tasmanian uncle who had left the island at the age of nine. Naturally the elephant's toenails came with us to Melbourne to serve as repositories of a type of sacral family nostalgia, a condition of wistful yearning that has always been associated with migration or exile.

In fact, the word 'nostalgia' was originally coined from the Greek in 1688 by one Dr Johannes Hofer to describe the melancholic feelings exhibited by Swiss soldiers forced to campaign far from the Alpine valleys and tinkling cowbells of home. Hofer thought it a potentially lethal disease, a malady of the imagination transmitted into the brain and viscera through an inflammation of the nervous system.[51] By the end of the eighteenth century, doctors had added a string of other displaced peoples to the nostalgically stricken, including British sailors on Pacific voyages, European students at foreign universities, and African slaves ripped from their homelands. It was, perhaps, a measure of their respective attitudes to the mother country that most British convicts to Botany Bay and Van Diemen's Land adapted relatively quickly to their new homelands,[52] whereas numbers of their French counterparts in New Caledonia are said to have pined to death for the loss of Paris.

Initially at least, my parents proved surprisingly resistant to the nostalgic condition. They belonged to that stalwart breed of first-generation migrants determined to live in the present. Trotting out the toenails at Christmas dinners was done, for them, in a spirit more ironical than wistful. Though never completely able to stifle their pride in this strange family heir-loom, it was also viewed as half a joke, something faintly ridiculous like the whole British-African Raj. Yet nostalgia is difficult to escape. Modern analysts suggest that the condition has ballooned from a *maladie du pays* into a *mal du siècle*. Some now see it as the central cultural malaise of modern man. Once a form of *Heimweh* or homesickness confined to a few, it is now socially pervasive, nebulous and insatiable. It has come to connote a yearning for some real or imagined time and place in the past that is suffused in sentiment and purged of pain.[53] It is also, of course, very big business: tourist, heritage, adver-tising and popular culture industries of every stamp try to stimulate the gush of backward-looking sentiment that will mobilise people's credit cards.

Modern diagnosticians associate nostalgia with the secular-isation and acceleration of time that began in the West with the French Revolution and has now reached such breakneck pace that we long to halt it by conjuring up frozen idylls of the past.[54] A psychic disorder rather than a medical disease, it is seen to afflict those who have been subjected to dislocating social and cultural shock, leading to a loss of self-confidence, identity and sense of self-worth. Those caught in transitional phases of the life cycle are thought to be especially susceptible, particularly the aged when faced with social obsolescence.[55]

Most analysts, or at least those who haven't already crossed into this twilight world, condemn the condition. At best, it is seen as reprehensibly escapist and conservative, a retreat from engagement with present and future realities. At worst, it is a reactionary ideology based on myths of community, race and country, and deployed by xenophobic figures such as Osama bin Laden, George W. Bush and John Howard.[56]

There is much truth in these claims, but it is also important to distinguish among the modalities of nostalgia. It has potential for good as well as harm. Though we will probably all feel its siren call at some point, we are not bound to succumb blindly. Nostalgia's powerful energy can also be harnessed or displaced into the creation of history, art and constructive social policy. Without some variants of nostalgia our heritage and conservation movements would probably lose much of their drive. Without nostalgia, historians would certainly have a reduced audience. After all, nostalgia is a crude form of historical consciousness that at least fosters dialogues between the past and present.[57] Not every nostalgic sentiment need be simple-minded or anti-intellectual: we can, surely, analyse and question, rather than simply wallow in our longing.

Now in their eighties, my parents have eventually succumbed to wistfulness for their African past. I do not know whether it is because they have crossed a key age threshold or whether they can afford to glance back now they have integrated their children within Australia. Either way, they began around a decade ago to exhibit yearnings for the flora and fauna of Africa. Among other symptoms, they started to make annual pilgrimages to the nature reserves and game parks of East and Central Africa. No doubt there was an element of escapism in this: they were certainly not exploring the slums of Soweto. But I am impressed that they have also channelled their yearnings into creative action. For a start, they took up flower growing—in the case of my father, a form of horticultural combat, I guess; he was collecting Protea blooms rather than elephants' toenails. Both of them have become passionate proselytes for South African Protea, out of which they established a prize-winning ecological garden. Perhaps more symbolically, they also helped to develop a large public garden in the Dandenongs that integrated South African Protea with the kindred genus of Australian Banksias. Above all, my father undertook the Herculean endeavour of scanning a lifetime's worth of African and Australian photographs into digital form and writing a memoir for his grandchildren. Gerontologists dub this a process of 'Life Review', and it is surely one of the most fertile of nostalgia's symptoms.

There is a good reason, I suggest, that the idea of nostalgia not be dismissed automatically by professional historians. It is a complex phenomenon with potentially positive as well as negative intellectual and social valencies. Quite apart from the fact that we will all at one time or another experience its lure, many of our wider public constituency are attracted to history precisely because of its imbrication with nostalgia. It has been famously joked that nostalgia isn't what it used to be—that in itself is a topic worthy of our historical attention. For my part, I suppose I can thank Teddy's elephant toenails for alerting me both to the onset of a nostalgic condition and to a rich subject for future analysis.

PART III

Cultural Institutions as Custodians of Memory and Tradition

5 THE HERITAGE OF 'OLD ENGLAND'

Michael Bennett

'Old England is no more than like a pleasing dream; when I think of it, it appears to have no more existence than in my own imagination.' Thus wrote Elizabeth Marsden in the 1796, two years after her arrival in New South Wales.[1] For her as for most early colonists, bond and free, England would remain home. The bonds of sentiment would be maintained by letters from family and friends, and by the ever more regular arrival of news, books and other cultural artefacts from the other side of the world. Many immigrants brought in their baggage material to nourish memories. Few can have been so purposeful as John Glover who, in his mid-sixties and with fading eyesight, arrived in Hobart in 1831 loaded with sketches of English scenes to paint.[2]

It is not hard to find evidence of nostalgic reflection among the first generations of Anglo-Australians. What is less clear, and what seems to have been little addressed in historical scholarship, is their sense of heritage.[3] There is a tendency to assume that the English colonists were conscious of their roots, genealogical and local, and that their sense of Englishness was historically informed. The contrasts they drew between 'old' England and Australia suggest that they saw the mother country as an ancestral, tradition-bound land, steeped in memories and monuments. This chapter looks afresh at what the first Anglo-Australians might have known about their roots, and how far their sense of an identity was nourished by a sense of common heritage. A key point to stress at the outset is that the relationship of English people with their national past, like most other aspects of English life, underwent marked change in the course of the nineteenth century. The nature and direction of this change have recently been matters of much discussion and debate.[4] The idea of 'old England' can easily obscure the fact that for colonial Australia, England was as much—if not more—a source of novelty, whether of ideas, technology or fashion. Among the novelties, one might argue, were new forms of engagement with the past.[5]

The current passion for genealogy encourages the belief that the early colonists were equally knowledgeable about their forebears. The family historian today, in making some new discovery about his or her ancestry, is often inclined to attribute their former ignorance to deliberate suppression. The 'convict stain' and the scandals that sometimes precipitated immigration to the colonies doubtless aided and abetted amnesia.[6] Still, it needs to be stressed that family memories in England, at least outside the charmed circles of hereditary wealth and privilege, were as—if not more—tenuous. Indeed, it is probable that a higher percentage of Australians of Anglo-Celtic descent can name their nineteenth century forebears than their distant cousins in the British Isles.[7] As regards the early colonists, the likelihood is that few were able to do more than name their grandparents and outline their circumstances. Some of the free settlers, especially the scions of the gentry class, took pride in their lineage. Fane Edge, whose first name reflects his association with the English aristocracy, may have brought to Norfolk Island his set of silver tablespoons with the Fane coat-of-arms.[8] A more common heirloom was the family bible. In the nineteenth century it formed the basis for recording family lore, but surprisingly few inscriptions in family bibles appear to date much back beyond the immediate family of the immigrants.[9]

If many colonists kept in touch with family and friends, few retained strong regional loyalties. According to Alan Atkinson, 'men or women coming from the same counties or regions in England rarely sought each other out'.[10] Sophie Dumaresq in early New South Wales had a soft spot for a convict servant from Yorkshire who spoke the dialect 'charmingly',[11] but a fair number of convicts seem to have moved between regions even before transportation forced them to share their lives with people of geographically diverse backgrounds. It was noted in 1820 that the accent of the native Australian was made up from an amalgam of dialects.[12] Incorporating elements from a range of regional cultures, Anglo-Australian culture soon became surprisingly homogeneous.[13] In this sense it was national identity, especially English or British as distinct from Irish, that seems to have been most important. Still, it cannot be assumed that this identity was maintained by an especially rich or robust collective memory.

The English colony was divided legally, between convict, emancipist and free, socially, by class and education, and above all by religion. Protestantism, it is true, was the real cement of English and British identity.[14] The Church of England and the Scottish Kirk were major cultural institutions. In the practice of religion, with imported bibles, service books and vestments, and in the building of churches according to designs brought from Britain, and sometimes even incorporating into the fabric odd stones and tiles dispatched from 'mother churches', the early colonists seem most clearly to have sought to keep faith with their heritage. Still, the established churches were losing their dominance as cultural institutions on both sides of the world, and organised religion was by no means tradition-bound.

The evangelical revival, along with broader social and cultural changes, had made Protestantism inherently unstable, effervescent and fissiparous. Like the Catholics, the Protestants had a sense of common heritage dating back to the Reformation and Wars of Religion, but their sense of religious identity was congregational and personal, and was sustained by more recent memories of schism, denomination, awakening and conversion.

The English colonists doubtless had more in common than they were inclined to admit. There was the English language, and a whole set of cultural practices, assumptions and tastes. English culture in the early colonies was necessarily thin and improvised. In this world, as imaginatively re-created by Alan Atkinson, familiar animals of hearth and farm loomed disconcertingly large as reference-points in culture as well as reminders of home.[15] The free settlers and the unfree convicts were united by their longing for 'home' comforts such as tea, sugar and tobacco. Yet such tastes were exotic and relatively recently acquired.[16] English literature provided a stock of cultural allusion that almost certainly extended beyond the book-owning literate classes. The story of Robinson Crusoe, with his struggle to maintain his identity as an Englishman and a Christian on a desert island, had considerable resonance in the early settlement.[17] Still, the institutions that supported more complex forms of cultural exchange and transmission in colonial Australia—newspapers and novels, subscription libraries and literary societies, masonic lodges and mechanics' institutes—were not relics of old England, but relatively new features of a complex and dynamic consumer culture.[18] A similar point can be made about the Anglo-Australian embrace of the English heritage of the law and constitution. While the convicts, emancipists and free settlers proved assertive in stressing their rights as 'free-born Englishmen', their concerns, agenda and organisational strategies were generally shaped by their immediate circumstances and relatively recent political developments. Still, the legal and constitutional struggles that took place in the early colony, along with their Protestant loyalties and anti-Catholic prejudices, provide the best evidence of popular historical consciousness.[19]

Few of the early settlers, convict or free, can have had a firm grasp of English or British history. It is not simply that few of them had more than a perfunctory schooling. The fact was that there was no place for national history in the curriculum of elementary schools or, for that matter, in grammar schools and universities in Britain until the late nineteenth century. For most of the population, whether in England or colonial Australia, history could have been no more than a bundle of half-remembered tales and historically located prejudices. The historical consciousness of the English-speaking peoples on both sides of the world was derived from speech and action more than schooling and reading. From the seventeenth century onwards the stories the English told themselves were being fused into a seductively simple plot of progress. According to this increasingly potent national myth, the Anglo-Saxon race was ever freedom-loving. Conquered by the Normans in 1066, the English regained some of their liberties in Magna Carta in 1215. Subject to the Roman Catholic Church, they broke free in the Reformation and defended the Protestant religion against foreign powers. The issues of political and religious freedom were locked together in the struggle that culminated in the Glorious Revolution in 1688 in which a constitutional monarchy, liberty under the law, and the Protestant religion were providentially secured. It was this view of the past, which many Scots shared, that formed the basis for the Union of England and Scotland in 1707, and nourished a common British identity that was increasingly meaningful not only for the English but also for the Welsh, the Scots and some Irish.[20]

The English calendar provided the lineaments of a national memory. After the Reformation the 'red letter' days of the Catholic Church were replaced by a calendar of thanksgiving for the preservation of Protestant England. The development began in the late 1560s with bells and bonfires to celebrate the accession of Elizabeth I on 17 November 1558.[21] It continued with the fiercely anti-Catholic and often oppositional festivities to mark the discovery of the Gunpowder Plot on 5 November 1605.[22] The importance of November in the political calendar was reinforced by the fortuitous landing of William of Orange at Torbay on that very day.[23] From 1689 congregations thanked God for discovering 'the snares of death that were laid for us' in 1605, and on the same day in 1688 for bringing William 'safely into his kingdom, to preserve us from the late attempts of our enemies to bereave us of our religion and laws'.[24] There were moves to counterbalance the tumultuous celebration of Gunpowder Treason day by the promotion of royal anniversaries. The anniversary of the execution of Charles I, king and martyr, was observed on 30 January with solemnity in Anglican circles. Royal Oak Day, commemorating the escape of Charles II after the battle of Worcester, remained popular in England from the 1660s until the nineteenth century. During the eighteenth century the tradition developed of celebrating the monarch's birthday: somewhat muted at first, it became a major event after George III's recovery from his first mental collapse in 1788.[25] It was the only secular holiday in the early years of British Australia.

The limitations of historical consciousness in 'old England' are most evident in the disregard for longer stretches of time. The Christian tradition ensured some chronological awareness, with marked interest in some quarters in ideas of millennium and in the concept of jubilee. In the seventeenth century such ideas assumed more secular form. The Luther jubilee of 1617, marking the centenary of Luther's nailing the ninety-five theses to the door of Wittenberg Cathedral, was obviously a counterblast to the papal jubilees. The celebrations to mark the centenaries of a number of German universities were more decidedly secular in inspiration. The Dutch shared this large historical sense, perhaps with implications for Australian history. When in 1642 Antonio van Diemen commissioned Abel Tasman's voyage in search of the South Land, he made specific reference to the Dutch taking over the task of exploration from the Portuguese and the Spanish.[26] He may well have had in mind that it was exactly two and a half centuries since Columbus had set sail across the Atlantic. In England it may have been remarked that the Glorious Revolution of 1688 followed a century on from the Defeat of the Spanish Armada in 1588, but there seems to have been no really self-conscious commemorations of this sort until the Shakespeare jubilee of 1769.[27] Thenceforward such celebrations become rather more common. There was the Handel festival of 1784, a quarter-century after his death and almost the centenary of his birth. In the wake of a 'jubilee of a poet and the commemoration of a musician', many people in 1788 felt it would be 'ungrateful in the extreme to [William III], our great deliverer from popery and tyranny, not to notice the close of the century which has experienced the beneficial effects of the system of government, the most perfect the world has produced, that was happily settled under his auspices'.[28] The London Revolution Society, founded somewhat earlier, held a centenary dinner on 5 November 1788 and set forward plans for more regular celebration of the Glorious Revolution and an extension of its principles and of the Good Old Cause.[29]

Monuments likewise have their roots in religion. They were constructed less to commemorate than to solicit prayers. One of the earliest of a more modern sort was the monument to the Great Fire of London in 1666.[30] Erected in the 1670s, its main purpose is not wholly clear. It commemorated the dead—though many more Londoners had died in the plague of 1665. It was more a monument to the loss of old London, and an expression of determination to rebuild in London's ground zero. It was also a warning for the future. In this capacity it was rapidly hijacked for sectarian ends. In 1681 an inscription was added that the conflagration was due to 'the treachery and malice of the Popish faction ... in order to the effecting of their horrid plot for extirpating the Protestant religion and old English liberty'.[31] For Englishmen in the eighteenth century this monument was quite simply *the* Monument. There were surprisingly few other public monuments of this nature.[32] In 1788 there was a well-supported proposal to build a commemorative column at Runnymede, 'a spot sacred to the liberties of the people', but nothing came of it.[33] It was not until the second decade of the nineteenth century that Britain began to acquire a larger range of public monuments. They include not only broadly supported plans for monuments to Admiral Nelson, but also more contested monuments to the rival statesmen William Pitt and Charles James Fox.[34]

The new culture of secular commemoration found echoes in Australia. Interestingly, it rapidly assumed a distinctive inflection. The celebration of the monarch's birthday remained a feature of the official calendar, but during the 1820s the anniversary of the arrival of the First Fleet began to assume special significance, not least for the Anglo-Australians who had been born in the colony. It was increasingly the occasion for dinners at which the toasts would be to the advancement of Australia and meetings at which petitions were drawn up to promote the interests and ambitions of the colonists. George III's silver jubilee in 1809, though proclaimed a 'universal jubilee' from the Thames to the Ganges,[35] and the centenary of the house of Hanover in 1814, cannot have had much resonance in New South Wales and Van Diemen's Land. Both were organised at the last minute, and the latter was subsumed in the celebration of what seemed, under Napoleon's Hundred Days, the end of the war with France. The concept of the silver jubilee, however, was later taken up in the colonies. In 1838 there were moves to celebrate the fiftieth anniversary of the foundation of New South Wales on 26 January.[36] A consciousness of the silver jubilee may have prompted Van Diemen's Land in 1838 to organise its own commemoration. A major regatta was organised, and a public holiday declared for 1 December, the day on which Abel Tasman had made landfall.[37]

As in Britain, there was a growing interest in monuments. The Anglo-Australians, however, sought their own heroes. In 1822 the Philosophical Society of Australasia set up a brass memorial to mark the landing-place of Captain Cook and Joseph Banks, 'the Columbus and Maecenas of their time', at Cape Solander.[38] In 1825 a tablet was set up in honour of the French explorer La Pérouse at Botany Bay. The initiative came from his fellow countryman and admirer Hyacinthe de Bougainville, but it had the active support of Governor Brisbane.[39] The interest in Abel Tasman in Van Diemen's Land is especially remarkable. Tasman was adopted early and surprisingly frequently as a Christian name, and in 1838 the date of Tasman's landfall was chosen as a public holiday. It was not until 1842, however, that the first public statue in Australia was erected. The person commemorated in Sydney was not the monarch, nor a British military or naval hero, but Sir Richard Bourke, the former governor.[40] Of all the men who ruled New South Wales, he had been the most liberal and sensitive to colonial aspirations. His monument is the counterpart, appropriately accented, to the memorialisation in many English cities of Lord Grey, Sir Robert Peel and other champions of moderate reform.[41]

The birth of European Australia—the first fifty years of English settlement—coincided with the beginnings of a major transformation in the manner and degree with which British people engaged with their past. According to Peter Mandler, this transformation needs to be understood in relation to the development of a 'mass-culture industry' using the new technologies of steam printing and engraving in steel.[42] Sir Walter Scott's historical romances in verse and novel form showed the market potential of history in the opening decades of the nineteenth century. The dramatic reduction in printing costs brought the attractive 1829 edition of the Waverley Novels within the range of tens of thousands of ordinary people. The 'People's Edition', issued in instalments from 1844, 'sold seven million weekly numbers'.[43] Scott had many imitators, but equally important was the salience of biography and history in the mass circulation non-fiction magazines like John Limbird's *The Mirror of Literature, Amusement and Instruction* in the 1820s, and Charles Knight's *Penny Magazine*, which was launched in 1832 and soon achieved a circulation of 200 000.[44] Naturally, the market for such works included the colonies. Biographies, histories and historical novels were among the most popular categories of books borrowed at the subscription library at Evandale, Tasmania, in the 1840s and 1850s.[45] While the reading public in colonial Australia was large and voracious, one should also not underestimate the importance of images. The great history paintings, reproduced in an array of books and magazines, may have been far more mesmerising and potent for image-starved Anglo-Australians than film and television are today.

The history boom in England was consolidated in the third quarter of the nineteenth century by the publication of a number of serious national histories. Thomas Babington Macaulay's *History of England*, published between 1848 and 1855, began to bridge the gap between popular and scholarly history. Edward Augustus Freeman's English history was history on an epic scale and a triumphalist account of the Anglo-Saxon race.[46] J. R. Green's *A Short History of the English People*, first published in 1874, was hugely popular. According to Mandler, 'it was, and remains the definitive romantic nationalist history'. By its third edition it had run to 326 000 copies.[47] The impact of such works on the intellectual formation of Australians in the late nineteenth century is worthy of further study. It illustrates the point that the reception of English culture, unlike the 'reception' of the English common law, was not a single event, nor even a series of events associated with waves of English immigration, but a continuous process of dynamic interaction. The Clarks who settled in Hobart in the 1830s brought little sense of British history with them. Andrew Inglis Clark, the self-educated lawyer, democrat and framer of the Australian constitution, learned his history from books published in England in the decades after his father's arrival in Van Diemen's Land.[48]

Pierre Nora has written about the chasm that modernity opened up between collective memory and history, and the manner in which 'sites of memory' function in maintaining group connectedness with the past.[49] In the English-speaking world it is hard to locate a time when collective memory alone sustained nationhood. In this sense, England in the late eighteenth century can certainly not be regarded as a wholly traditional culture. By the same token, it was largely lacking— or at least was only beginning to develop—the monuments, sites of memory, and institutions necessary to sustain national identity. The calendar provided only the most meagre mnemonic framework. An evocative and contentious site in the late seventeenth century, the London Monument, rapidly became merely a landmark and a place of assignation. Established in 1753, the British Museum was for fifty years only accessible to the well-heeled and persistent.[50] In times of popular commotion it served as a redoubt for the statesmen and gentry who resided in the neighbouring squares.[51] The rules of admission were liberalised in 1810, and more than a thousand people a day viewed the Elgin Marbles when they were first exhibited in 1816.[52] By the late 1830s there were complaints about the large number of unaccompanied children running about the museum.[53] The increasing accessibility of the collections fits with the notion of a 'mid-nineteenth century reconceptualisation of museums as cultural resources' to be deployed in nation-building.[54] It needs to be borne in mind, however, as Graeme Davison points out in the next chapter, that the museum, with its focus on world antiquities, was very far from being a store-house of national memory.

England was not only changing rapidly, but was exceedingly brash and present-oriented. Anglo-Australians may have represented it as 'old England', combining a commitment to a new start with nostalgia for what they had lost. Manning Clark, in his imaginative depiction of a Devonshire farmer transplanted to New South Wales, illustrates some of what informed this view: he 'reflected wistfully on his new way of life in a country where no holy bells knolled him to church on Sunday … where the churchyard contained no inscription on the tombs of his family or his friends to remind him of man's great hope during his journey through life'.[55] Yet in the nineteenth century Australians looked to Britain more for news than for history, more to engage with the present and forge a future than to wallow in the past.

One major new development in mid-Victorian Britain was a massive growth of interest in past times, and the projection of a more coherent view of national history. As David Lowenthal has written, 'to secure themselves against the evils of rampant change and the dangers posed by the new industrial order, Victorians took refuge in one or another past, pasts not so much preserved as extravagantly recreated in architecture, art, and literature'.[56] In Britain, as elsewhere in Europe, monuments were being constructed, commemorative rites and cultural institutions established, and traditions invented to support, and occasionally subvert, nation-building.[57] This new sense of English and British heritage, communicated through print and by migration, but accessible in Australia only virtually or through simulacra, stimulated, provoked and enormously complicated Anglo-Australian aspirations, political and cultural, in the late nineteenth century.

6 WHAT SHOULD A NATIONAL MUSEUM DO? LEARNING FROM THE WORLD

GRAEME DAVISON

National museums have recently been in the news, not just in Australia but also in other Western democracies where the ructions of national politics have echoed in the corridors of their cultural institutions.[1] This is a measure of the heat generated by issues of national identity in the age of global terror, as well as of the high regard in which museums are now held as repositories of the national past. When people in the United States and Australia are asked to rank the sources of information about the past that they most trust, museums come close to the top of the poll, well ahead of history teachers and far ahead of politicians, who come last.[2] Why people feel that way is less clear. Perhaps it is the appearance of reliability that comes from a tangible, rather than a discursive, past. For the ever-growing numbers of international tourists, museums are pre-eminently the places where the nation is on show.

Because they are also trusted and visited by large numbers of children on compulsory school excursions, they are likely to be scrutinised by those who fear that the nation's youth could be led astray. And because they are usually funded by taxpayers, the people's representatives feel a special responsibility to keep an eye on what they do. All these circumstances have loaded national museums with an almost unsustainable weight of expectations.

On the whole, this increased level of public scrutiny is a good thing, as long as it is the public, and not just a few politicians and journalists with barrows to push, who do the scrutinising. Too much of the recent debate about the National Museum of Australia has been conducted in narrowly political terms, with critics checking out exhibitions and public programs against preconceived standards of correctness, totting up mentions or omissions of stock heroes and villains, and looking for coded messages in everything from labels to layouts. The 2003 review of the museum's exhibitions and public programs chaired by John Carroll manages, for the most part, to avoid such simplicities, yet its scope remains disappointingly narrow. One of its most conspicuous omissions is an almost total lack of reference to the experience of national museums outside Australia.[3] This is not entirely Carroll's fault: when I asked him about it, he explained that the Department of Communications, Information Technology and the Arts had declined a request for funds for an overseas tour. This was a pity, since exposure to even a few other national museums might have led him to question some of the assumptions that seem to have shaped his report. This chapter reviews some of the sights on the tour John Carroll was not allowed to take.

One of the assumptions shared by Carroll and the museum itself is that the prime purpose of a national museum is to define or express a sense of national identity. According to this view, the museum is a bit like a national church, charged with the mission of inculcating patriotism, or at least of encouraging reflection on the character of the nation and its peoples. Here is what the National Museum of Australia says about itself on its website:

- The National Museum of Australia explores the land, nation and people of Australia.

- The Museum celebrates Australian social history in a unique way by revealing the stories of ordinary and extraordinary Australians, promoting the exploration of knowledge and ideas and providing a dynamic forum for discussion and reflection.

- With a history of challenging convention and encouraging debate about who we are as Australians and what shapes our national culture and psyche, the Museum is sometimes controversial and never dull. For every Australian visitor, there is something to remember, share, enjoy or learn. For overseas visitors, there is the chance to experience, through sight, sound and touch, what Australia used to be, what it is now and what it could be, motivating them to travel further in Australia, having had a taste of a living, dynamic and futuristic museum.[4]

The statement is carefully balanced: the museum will celebrate *and* challenge; it embraces the ordinary *and* the extraordinary; it tells stories *and* encourages debate; it looks backwards *and* forwards. Centrally and most controversially, however, it encourages 'debate about who we are as Australians and what shapes our national culture and psyche'. It is this part of its mission that gives the museum its primary rationale and exposes it to the greatest political risk.

During the recent controversy surrounding the museum, when I was invited by Dawn Casey and Tony Staley to examine the complaints made by a member of its council, David Barnett, about its interpretation of Australian history, I was struck by Barnett's incidental remark that the Prime Minister had instructed a previous chair of the museum's council that the museum was *not* to attempt to define Australian national identity. In view of the museum's previous statements of its goals, this struck me as odd, an indication that Barnett had perhaps misinterpreted Howard. With 'Nation' as one of its guiding themes, how could the museum avoid the issue of national identity? I wondered. Did the Prime Minister think that issues of national identity did not belong in the national museum, or was it—as some of his recent statements suggest—that he considered our national identity so settled and understood that there was no need for the museum to foster debate about it? Either way, it was clear that in making 'national identity' part of its remit, the museum was guaranteeing that it would remain 'controversial and never dull'—perhaps, as Dawn Casey's experience suggests, more controversial than it bargained for.[5]

We can see how distinctive is the National Museum of Australia's conception of its mission if we place it in historical and comparative context. A hundred and fifty years ago, when many national museums were established, and were given that troublesome title 'national', their founders would not usually have aspired to define or debate national identity. The prime or ostensible purpose of the museum, and what gave it the name 'national', was that it was expected to serve a national *purpose*, namely to educate, enlighten and civilise the people by exposing them to scientific specimens of the natural world and to the heritage of humanity. Their primary function was to collect, study and display. Only secondarily did they 'instruct', and as for celebrating or challenging, that would have struck most nineteenth century museum directors as quite odd. In 1829 James Smithson, in endowing what would become a prototype of modern national museums, the Smithsonian Institution, directed only that it should be devoted to 'the acquisition and diffusion of knowledge among men'.[6] Knowledge was assumed to be global, not national, and it should be diffused internationally as well as nationally. Only in the late twentieth century did the Smithsonian, in company with many other national museums, hoist the contentious phrase 'national identity' to its masthead.

In 2000 the retiring Secretary of the Smithsonian Institution, Michael Heyman, reflected on the spectacular growth of visitation during his tenure. In part, he argued, this reflected a growing 'need to represent our national pride'. Museums had

> come to be places of validation in a society that has seen the erosion of many social institutions traditionally representing trust and authority. While religion and family retain their strong foundations for many Americans, other Americans are experiencing uncertainty and drift. Museums have always been places where society asserts that certain things are important. But increasingly, all of society, not just traditional elites, look to museums and similar organizations to recognize values, to represent permanence in a changing world, and in general just to sort out what matters.[7]

Under Heyman's successor, Laurence Small, the pressure on the Smithsonian to act as a kind of national church, inspiring patriotism and honouring national achievers, has grown even stronger.[8]

Today, nevertheless, the National Museum of Australia and the Smithsonian are unusual among national museums in their almost exclusively national focus. Here is a selection of 'mission' or 'vision' statements from a range of other national museums:[9]

- National Museum of American History:
    The National Museum of American History dedicates its collections and scholarship to inspiring a broader understanding of our nation and its many peoples. We create learning opportunities, stimulate imaginations, and present challenging ideas about our country's past.[10]

- Canadian Museum of Civilization:
    To increase, throughout Canada and internationally, interest in, knowledge and critical understanding of and appreciation and respect for *human cultural achievements and human behaviour* by establishing, maintaining and developing for research and posterity a collection of objects of historical or cultural interest, *with special but not exclusive reference to Canada*, and by demonstrating those achievements and behaviour, the knowledge derived from them and the understanding they represent.[11]

- Deutsches Historisches Museum:
    The museum shall ... strive to help the citizens of our country to gain a clear idea of who they are as Germans and Europeans, *as inhabitants of a region and members of a worldwide civilization.*[12]

- National Museum of Ireland:
    The National Museum of Ireland is charged with preserving and making accessible the portable, natural and cultural material heritage of Ireland while responsible for communicating to both the people of Ireland *and visitors* an understanding of our heritage. The museum also serves to deepen cultural ties both within Ireland *and with other countries as well as opening a window on the world's material heritage through which Irish people may appreciate their own culture in its European and global context.*[13]

- National Museum of Scotland:
    We preserve, interpret and make accessible for all, the past and present of Scotland, *of other nations and cultures*, and of the natural world.[14]

- Danish National Museum:
    The National Museum is Denmark's central museum of cultural history, comprising the histories of *Danish and foreign cultures, alike.*[15]

- Museum of New Zealand: Te Papa:

    Te Papa provides museum services that contribute
    to the Government's outcome of preserving and
    presenting the taonga (treasures) of our peoples,
    interpreting the heritage of New Zealand for national
    and international audiences, and helping establish New
    Zealand's place in the world through *contextualising our
    heritage within the heritage of other cultures.*[16]

In some cases, such as the Canadian, Danish and Scottish
museums, the institution collects beyond the bounds of the
nation-state, and in all, except the American, it aspires to interpret the history and culture of the nation in its regional or
global context. While museums are almost everywhere expected
to contribute to the visitor's sense of 'identity', most balance
the cultivation of national identity or citizenship against awareness of the 'human race' or of a 'worldwide' or 'global' community. In this, they are no more than reflecting contemporary
realities, for just as the foundation of national museums in the
nineteenth century followed the global spread of nationalism,
so their transformation in the late twentieth century was a
response to the international spread of multiculturalism.[17]

'National identity' is the most recent in a long and often
tangled lineage of ideas that has governed our thinking about
national selfhood. A hundred years ago it would have been
more common to speak of 'blood', 'race', 'kinship', 'folk' and
'character'—words that remind us of the close connection
between the development of museums and the nineteenth
century discourse of race and colonialism. Only since the
1970s, first in the United States and then almost everywhere,
has 'identity' become the standard way of thinking about our
connection to the nation.[18] If we look for the intellectual ante-
cedents of the twentieth century national museum, with its
focus on the lives and material culture of 'ordinary people', we
may find the closest approximation in Scandinavia, where for

almost two centuries both national and regional museums have collected objects representative of the nation's distinctive crafts and folk traditions.

In 1884 the director of the Danish National Museum, J. J. A. Worsaae, noted the strong connection between the history of nationalist movements, which grounded their sense of national distinctiveness in folk traditions and languages, and the development of museums. 'It is significant', he observed acutely, 'that the zeal to create national collections of antiquities and to preserve national monuments first appeared, and was most ardently pursued in smaller countries, where the nationality and independence of the people appeared to be particularly threatened, e.g. in Denmark, Hungary, Ireland, Scotland and Holland'.[19] The threats he had in mind were primarily external: Danish independence threatened by Swedish, Hungarian by German, Irish and Scottish by English. But his reasoning has a more general application, for the 'museumising imagination', as Benedict Anderson calls it, can be stimulated as much by internal threats to the integrity of the nation as external ones.[20]

Some of the most interesting new history museums in the world are in countries undergoing new experiments in nation-building. Over the past year I have visited several museums in the United Kingdom (including the Museum of Scotland in Edinburgh and the Museum of the British Empire in Bristol), in South Africa (the Voortrekker Monument, Museum Afrika, the Apartheid Museum and the Hector Peterson Monument and Museum), and in Germany (the Jewish Museum and the Deutsches Historisches Museum in Berlin). Each, of course, is a response to specific national circumstances and the stresses of nation-building, and hence the pressures on the museums are very different in each case. However, each, I believe, contributes something in answer to the question: What should national museums do?

The Museum of Scotland, the newest and most glamorous of the stable of museums now collectively known as the National Museum of Scotland, is one of the most conspicuous symbols of Edinburgh's new status as a national capital. While this represents a victory for Scottish nationalists, even they, I am sure, would not suggest that their fight for national independence has quite the dramatic significance of, say, the struggle against apartheid in South Africa or the reunification of Germany. The museum was born of both pragmatism and politics. In 1981 the Secretary of State for Scotland had decided to merge two previously distinct institutions, the Royal Scottish Museum and the National Museum of Antiquities of Scotland, and to house their collections in a specially built new building. The National Museum of Antiquities had long styled itself as a 'national museum' but only in the limited sense of being open to the public and situated in the national capital. Once the project got under way, however, the nationalising imperative grew stronger. A committee of inquiry recommended that the new museum should not be a mere repository of collections but should 'contribute to the interpretation of Scottish culture'. By 1989, a feasibility study of the new building anticipated that 'a new national museum will be seen as a symbol of national identity'. And by the time it opened, and the exhibits were installed, it had been accepted that its galleries should follow a broadly narrative sequence reflecting the history of the nation as a whole.[21] 'The museum presents, for the first time, the history of Scotland—its land, its people and their achievements', the visitor is told.[22]

To an Australian observer, that formula—'land, people and achievements'—has a familiar ring, although, unlike the National Museum of Australia, the National Museum of Scotland is able to ground its interpretation in the rich collections of objects assembled by the museums that preceded it. When I visited the museum in 2005, I was conducted around by a volunteer guide, Robbie Cramond, a sprightly 80-year-old who I later discovered was actually one of the museum's founding fathers. We had hardly started out before one of my fellow visitors wanted to know: 'Are all the objects in the museum real?' Robbie was able to assure her that, with the exception of some obviously modern sculptures, yes, all the objects were original and authentic. But while all the objects were authentic, the way in which they are now interpreted in the Museum of Scotland is very different from the significance they had when they were first collected. On the ground floor of the museum, rocks, plants and fossils collected for the former natural history museum are now deployed to tell the story of the making of the prehistoric 'Scottish landscape'. In one of the exhibits a map of Scotland, chopped off at the English border, is superimposed on a map of the continental landmass of several million years ago. An absorbing video on ancient flora concludes: 'That's what happened to Scotland in the first million years or so'. Behind this kind of retrospective nationalisation there often lurks a desire, admirable enough in itself, to invoke a sense of national pride to conserve ancient and endangered habitats. But it also plays upon one of the oldest, and most frequently abused, of national myths, the supposedly indissoluble link between a people and its land.

The National Museum of Scotland, it must be said, is at pains to avoid anything in the way of ethnic essentialism. Visitors enter the first-floor gallery on 'The Kingdom of the Scots' through a portal bearing inscriptions from the Declaration of Arbroath (1350), and displaying objects, such as the Monymusk Reliquary and a small statue of St Andrew, which testify to the Scots' sense of themselves as a people with their own long-held traditions. This gives way, however, to an impeccably pluralist account of the making of the Scottish people in which the arrivals of the Picts, Angles, Britons and Caledonians are seen as anticipating the modern migrations of Lithuanians, Poles, Italians and Pakistanis. Here, as in the rest of the museum, the deep religious antipathies that shaped so much of Scottish history, between Catholics and Calvinists, Hanoverians and Jacobites, are represented perhaps more neutrally than some patriotic Scots might wish. Above an excellent exhibit on the Battle of Culloden, the tattered banners of the British and the Jacobites are hung side by side in what our guide Robbie Cramond explained was intended as a gesture of reconciliation. The effect, intentionally or not, is sometimes to drain the story of its passion, to tie up ends that should perhaps better be left loose.

The difficulties of representing the nation are even more profound when, as in post-apartheid South Africa, the monuments and museums of the old regime are still so palpably present in the land. The Voortrekker Monument in Pretoria, erected in 1949, is a powerful manifestation of the Afrikaners' sense of themselves as a people called, like the people of Israel, to possess a Promised Land. In larger-than-life statues of the Afrikaner leaders, in an impressive frieze of carved panels, and in tapestries narrating the story of their heroic trek from the Cape to the Transvaal, the Voortrekker Monument transformed an episode in the history of white settlement into a powerful national myth. The monument in turn created a place of commemoration as evocative, still, to many white South Africans as the Shrine of Remembrance or the Australian War Memorial are to Australians.

After the fall of apartheid there were some black South Africans who urged the destruction of the monument. Others proposed that it should remain, but that on a nearby hill there should be erected, as a counter-monument, a gigantic statue of Nelson Mandela's raised fist. Mandela, who had not been consulted, declined to allow this proposal to proceed, but in the meantime, interestingly, the Voortrekker Monument is being subtly reinterpreted.[23] In an important 1998 speech at the reopening of the British Settler Monument in Grahamstown, Mandela made a distinction between three kinds of national monument: 'those which stand as mute pointers to a fixed and ever-receding past'; those which, while nurturing 'a particular tradition of our land', enrich the life of the nation; and those which 'open the past to scrutiny, recalling it in order to illuminate and transform it into a part of our living and changing society'. The British Settler Monument, he went on to say, belonged to the second category, of monuments that while nurturing 'a particular tradition', enriched the whole; but it was places like the Voortrekker Monument, surely, that he had in mind as belonging to 'a fixed and ever-receding past'.[24] Yet the museum has not been closed and in the museum section an attempt is quietly being made to reinterpret the Great Trek, not as the master narrative of the Afrikaner nation, but as one stream in the broader history of world migration.[25] It is hard to believe that the attempt will succeed, but it is perhaps one way of neutralising a once-powerful national monument without actually destroying it.

The most telling indications of how national memory is changing in South Africa are not in these attempts to recuperate the old, but in the several new museums that now give historical form to the previously repressed memories of the apartheid era. Probably the most popular of these is Robben Island off Cape Town, the notorious place of exile and punishment for the political victims of apartheid including Nelson Mandela, which has now become a place of pilgrimage for the whole world. More than a million and a half people, about one-third from South Africa, the rest chiefly from the Western English-speaking democracies, have visited Robben Island since 1997.[26] In the new master narrative of South African history, sites of suffering, exile and death have come to play a powerful new role in the national imagination. Johannesburg's Museum Afrika currently shows a simple, but powerful, exhibit on the history of the Treason Trials in the 1950s and 1960s. The centrepiece is a gallery of photographs of all the main protagonists: the accused, the prosecutors, the judges, the witnesses. A notebook and pencil attached to each portrait enables visitors, including relatives of the accused, to write their personal responses. Some are from relatives of the accused expressing pride and gratitude for their sacrifice, but some—directed at a few of the accused who became witnesses for the prosecution—tap a reservoir of unrelieved bitterness.

Orlando, on the edge of Soweto, the site of the 1976 student uprising, in which South African security forces opened fire on students protesting the imposition of Afrikaans in local high schools, is now the home of a handsome new museum dedicated to the memory of Hector Peterson, the 13-year-old schoolboy who was the first to be shot. The most ambitious of these new museums is the Apartheid Museum, a privately funded museum located next to a new casino between Johannesburg and Soweto. As they enter the museum, visitors are given a plastic pass randomly assigning them an identity as either black or white. They walk down separate corridors past the signs that routinely structured everyday life in South Africa along racial lines. Many of the galleries in the museum have a similar parallel structure, with the experiences of oppressors and oppressed delineated on opposing walls. As in the Hector Peterson Museum, much of the story is told in photographs and film: save for a few handbills and documents retrieved from state archives, the victims of apartheid did not accumulate much in the way of material culture. Nevertheless, the effect is deeply moving. The museum opened while the Truth and Reconciliation Commission was sitting and its narrative logic reflects the imperatives that also guided the commission. The story of national division that structures much of the museum is nevertheless set within a master narrative that begins and ends with the promise of racial harmony. Johannesburg, we are reminded, began as 'the most cosmopolitan city in Africa', 'a robust blend of nations, races, cultures and languages'. The museum ends with an uplifting evocation of the dramatic final scenes of the apartheid era—the liberation of Mandela and the first post-apartheid election.

Apartheid, the museum's narrative suggests, is a nightmarish aberration from the true path of South African history. This is the hopeful message inscribed on the museum's website:

> The Apartheid Museum, the first of its kind, illustrates the rise and fall of apartheid: The racially prejudiced system that blighted much of its progress and the triumph of reason which crowned half a century of struggle ...
>
> The museum is a beacon of hope showing the world how South Africa is coming to terms with the past and working towards a future that all South Africans can call their own.[27]

But as impressive as the Apartheid Museum is, one cannot help wondering who it is for, and what it contributes to the process of national reconciliation. It is ironical that the Voortrekker Monument, dedicated to commemorating a 'fixed and receding past', still appears to attract more visitors than the Apartheid Museum. It was a Saturday, admittedly, when I visited the Apartheid Museum and on Monday the busloads of schoolchildren would perhaps create a different impression. All the same, I was left to wonder how long, in a city where murder and AIDS are daily realities, and where many of the gross inequalities of the apartheid era persist, the museum's triumphalist interpretation of the nation's past will remain plausible.

Germany is another country whose sense of itself has been formed against the background of not one, but two, national nightmares. As you walk through present-day Berlin, now surely one of the most striking showcases of contemporary European architecture, you are constantly reminded of the successive catastrophes of Nazism and Communism. As in Mandela's South Africa, the relics of the old eras have not been expunged, but often carefully preserved. Some of the simplest, yet most powerful, forms of commemoration are those begun under unofficial auspices, such as the improvised monument to the victims of the Wall, close to the Reichstag, and the outdoor museum known as 'The Topography of Terror' on Wilhelm-strasse, where, close to the site of the former Gestapo head-quarters, and in the lee of the only remaining section of the Berlin Wall, a gallery of photographs reminds modern Berliners and visitors of the crimes once perpetrated on the spot.[28] These simple, and apparently spontaneous, acts of remembering give context to the more institutional responses, the most important of which, like Daniel Libeskind's now famous Jewish Museum, the Monument to the Murdered Jews of Europe and the newly reopened German Historical Museum (the Deutsches His-torisches Museum), constitute possibly the most sophisticated working through of the purposes of national remembering that I have seen anywhere. Like the new museums in South Africa, these museums come after the long period of national soul-searching that became known in Germany as the *Historikerstreit*. A generation before Australia's 'history wars', Germans were obliged to wrestle with the issues of national guilt and trauma. Now, some critics suggest, Berlin is in danger of being bur-dened with 'an inflation of monuments'.[29] In different ways, the Jewish Museum and the new German Historical Museum offer suggestive models of how nations can think about the past, avoiding the simplifications of either triumphalism or cata-strophism, offering us space for reflection before we are hastened to judgement or pushed towards a preconceived conclusion.

An astute American observer, Stephen Weil, argues that contemporary museums are less ideologically programmed than their nineteenth century counterparts. 'The museum [he writes] was established to "raise" the level of public under-standing, to "elevate" the spirits of its visitors, and to "refine" and "uplift" the common taste.' But this improving ethic, he argues, is now on the way out and somewhere in the mid-twenty-first century the relationship between the museum and the public will have undergone a 180-degree turn: 'The museum's role will have been transformed from one of mastery to one of service.'[30]

Perhaps Weil was right when he wrote about the trajectory of American museums, but looking elsewhere, and even at recent developments in the United States, there seems to be at least as much evidence to the contrary. Museums were once designed as empty boxes ready to be filled with whatever the museum director wanted; but now the building, for good or ill, is often part of the interpretation, can even be the interpretation itself. (What this means for their reputation as authoritative sources of knowledge about the past is as yet unclear, since they still draw part of their authority from an older conception of the museum as a scientific and objective source of knowledge.) While the National Museum of Scotland is configured as a tower that the visitor ascends, chronologically, from prehistoric basement to contemporary attic, and the Apartheid Museum follows two parallel paths, joined at the beginning, separating and then converging at the end, Libeskind's Jewish Museum is famously configured around three intersecting underground pathways, each representing a response to the ineffable reality of the Holocaust. One, the path of exile, leads towards a kind of walled garden; the second, the path of annihilation, terminates in the emptiness of a hollow tower; while the third, a figurative Jacob's Ladder, leads visitors up a long stairway to the top of the building where they begin a slow descent, through the various historical galleries, until they arrive back at the intersection where they began.[31]

In keeping with his deconstructivist philosophy, Libeskind is seeking forms to suggest the fragmentation, disturbance and silences of the past. Not everything in the rest of the Jewish Museum follows Libeskind's lead, but as an architectural model for thinking about the past, especially about a past in which the contradictions simply do not lend themselves to a simple resolution, it surely deserves our attention. Conservative critics of the National Museum of Australia waxed hot over its alleged mimicking of Libeskind's Jewish Museum, and the supposed coded message that the fate of the Aborigines was a genocide comparable to the Holocaust in Europe. But the lessons of Libeskind's architecture are much more subtle and wide-ranging than this. For it is the master narratives of national history, not just the events of the Holocaust or the Australian frontier, that it brings into question.

One of the striking consequences of the reunification of Berlin has been the amazing revival of the great complex of nineteenth century museums, the so-called 'Museum Island' along Unter den Linden. The Deutsches Historisches Museum inhabits the baroque Zeughaus, home of the former German military museum and, in the former GDR, the Museum of Marxist-Leninism.[32] Now, a brand-new building by the American architect I. M. Pei is home to an impressive new exhibition, *Myths of the Nations. 1945: Arena of Memories*, possibly the most ambitious attempt of German historians and museologists to confront the implications of the past half-century for national self-understanding. The exhibition is remarkable in several ways: for its breadth (it attempts to survey the making of national memory, not just in Germany, but in all the combatant nations since 1945); for its imaginative use of graphic materials, especially cinema and popular art (I counted about sixty projectors showing short film clips); but above all for its bold approach to the central problem of historical memory. Here is a portion of the exhibition's opening statement:

> Almost sixty years after the end of World War II it is possible to piece together a history of the images and ideas that Europe, the USA and Israel formed of the Second World War and the genocide. Nowhere have the memories of the war faded. On the contrary, they are constantly being renewed in ever-changing variations ...

Memories are in a constant process of realigning themselves. The critical re-appropriation of past events that were previously considered taboo was informed in the West by the paradigm of the genocide of European Jewry ...

Altogether, the memory of World War II and the genocide is a central component of a newly developing European public opinion. It can nevertheless not be assumed that the West's categorical imperative to remember will automatically be taken over in the Eastern parts of Europe. The diverging historical constructions vis-à-vis the Second World War will continue to confront each other in a hotly contested 'Arena of Memories'.[33]

By bringing the issue of historical memory to the forefront, and placing the German experience alongside that of the other combatant nations, the exhibition is able to confront the demons of Germany's Nazi and Communist past, yet escape the trap of collective guilt. It throws a searching light upon the political uses of the past among Germany's former foes, for example the way in which during the Falklands War Mrs Thatcher invoked the images of national solidarity associated with the Battle of Britain, and modern Israel's claim to a monopoly of the moral capital of the Jewish Holocaust.

I must admit that, after the recent public controversies surrounding the National Museum of Australia, I had rather lost heart about the prospects of building a national museum around the examination of national identity. When I was asked to advise the museum on its response to the Carroll review, I even suggested that, in the current circumstances, the museum might prudently lower the risk of political attack by giving less emphasis to the concept of 'nation' and orienting its permanent galleries around its other two central themes: land and people. However, exhibitions like the Deutsches Historisches Museum's inspiring *Myths of the Nations* show that, in a country with the courage to face its past, and the imagination to look beyond its own borders as well as within, the national museum can become a place, not just for celebrating the nation's triumphs, or even for purging its collective sins, but also for confronting the ways in which the nation is itself constituted and reproduced through its collective memories. I would like to think that some day, not too far off, the National Museum of Australia would have the opportunity, the intellectual courage, and the resources to attempt something similar.

7 REFLECTIONS OF A NATIONAL MUSEUM DIRECTOR

Dawn Casey

The director of a national museum in the early years of the new millennium faces numerous and often contradictory demands. There are many different views about what the proper role of a national museum is, just as there are many ways in which these views can be interpreted. James Gardner, associate director of curatorial affairs in the Smithsonian's National Museum of American History, suggests that national museums must present 'multiple points of view':

> Rather than try to concoct a simple story of shared experiences, we should share many stories, from multiple points of view, exploring the complexity and richness of the American past— seeing difference and contest as a strength, not something to be plastered over with an idealised story of shared values and goals.
>
> Different voices give us a fuller picture of American history, each story telling us something about all the others. Just because

we are a national museum that does not mean that we are obligated to tell a celebratory story—[we have a] responsibility to help our visitors understand that history is diverse and contested. We have an obligation to interpret history, not present the past as we wish it had been.[1]

During my time as director of the National Museum of Australia in Canberra, between 2001 and 2003, the museum, like many others internationally, followed this approach. At the 'National Museums: Negotiating Histories' conference held in Canberra in 1999, prior to the opening of the museum, I said:

> A cornerstone of the National Museum's mission will be to explore and portray an Australian heritage that includes recognition of the achievements of a culturally diverse society.
>
> As is the case with other national museums, the initial choice must involve just how we position these different cultures and values within the museum.[2]

The Pigott Report of 1975 which led to the establishment of the National Museum of Australia recommended that the 'continent', rather than the 'nation', be the focus:

> Virtually every nation has its national museum, but here the argument is particularly powerful. For the nation covers a whole continent; and moreover that continent, because of its long isolation from the other land masses, has had an unusual natural history and human history …
>
> It should be stressed that a continent, rather than a nation, is the ideal focus for a museum, because the natural boundaries are more permanent and powerful than man-made boundaries. Hitherto, because of national boundaries, no continent has constituted the central theme of a large museum … A new national museum will illuminate new fields of knowledge and also link traditional fields in revealing ways.[3]

In relation to Aboriginal history, the Pigott Report was clear:

> The argument for a major display of Aboriginal history is over-
> whelming. The chronology of the human occupation on
> Australia is dominated by Aboriginals. If the human history of
> Australia were to be marked on a 12-hour clock-face, the era of
> the white man would run for only the last three or four minutes.[4]

However, for those who aspire to manage today's museums, the
complexity of decision-making goes well beyond the intellectual framework for exhibition development and research and
collecting policies.

One cannot talk about content in isolation when there are
also visitors, governments, which provide the funds, and governing boards to consider. There have been profound changes in
museums worldwide during the last decade which continue to
shape them today. The transformations have occurred not only
within the museums themselves but also within the broader
context in which they operate internationally.

The significant decline in visitor numbers in recent times,
economic pressures brought about by the ever-increasing
operating costs and the decline in philanthropy, together with
the more exacting requirements of governments and boards of
trustees to run more cost-effective and commercially oriented
organisations, have meant a shift in emphasis for management.
Museums began seriously to survey their visitors and made
a conscious effort to be more people- and particularly child-
friendly and to improve the 'visitor experience'.

The British Museum, and the Metropolitan Museum of
Art and the Natural History Museum in New York, were
among the first to realise the advantages of having shops and
cafés, not just to improve the visitor experience, but also to
raise much needed revenue. The shops now look like gift shops
rather than libraries, with exclusive merchandise ranging from
posters to exquisite jewellery. And there is always the tote bag

to carry home newly purchased museum books and gifts, an exclusive memento in itself.

During the last decade a number of new museums opened around the world and older ones that had previously focused on natural history were redeveloped. These include the Canadian Museum of Civilization, the Jewish History Museum in Berlin, Te Papa in New Zealand, the Holocaust Museum, the National Museum of Australia, the Melbourne Museum, the Guggenheim Art Museum in Bilbao, the National Museum of Native Americans in Washington, the Tate Modern in London, the Natural History Museum in New York, the Imperial War Museum in the United Kingdom and the National Museum of Scotland.

These new and redeveloped museums also reflected a changing world that saw the reunification of countries, the emergence of new national identities, post-colonial recognition of the rights of Indigenous peoples, and projects of urban renewal. While some of the new museums are not explicitly national in orientation, they have incorporated themes of national significance and they project an image of what one might expect of a national museum.

New museums have also moved away from an image as élite institutions whose messages are only comprehensible to a select few. They offer a popular ambience with cafés, shops, restaurants, technologically enriched exhibitions and public programs developed by multi-disciplinary teams, and exuberant architecture. They have also become major tourist destinations in their own right.

In some cases the architecture reflects the content of the museum. The Canadian Museum of Civilization reflects native Canadian totems and the significance they place on circles. The architecture of the Jewish Museum of History and the Holocaust Museum emulates the horrific journey taken by the Jews to the death camps.

The new National Museum of Australia, which opened on 11 March 2001 as the government's gift to the Australian people as part of the Centenary of Federation celebrations, was a natural fit in the new international museum landscape. However, it also fuelled the 'history wars', with members of the museum's board, museum traditionalists and professionals engaged in a frenzy of debate. Participants in the debate were not divided neatly along traditional political lines, however, as museum traditionalists and professionals were often left-leaning in their politics. Some museum professionals from the left, although they had been at the forefront of the intellectual and cultural shift to improve museum practice to reflect the multicultural nature of society in the twentieth century and the recognition of Indigenous peoples, did not accept that inclusiveness meant more than consulting people and creating separate spaces for children's exhibitions.

I suspect they were so proud of what they had achieved that they did not recognise the extraordinary transformation in museology that was taking place, which was reflected in the opening of Te Papa, the Melbourne Museum and the National Museum of Australia. Hence many who entered the debate immediately following the opening of the National Museum were sitting on the same side of the fence as those from the far right.

There were a few museum professionals and academics who recognised the need for change. In 1994 Roland Arpin, executive director of the Musée de la Civilisation in Quebec, gave a contemporary museological answer to the question of how museums can help people to understand the world:

> It's not enough to simply exhibit, we must exhibit for someone; it's not enough to simply interpret, we must interpret for some-one. These 'someones' are not a homogeneous mass but different people requiring different museum experiences. Young or old, well-educated or not, careless or attentive, hurried tourist or

devoted museum-goer, the variety of our visitors demands that our codes, messages, information and means of communication be varied, appropriate and adaptable, even within the course of a museum visit.

... An interactive museum is not simply an institution that provides a few sensory experiences. An interactive museum is above all one that 'connects' with its visitors in all their panoply of difference. The museum thus becomes a place where explanations are available; where, faced with multiple ideas, values and beliefs, visitors can find reference points and touchstones to help them move beyond appearances and truly understand the phenomena that surround them.[5]

In Australia, Graeme Davison identified five characteristics of modern national history museums. He argued that such museums:

- Challenge standard narratives of national history
- Question the racial and evolutionary categories and hierarchies which previously governed the collection of museum objects
- Show a heightened consciousness of the museum's clientele, real or potential
- Are experimental in museum display technique, often involving a merging of electronic and concrete imagery and
- Adopt a pluralistic, internationalist perspective.[6]

American commentator Stephen E. Weil from the Institute of Museum and Library Services highlighted the rapid evolution of the last decades by imagining the character Rip Van Recluse, an old-fashioned curator in a New York museum who dozed off at his desk fifty years ago and wakes up in the present time. His astonishment at the museum of today is particularly instructive. Inward or collection-based museums have become outward looking and service-based; museums are responsibly entrepreneurial and have learned to justify the efficiency and effectiveness of their programs.

The debates surrounding Te Papa, the Melbourne Museum and the National Museum of Australia should have provided the opportunity for academics and museum professionals to have a reasoned discussion about the merits or otherwise of this new museology. But in the case of the National Museum and the Melbourne Museum, the 'cultural commandos' of the 'history wars' hijacked the debate, making the museums tangible examples to further galvanise the 'ordinary people' against the left-leaning politically correct 'élites'. Or so they thought!

The criticism of those on the left was music to the ears of David Barnett and Christopher Pearson and was linked by Pearson with the attacks made by people such as Keith Windschuttle, Miranda Devine, Piers Ackerman, Alan Jones and Gerard Henderson to provide the ammunition for the museum's council and the government to instigate the review headed by Professor John Carroll, a sociologist at La Trobe University. The review was driven by political ideology, as evidenced by the lack of representation on the review panel of practising historians, Indigenous people or international museum expertise as was the case with the reviews of Te Papa in Wellington and the Jewish Museum in Berlin.

Initially, the Coalition government led by Prime Minister John Howard had approved the new Museum of Australia's aims. An advisory committee led by Jim Service recommended that the government build the museum, and funding was announced in December 1996. The Service Report stated:

> There are many identities and voices contributing to our picture of ourselves and our nation. By developing and interpreting its collection through a range of exhibitions and outreach activities, the NMA focuses on balancing these personal and sometimes untold stories within the pattern of well known historical events, in a way which is relevant to contemporary and future audiences.[7]

The report also recognised the significance of new technological and market imperatives:

> Museums are continually changing and developing new display techniques using the latest technology to provide engaging experiences … museums are positioning themselves in the leisure and entertainment markets to attract wider audiences … to fulfil the role of educator they first need to entertain and capture the imagination of potential visitors … they can attract new audiences by … marketing themselves and being responsive to visitor need.[8]

The Prime Minister, speaking at the opening of the museum in 2001, endorsed the emphasis on diversity and innovation:

> What [the Museum] does unusually, and I think very attractively is seek to interpret the history of our nation. Not only in terms of events and objects but also in terms of the life experience of people from different backgrounds, Indigenous people, people who came to this country having been born elsewhere, and people who have been born in this nation …
>
> It will I think over time change the way in which people view museums, because this museum and what its concepts seek to do is to interpret and relate history and the experience of our country in a somewhat different way. Quite properly and inevitably there will be debate in the future about that way of interpreting our history and that way of relating those events. But importantly, it represents a quite different way of presenting the history and culture of a nation.[9]

However, just two years later, the Prime Minister declared that there was no longer any need for 'navel gazing'—Australians knew who they were. In his closing address to the Liberal Party National Convention in 2003, he said:

> We no longer navel gaze about what an Australian is. We no longer are mesmerised by the self-appointed cultural dieticians who tell us that in some way they know better what an Australian

ought to be than all of us who know what an Australian has always been and always will be.

… We have ended that long seemingly perpetual symposium on our self-identity that seemed to occupy the 10 years between the middle of the 1980s and the defeat of the Keating Government in 1996.[10]

There was no need for any sense of shame about the past—and, in particular, past treatment of Aboriginal people. As Robert Manne pointed out in *Whitewash*: 'More deeply in the Howard years a counter-revolution in the sensibility concerning the dispossession of the Aborigines—no less real than the revolution which had begun in the late 1960s and early 1970s, in the days of Stanner and Rowley—was swiftly gathering momentum'.[11]

Indeed, the Prime Minister assumed a leadership role in the 'history wars' and the formulation of a new approach to the 'Aboriginal problem'. The Coalition government weakened legislation aimed at protecting Indigenous sites of significance, reduced reconciliation to practical issues of health, education and housing, and adopted an Orwellian approach to the use of language relating to Aboriginal and Torres Strait Islander peoples:

- Australia was 'settled', not 'invaded'.
- Aborigines were 'dispersed', not 'massacred'.
- Children were 'removed' for their own good, not 'stolen'.
- 'Some' Aboriginal people and children, not 'generations', suffered from the impact of 'settlement', not 'colonisation'.
- The word 'genocide' was banned in relation to Australian history.

To further reinforce their view of the place of Indigenous Australians in this country, government decision-makers have not appointed any Indigenous people to the boards of the Australian Broadcasting Corporation, the National Museum of

Australia, the National Maritime Museum, the National Library of Australia or the National Gallery of Australia since they came to power.

As we know, however, the revolution is not only about returning Indigenous Australians to being once again 'the miserablest people in the world, lacking goods for trade, who neither farm or husband animals and who epitomise the negation of an ordered society',[12] it is also about using any means available and every opportunity, including the National Museum of Australia, to perpetuate the myths that represent what it means to be Australian.

Myth one: Australia is a sporting nation. We have a natural, inherent passion for ball games, team games, physical fitness and the great outdoors. We produce more international stars per head of population than other countries. Our heroes are rugby players, Olympic athletes, tennis champions and cricket captains, and we strive to be like them. When we are little we play cricket in the back yard, when we are older we play in the school teams, and when we grow up we go to the gym or the pool every week to keep fit, in between hiking for miles through the beautiful Australian bush.

Myth two: Australia is a tolerant and egalitarian nation. In this country, Jack is as good as his master. We do not stand on ceremony, and anybody is welcome if they are prepared to do their share of the work. We are democratic by nature. We do not care who you are or where you come from, there is plenty of room for all. Our motto is 'the fair go', and we always sympathise with the underdog.

Myth three: Australia is a Christian country. It is true that the Constitution specifically forbids the Parliament to make any law in respect to religion,[13] and most of us never go to church, but somehow we are all Christians underneath. By default we write 'Church of England' on the census form, unless we are Catholic. We know our Bible stories, we are kind to animals, and we love our neighbour—some of the time.

Christianity is just part of our background culture. Which of course means that, sadly, those Muslims and Jews and Hindus and Buddhists can never be properly Australian. They just do not fit in.

Myth four: Australia has a peaceful history. During the Centenary of Federation celebrations, the nation was praised as having been created 'without bloodshed'. Wars, revolutions and mutinies are things that happen somewhere else—in those unhappy countries where refugees come from. Life here is traditionally peaceful and easy-going, we have a robust parliamentary democracy and a laid-back, tolerant approach to life.[14]

In reviewing David Barnett's allegations at the request of the chairman of the National Museum, Graeme Davison detected an underlying suggestion that the museum labels expressed 'a kind of systematic bias in the interpretation of Australian history', the bias of 'political correctness'. He said that Barnett 'gives the impression—which I am sure he does not really hold—that the museum should follow the historical views of the government of the day'. Davison hoped that this was not the view of Tony Staley and his council, who would surely appreciate that the historical interpretations presented in the museum must 'survive changes of government and councils'.[15]

And although Davison did not find the systematic bias of 'political correctness', the 'cultural commandos' were still not satisfied. It was not what they wanted to hear. Regardless of how scholarly and professional Davison was, and even though he was considered by many as not aligned to the left or right, his disagreement with the views of Barnett and others meant by implication his opinions were not accepted. Or, as he wrote in *The Historian's Conscience*: 'In the midst of the debate the *Australian* had described me as a "middle of the road historian", a title I could wear with equanimity, if not with pride. By the end of the affair, I observed—to another newspaper—

that there now seemed to be rather more lanes on my right than when I'd set out.'[16]

The other and more insidious reason was that Barnett in particular wanted to change the 'role' of the National Museum —a change to be enshrined in legislation—as confirmation, no less, of the conservatives' victory in the 'history wars'. The terms of reference for the review headed by John Carroll requested consideration of future priorities, including the continuing relevance of the National Museum of Australia Act in the development of permanent and temporary exhibitions and scholastic and public programs.

And although Carroll brought along his political ideology in his chairmanship of the review, he did retain his professional integrity, much to the chagrin of Pearson and others, and did not recommend changes to the Act, but even more annoyingly he did not recommend dramatic change to the Gallery of First Australians. Nor did he accept the idea that there was a systematic bias of political correctness.

Graeme Davison was right when he said that the main reason we failed to arrive at consensus around the National Museum board table was 'that the museum's critics were not really pluralists at heart. For them, the issues were not finally about scholarly expertise, or balance, but about whether the museum reflected the right political values.'[17]

From my perspective, it was clear that most of the critics— I hasten to add, however, that there are not very many—are of the view that national museums should celebrate, unify and inspire the nation. The inclusion of difficult or unpleasant material indicates poor taste or, worse, a lack of national spirit. Contested stories have no place, because people look to a national museum for the pure and simple truth—just the facts thank you, not the opinion.

But the truth is rarely simple. The interpretive path taken by the world's newest museums reflects awareness of the complexity of history, the elusiveness of truth and the validity of alternative viewpoints. Museums have in fact benefited greatly from history's increasing recognition of the perspectives of Indigenous peoples, women, and immigrants—a multitude of previously overlooked or suppressed voices. Including their stories increases the scope both of our collecting areas and our audience reach and adds enormous interest to exhibitions about even familiar historic events.

One result of the increased emphasis on diversity has been the popularising of history for a variety of audiences of all ages. There should be no going back to the grand, simple narrative of national progress, however much some of our critics may long for it. The national story is complex and emerges not from a neat time-line, nor from a list of facts, but from the interplay of many stories and points of view. These can range from the profoundly tragic, through the ironic or quirky, to the absurd or the joyful. They are the sum of us. As museums strive to arrive at fresh insights into social, cultural and environmental history, they depict a complex world that includes of many viewpoints, not because they are 'politically correct' or perversely wish to rewrite history, but because they are intellectually respectable.

Did we get everything right at the National Museum of Australia? No. There are some things that can be improved, but there is no doubt it has more than lived up to expectations and is respected internationally by museum experts. And the Australian public love it. Although the federal government declined to renew my contract, I am pleased to report that under my leadership the museum achieved the following:

- The annual operating budget increased from $4 million to $43 million and the number of staff from 40 to 210 plus 200 volunteers.
- The museum attracted approximately two million visitors to its exhibitions, programs and events. This included

approximately 150 000 schoolchildren and was three times the number of visitors expected.

- Ninety-five per cent of 10 000 visitors surveyed indicated they were 'satisfied' or 'very satisfied' with their museum experience.

- An independent analysis of the media coverage for 2000–01 and 2001–02 found that in the first year the museum attracted media coverage valued at $13 million, and $6 million in the second year. In the first year, 80 per cent of coverage was positive and 8 per cent negative; in the second year, 93 per cent was positive and 2 per cent negative.

- Seven major travelling exhibitions, ranging from 600 to 900 square metres, were developed. One of these included a 500-square-metre exhibition developed for Guangzhou in China.

- Eight small temporary exhibitions of 250 square metres were developed, with four of them travelling to several other venues throughout Australia.

- The retail shop had a $1 million turnover and was on track for a 9 per cent net profit of gross sales and in excess of $800 000 revenue raised through catering and venue hire.

- The museum obtained approximately $3 million in sponsorship and philanthropy, including cash and in kind.

- The museum attracted Getty and Australian Research Council research grants in excess of $1 million.

Finally, for those of you who aspire to becoming a director of a new national museum, let me just remind you of Judy Horacek's cartoon featuring a Dodo, with the observation: 'Life's a bitch and then you're extinct'.

8 THE ARCHIVE UNDER THREAT

JOHN FROW

This chapter is about the archive, by which I mean any place in which the vestiges of the past are stored. The archive is a repository of public memory, and it comes into existence by an act of construction and collection—but also by acts of selection and exclusion—usually stretching over very long periods of time. The making of an archive takes place under particular economic, political, cultural and legal conditions of existence; my concern here is with the way in which changes in those legal conditions are currently transforming the quality of our dealings with the archive in the digital era, and thus the quality of 'publicness' of our public memory.

Our understanding of what constitutes an archive has of course changed considerably in recent times, extending it from collections of government records, of public or private correspondence, of published or manuscript writings in general to more ephemeral and more popular materials, to oral records, to items of material culture, and most recently to electronic data; we are also more deeply aware of the complicity of the process of archive-formation with the history of class, state and imperial power.[1] These extensions have unsettled the very notion of a historical record. Francis Blouin writes:

> It could ... easily be said that a century ago archives and history occupied the same conceptual and methodological space. This sense of partnership in the study of the past has undergone a variety of stresses and strains over recent decades, to the point that what constitutes the archive has become a question fundamental to how our knowledge of the past is acquired and shaped.[2]

The focus of this chapter will eventually be on the digital archive and on the archiving of scientific knowledge in scholarly publishing; but let me begin by seeking to define the archive more carefully in terms of its institutional and particularly its legal conditions of existence.

In the first instance, then, an archive is a repository of copies of works: that is, of copyrighted and once-copyrighted materials that have been acquired by deposit or gift or puchase, and which are available for public consultation or borowing under specific forms of legal exemption from the limitations of copyright. In the areas of the world governed by the World Intellectual Property Organisation convention, there are three main areas of exemption that make it possible for libraries to make copyrighted works publicly available. One is the *first-sale doctrine*, which stipulates that once the work has been legitimately copied and published, the author's rights in relation to that physical copy are exhausted. The second is the provisions for *fair use* or *fair dealing*, primarily for educational and scholarly purposes. And the third is the *libraries exemption* (given in Australian law in sections 49–53 and 110A and B of the *Copyright Act 1968*), allowing copying by the so-called prescribed libraries under certain very strictly circumscribed circumstances: in simple terms, what is allowed is the making of single copies of articles or short extracts from books for research or private study, and of replacement copies for preservation purposes or where an item has been lost, but only where the item is no longer available on the market.

A second and broader specification would say that an archive is a repository of *information*, taking the form of copies of works that are regulated by a particular intellectual property regime. Information has in most societies been culturally framed as an inappropriate object of private and exclusive ownership, although in the societies that we think of as constituting Western 'modernity' this ethos has coexisted with the partial monopolies granted by copyright law and other forms of intellectual property rights. There has, however, been increasing commercial pressure for the privatisation of these categories and their removal from the commons.

The characteristic structure of information is that of gift exchange without monetary recompense but in contexts of calculation and strategic manoeuvre.[3] The barter of information, and the estimation of who knows what, condition the forms of its reciprocity but can never endow it with real scarcity, since its most important quality is its inexhaustible reproducibility: if I tell you something I still 'possess' it myself, and so on indefinitely. Although the category of intellectual property is grounded in an extension of the concept of real property, the fact is that, unlike land or material goods, information is not consumed by use.

Thomas Jefferson put this much more eloquently than I can in a letter of 1813:

> If nature has made any one thing less susceptible than all others of exclusive property, it is the action of the thinking power called an idea, which an individual may exclusively possess as long as he keeps it to himself; but the moment it is divulged, it forces itself into the possession of everyone, and the receiver cannot dispossess himself of it. Its peculiar character, too, is that no one possesses the less, because every other possesses the whole of it. He who receives an idea from me, receives instruction himself

without lessening mine; as he who lights his taper at mine, receives light without darkening me. That ideas should freely spread from one to another over the globe, for the moral and mutual instruction of man, and improvement of his condition, seems to have been peculiarly and benevolently designed by nature, when she made them, like fire, expansible over all space, without lessening their density in any point, and like the air in which we breathe, move, and have our physical being, incapable of confinement or exclusive appropriation. Inventions then cannot, in nature, be a subject of property.[4]

This indeterminacy of the positioning of information (its ability to exist in many places simultaneously) gives rise to a more general indeterminacy inherent in the fact that information is structured as an open system with multiple users.

Two obstacles to commodification develop immediately from this radical indeterminacy. The first is the problem of defining and enforcing exclusive property rights (which are the precondition for capital investment) in something both intangible and diffuse. The simple solution to this problem is to treat information as a secret. The more complex solution, and the one that has been worked out in great detail by Western law over the last three centuries, is to restrict access to and use of information without necessarily restricting possession of it; thus copyright law restricts only the making of unauthorised copies, patent and trademark law restricts commercial exploitation, and so on.

The second obstacle is the problem of attaching exchange value to an entity that has an almost limitless use value: that is, of making an abundant good scarce. The uncertainty that flows from the indeterminacy of uses (the unpredictability of the 'take' of any information product) entails considerable risk for capital investment. At the same time, the relatively high costs of initial production and the relatively low costs of subsequent copying of information goods make predictability imperative. The problem of the minimisation of risk can be solved in part by the production of scarcity through control of the right to copy, which in turn is regulated by the legal institution of authorship, the single most important channel for the creation of textual desire and the minimisation of market uncertainty.

For all libraries except deposit libraries, a condition of their successful existence is that they negotiate a path between the costly scarcity induced by this strategy and their role of making information broadly accessible to a public. A third specification of the archive, then, would look at the way libraries and other repositories work both as concrete institutions and as a model of one set of social relations for the circulation of knowledge: the so-called library model of knowledge management, in which a hybrid mode of free or nearly free lending threads a middle way between the economy of the commodity and the economy of the gift.[5]

A library in this sense is a collection of informational materials, traditionally but not necessarily printed matter, which have typically been bought in the market but which, in most public library systems, do not circulate as commodities. But neither do these materials circulate as gifts; they are, rather —to use Marcel Mauss's term—prestations, 'gifts' that return without conferring any rights of ownership or permanent use.[6] While the 'library model' thus tends to collapse rather than to dichotomise the categories of gift and commodity, it does nevertheless represent a genuine alternative to the privatis-ation of the commons in information. This model is, however, under threat.

Public libraries as we know them came into being as part of that massive expansion of state institutions in mid-nineteenth century Europe and North America that also gave rise to the public schooling system, post offices, railways and public hos-pitals, and which set an ethos of public service against the monopolistic tendencies of the uncontrolled market.[7] Their present existence is framed by a tension between that expanded model of the state and its role in the provision of free (that is, subsidised) public services and a more restrictive view of the state that seeks to open the provision of information to market forces. To put it crudely, a model centred on the informing of citizens has been replaced, at least in part, by a model of choices made by consumers. The causes of this shift are many and complex, but a major one in the case of the public library system has been the change in the status of information itself from being 'economically valueless, mainly government produced and largely public, to being value-added, commercially sensitive and high cost'.[8]

In an American study, Herbert and Anita Schiller identify a 1982 US government report as a turning point in the progressive weakening of the 'library model'.[9] Announcing an end to the principle of co-operation between the public and private information sectors, the report represents 'the private industry's challenge to the right of the public sector (government, libraries, universities, etc.) to engage in *any* activities the industry regards as its own province'—that is, any activities that might have a commercial potential.[10] Since then the pressure has been on the public library system (perhaps the most genuinely popular of all cultural institutions)[11] not only to implement various local forms of commercial practice—'charging users for information, relying on private vendors for databases, contracting out functions to private firms, and so on'[12]—but more generally to relinquish its primary role in the provision of information.

The focus of my chapter is on the tension between this impetus to make information scarce and expensive, and the electronic revolution—a revolution in the technologies of proliferation and dissemination—which has generated the possibility of a vast increase in the accessibility and visibility of information, and in particular of a transformation of the archive into something like a model of the public domain in which knowledge circulates freely: a model, let me add, that corresponds closely to that Enlightenment ideal of open knowledge systems which underlies the Western scientific ethos.

My concern here is not with the totality of the electronic revolution but with its specific effects on archives; in particular, I am not directly concerned with the Internet except as it concerns the storage and retrieval of research materials. Two main areas are of direct relevance: the effect of intellectual property law on the workings of the archives stored in public and research libraries; and the role of intellectual property in the current crisis in scholarly and scientific publication.

At the centre of the electronic revolution is the technology of digitisation: that is, the transformation of analogue print or visual or auditory materials into a common machine-readable form. The digital in this sense is a 'copy' of an original, produced by the keying in or scanning of documents, by downloading or transferral from another database, or by the networking of material. This means in turn that the distinction between 'reading' and 'copying' that governs the use of print becomes far more difficult to define and enforce in the digital domain, and it means that one of the salient effects of digitisation is the creation of new forms of property relation: its proliferation of copies at virtually zero cost tendentially undermines the tight control of copying that is at the centre of Western intellectual property regimes.

Despite these consequences, however, the institutions of intellectual property continue to work within a framework designed for print and for the figure of the individual author who supposedly uses publishers as mere intermediaries. Among other things, this means that many copyright exemptions for print have not been extended to digital copying. Libraries' limited rights to copy print materials for their users are largely not available for electronic copying; any use of copyright digital information must be licensed by the copyright holder, although in Australia a limited right of copying was granted under the Digital Agenda amendments of 2001.

In the United States and Australia, digital copying is allowed for preservation (that is, for 'archival purposes', effectively the replacement of an owned original copy), but this archiving right does not include the right to convert print and other non-digital media to electronic form for storage and retrieval purposes; libraries have no right to lend digital copies of works, which means the first-sale doctrine does not apply to them. Similarly, the European Commission Directive on the harmonisation of copyright makes it possible, at least in some countries, for libraries to digitise materials in their collection but not to communicate it to the public without explicit permission—something that is very difficult to obtain in the case of older materials or material published outside mainstream sources, and especially given the fact that in the current circumstances of commercial uncertainty publishers have often been unwilling to give any permissions for digital reproduction. Finally, there is no Australian, US or European right to make back-up copies of audio and videotape recordings: libraries can only replace damaged copies, and only if there is no market alternative. The general effect of this is a de facto prohibition on electronic browsing, since only the copyright holder may 'communicate to the public'; there might well be cases where the paper form of a work could legally be made available to the public but not the electronic form.

Digitisation takes place at the two levels of metadata and data. The category of metadata includes the making of catalogues, the construction of search engines, the downloading of content from search engines, abstracting, and the creation of bibliographies. That of data refers to the digitisation of existing content, or the creation of new digital content, as part of the archival function of libraries. Carol Henderson, the president of the American Libraries Association, recently wrote about this:

Libraries ... recognize that a key societal function of libraries—the archival function—is at risk because electronic information is so seldom actually available for purchase and permanent retention or preservation. Libraries play this archival role because history has shown that it is not economically viable for profit-based businesses to do so. The disappearance of much electronic information after a very short period of time, the fragility of digital bits, and the short life of hardware and software suggest that this role of libraries will be more needed than ever before, but harder and harder for libraries to accomplish.[13]

There are a number of issues at stake here:

- University libraries often need to pay several times over for archiving rights to electronic journals: for the journal subscriptions; for the photocopying licence to enable them to make copies for teaching purposes; for clearance to include the same material in study packs. Yet, after these various levels of licensing, they still do not necessarily have a collection of archived back issues.

- Increasingly, libraries are purchasing or leasing digitised materials that are based on collections held in other libraries: it is the intermediaries that are profiting from this exploitation of the value of special collections.

- As resource archives, libraries increasingly make use of digitised teaching resources, especially multimedia resources. A key problem here is that a CD-ROM, for example, may incorporate the rights of multiple authors, including the developer of the underlying software; and any authors whose work is incorporated in another work become copyright holders: for example, in the case of a sound recording of a musical performance, the owners of the copyright in the 'underlying works' represented by the music and the lyrics will have to give their consent before the recording can be lent to the public by a public library.

- Distance education raises particular problems to do with the provision of digital materials, since these require the making of copies and, in addition, may render the provider liable as an online service provider.
- One of the most important activities of libraries is document delivery. Under the constraints of current intellectual property law, this can only be construed as a commercial activity, licensed by copyright holders and thus dependent on the granting of permissions.
- The lending of software (at least where the software is less than fifty years old) is prohibited in most contemporary intellectual property regimes, even though it is clearly a 'literary work' in the sense of the relevant Acts. There is no exemption for fair dealing in the case of software, and there are problems in lending books that have software attached.
- Finally, there is a different set of problems associated with image archives and with the collection and holding of material objects, where other kinds of intellectual property rights obtain and where, crucially, the dimensions of work and copy coincide.

The most general level of the transformation of the function of the archive concerns the evolution of new conditions of access, or restriction of access, for digital material. More than 50 per cent of the fee income collected on behalf of authors in the developed countries derives from photocopying royalties from the print medium; significant moves are now under way to extract royalties from digital reproduction: from the licensing of digital archive copies, of works made available to disabled people, of the first digitisation of a work, and of value-added services such as the provision of course packs. In one sense, the use of a licence mechanism is a technical question about the facilitation of permitted exemptions to the limitations of copyright; but in another sense it has economic consequences that are potentially crippling for public libraries and other archives.

This brings me to my second area of concern: the transformation of scholarly and scientific publishing. In many domains, especially the sciences, print publication is in the process of being phased out, to be replaced not just by electronic journals but also by powerful electronic interfaces. Publishers such as Reed-Elsevier (Science Direct) and OCLC (First Search) deliver content—both metadata and data—from vast archival databases. First Search, for example, references more than 5.9 million online full-text articles from over 3500 electronic journals. Libraries are licensed intermediaries for these databases, but in one sense act merely as brokers to squeeze better deals from publishers. One consequence of this is that 'the ability to click from abstract or citation to the full text of an article is prompting a shift in the way that journals are used. Scientists often care less about the journal title than the ability to track down quickly the full text of articles relevant to their interests. Increasingly, users view titles as merely part of hyperlinked "content databases" made up of constellations of journal titles',[14] and new forms of publishing and research practice have developed accordingly. In high-energy physics, for example, the Los Alamos e-print archives have become the primary vehicle of publication. Here, articles are published as pre-prints, with peer review coming *after* publication; a similar model is currently being developed for the biomedical sciences.

These moves are of course in part a response to the crisis in the publishing of scholarly serials, which saw a 291 per cent cost increase between 1986 and 2000. Science publishing is now dominated by three huge conglomerates: Elsevier, Thomson and Bertelsmann. Elsevier controls something like 1500 journals, including key journals and databases in medical science, biology and business; it had profits of US$500 million on sales of $1.1 billion in 1997 from its scientific activities alone. Its title *Brain Research*, to take one example, doubled in cost between 1992 and 1996 to US$15 000 annually. The US

Association of Research Libraries calculates that its 114 member libraries spent 142 per cent more on journals in that year than ten years before but ordered 6 per cent fewer titles.[15]

The effect on the budgets of research libraries has thus been catastrophic: they are massively distorted towards the costs of scientific journals and database licences, and there have thus been extensive cut-backs in monograph purchases—which in turn hurts scholarly publishers, which in turn makes it much harder for young scholars to publish, and so on down the line.

The situation has generated a number of attempts to circumvent it by means of alternative forms of organisation of publishing. In 1995 Stanford created High Wire Press to return scholarly publishing to non-profit organisations. SPARC, the Scholarly Publishing and Academic Resources Coalition, set up in 1997 by the US Association of Research Libraries, is under-writing the launch of titles directly competing with expensive titles, with its members committed to buying each of them; its electronic chemistry journal, *PhysChemComm*, for example, sells for US$353 and competes directly with Elsevier's *Chemical Physics Letters* at US$8000. The Public Library of Science has similar aims: academics who have signed up to this initiative have promised to publish in, edit or review for, and personally subscribe to, only those scholarly and scientific journals that have agreed to grant unrestricted free distribution rights to any and all original research reports that they have published, through PubMed Central and similar online public resources, within six months of their initial publication date. Finally, George Soros's Open Society Institute has recently sponsored the Budapest Open Access Initiative. The preamble to its manifesto says:

An old tradition and a new technology have converged to make possible an unprecedented public good. The old tradition is the willingness of scientists and scholars to publish the fruits of their research in scholarly journals without payment, for the sake of inquiry and knowledge. The new technology is the Internet. The public good they make possible is the worldwide electronic distribution of the peer-reviewed journal literature and completely free and unrestricted access to it by all scientists, scholars, teachers, students, and other curious minds. Removing access barriers to this literature will accelerate research, enrich education, share the learning of the rich with the poor and the poor with the rich, make this literature as useful as it can be, and lay the foundation for uniting humanity in a common intellectual conversation and quest for knowledge.[16]

The initiative goes on to call for an extension of such access to all of the scholarly and scientific literature, through two mechanisms: self-archiving, and the development of alternative journals that do not charge subscription or access fees and do not use copyright to restrict use of the materials they publish.

What is at issue here is the lopsided market situation in which the costs of generating intellectual property are met by, mostly, public institutions, and the intellectual property rights are then donated to publishers who resell them to university libraries at a high cost. John Sutherland, writing in the *London Review of Books* in 1999, put it this way:

It's a sweet deal for the publisher, who pays none of the costs of originating his material. Those costs, which can run into millions of dollars and years of salaried time, are picked up by the authors' institutions or by grant-awarding bodies. Authors are paid nothing for the publication of their work. Nor do journals normally pay for the confidential peer reviews which guide their selection. The publisher thus gets an excellent product gratis, and all he has to do is package it. And, sweetest of all, his running costs and overheads are covered by subscriptions, the level of which he himself sets. Effectively, this means that he can make universities pay through the nose for something that the universities have paid to produce in the first place.[17]

Any solution to this problem rests with the universities making use of the market leverage given them by the intellectual property rights that they themselves generate. Caltech, to take one example, has announced that in the short term it wants all its faculty to agree that they will publish in journals only on the basis that they and Caltech, as joint copyright holders, lease the material to the publisher for a limited period, with a proposed reversion after two years. MIT has released its online courseware into the public domain. More generally, it seems to me likely that any solution to the crisis in the cost of scientific publication will come only when the world's major research universities use their collective market power to overcome these market distortions, as well as using their political leverage to restrain the claims that publishers are making to extensive intellectual property rights.

What I have been describing are two distinct but inter-related areas of struggle over control of and access to the archives that are the repository of our cultural memory. The situation is not yet a disaster, and in many ways it is counterbalanced by the construction and release of immense new research archives in electronic form, as well as by the multiplying resources of the Internet, including, to name just two areas, resources for genealogical research and for the study of local history.

At the same time, however, we are witnessing the gradual marginalisation of those without privileged access to research archives—and particularly that majority of people in the poorer parts of the world who can no longer, or could never, afford the entry fee at the doors of the digital archive. The paradox with which we are living is that there is simultaneously a massive expansion of the world's archival reserves, and a closing down of the public domain as the commons in information is converted into privately owned holdings from which rent can be extracted, and as the archives that have been bequeathed to us, and that we ourselves have in part helped to construct, are removed from our control.

9 THE ART MUSEUM AS MONUMENT: CULTURAL CHANGE CONTAINED

IEN ANG

Museums are monuments for cultural value: they represent what society cherishes and considers worthy of public presentation. Through their displays and their day-to-day operations they raise questions about knowledge and power, identity and difference, and permanence and transience.[1] But as society undergoes rapid change, how and what museums can, should and do represent is subject to fervent debate. Thus, museums are sites where cultural change is being played out, sometimes consensual, sometimes conflictive. But if this is so, where does this leave the image of museums as inherent guardians of the status quo, upholders of tradition and privilege?

One of the key transformations in Australia's recent history has been the ascendance of cultural diversity, both as a social fact and as a cultural norm. Indeed, the ongoing controversy around multiculturalism is at least in part reducible to the great philosophical and practical challenges posed by the recognition of diversity within the national body, and the far-reaching (and as yet unthinkable) consequences if the principles of multicultural democracy were taken to their full conclusion in public life.

The social and political significance placed on cultural diversity today is apparently deeply antithetical to what museums stand for, especially art museums. While the public display of art was always associated with its potential benefit for the general public, this claimed civic role has been contradicted by the art museum's historical function as a marker of class distinction.[2] Large sections of the population have never been part of the art museum audience: they were effectively excluded from the cultural world of the art museum. In other words, there was no place for cultural democracy in the art museum.

Take the Art Gallery of New South Wales, for example. Founded in the 1870s, it is in its origins a prime exemplar of the classic nineteenth century model of the art museum. Today it remains one of the most authoritative flagships in the cultural infrastructure of metropolitan Sydney. The Art Gallery's status as a seat of cultural power is reinforced by its physical monumentality. Its imposing façade resembles a Greco-Roman temple and its interior is dominated by a huge, cathedral-like central foyer flowing into grand halls and galleries, where precious works of art are solemnly displayed for visual contemplation and aesthetic appreciation. The whole ambience of the museum, exterior as well as interior, has a formality that incites visitors to be impressed, if not awed. Even if the Art Gallery of New South Wales were to decide to shed its elitist legacy, then its very architecture and its dominant associations would be an enormous barrier.

In her book, *The Museum in Transition*, Hilde Hein observes that traditional aesthetic theory, the epistemological foundation of the art museum, inevitably contributes to the intimidation of the visitor. 'The mythology of the art museum is so infectious', she writes, 'that once within its walls, an object mysteriously attains the imperious status of artwork, and visitors feel compelled to confirm its judgment within the parameters of their own experience. Where this resonance is lacking, people take its absence as a personal defect.'[3] Hein believes that art museums are *inherently* conservative, hierarchical and elitist. If she is right, then the very idea of democratising the art museum, opening it up to a broader and more diverse range of audiences and experiences, is a contradiction in terms.

But this is precisely what all museums and galleries have increasingly been compelled to do in these multicultural times. So widely accepted have the principles of 'access and participation' and 'social inclusion' become in arts and cultural policy thinking that relevant professional organisations now routinely assist museums with the task of becoming more responsive to cultural diversity. For example, Museums Australia, the peak national association representing the nation's museum and gallery sector, has a cultural diversity policy, which states: 'all Australians have the right to see elements of their culture preserved and interpreted in museums. Museums accept their obligation to effect this principle through all program areas and in relevant museum practices.'[4]

In their seminal publication, *Exhibiting Cultures*, Ivan Karp and Stephen Lavine have argued that museums, especially art museums, to serve the needs of multicultural audiences must abandon their image as temple and adopt the notion of a museum as forum, a place where visitors have the opportunity to learn about different cultural traditions and perspectives.[5] The art museum then would no longer operate as the arbiter of 'good taste' but as a facilitator in the communication of different forms of cultural expression that reflect the values, interests and experiences of particular communities. This is the notion of the museum as a cross-cultural 'contact zone'.[6]

Edmund Capon, the distinguished director of the Art Gallery of New South Wales, is acutely aware of the need to attract a more culturally diverse range of visitors. He puts it succinctly:

> Our problem is very clear. It is that we don't get the Chinese community in here. We don't get the Indian community in here. We don't get the Vietnamese community in here. We just don't do it. Somehow, you see, we're perceived to be a kind of European cultural institution.[7]

His concerns are echoed by Brian Ladd, the gallery's director of public programs, who observes that there is a huge cultural gap on a number of levels:

> The gallery doesn't attract large audiences of committed individuals from non-European communities ... The reasons vary. Many in these communities do not know about the gallery or where it is. And if they do, it may have little if any relevance to their lives. Visiting the gallery can also be a daunting experience if you're not familiar with Western museums. First-time visitors often feel intimidated by the architecture and overwhelmed by the large and relatively empty spaces. These negative experiences can put people off returning to the museum.[8]

Articulated here is a clear awareness of the lack of universality of the art museum's appeal, its intrinsic cultural bias. Capon reasons that people of Asian backgrounds are generally unfamiliar with the very idea of the art museum. He explains that there is no great tradition of the art museum in Asia, where cultural objects are valued for their historical or civilisational importance—signifying a glorious national past, for example—rather than for their artistic excellence per se. From this perspective, one could understand why Asians do not flock to art museums once they have migrated to the West—it is not part of their cultural habitus.

If this is so (and of course we are dealing with a general-isation here that itself merits further research), then it poses a considerable challenge for an institution such as the Art Gallery of New South Wales, at least if it wants to attract Asian audiences into its space. While Asian art is one of the gallery's main priorities, reflecting Capon's own love of Chinese art, attracting Asian audiences to its Asian art exhibitions has required the development of some highly intensive affirmative action initiatives. In this respect, the gallery has often applied the principle of what can be called the 'ethnic bind': the idea that particular groups of 'ethnics' would be interested in par-ticular exhibitions because they feature art from their own cultural heritage. Thus, when the gallery staged *India: Dancing to the Flute* in 1997, an exhibition of music and dance in Indian art, its marketing strategy included a thorough direct market-ing campaign among Sydney's multifarious Indian community organisations and associations. Similarly, for the *Masks of Mystery* exhibition in 2000, featuring Chinese bronze figures from the ancient Shu Kingdom, the gallery invested heavily in wooing the Chinese community of Sydney.

But persuading these ethnics to come to the Art Gallery could not happen by selling art for art's sake. Through trial and error the gallery has learned that to get Asian audiences in it has to surround the exhibitions with relevant cultural events and performances. Thus, *Dancing to the Flute* was accompanied by an extensive program of Indian music and dance perform-ances, while during *Masks of Mystery* Chinese audiences were drawn into the gallery in large numbers by free performances of ancient Chinese bells.

Interestingly, then, these Asian exhibitions have led to a significant reconception of standard exhibition programming. The very fact that Asian art was seen as difficult to sell, together with the instinctive assumption that this art should be of interest to particular ethnic audiences if only they could be persuaded to come and visit, has led to an emerging practice within the gallery to surround the objects of art with live cultural performances.

This, of course, is a rather major departure from conventional practice for an art museum. After all, one could not imagine exhibitions of European art being presented in a similar way. The irony is not lost on Ann MacArthur, the Asian programs co-ordinator at the Art Gallery: 'You know, just because you do an Asian exhibition, you've got to do it all singing and dancing, and Aboriginal art gets the same emphasis on performance. But you don't hold a mass if you're having a European icons show and no one is dancing the cancan for the *Renoir to Picasso* show. It's just funny.'[9]

In other words, whereas European art is allowed to maintain its elevated status as autonomous high art, Asian and Aboriginal art have somehow to be brought down to the level of popular culture. One could reject this unequal development as a case of abject Eurocentrism, relegating non-European art to the inferior realm of the folkloric, but it is also possible to interpret it in a more favourable light. As MacArthur puts it, 'in one way I see it as positive because you can point out that visual arts is not separate from performing arts in those traditions ... They don't have to be separate disciplines.' Indeed, one could make the point that this is an unsettling of the aesthetic codes of Western conceptions of art: the strict separation of artistic disciplines, as well as the strict dichotomy between art and life.

The imperative to bring art and cultural experience together in exhibitions is increasingly recognised by the Art Gallery of New South Wales. As Capon puts it, 'it's got to be promoted and sold as an exhibition with an experience, it cannot be just about objects'. This philosophy was one of the key considerations behind the gallery's decision to mount a blockbuster exhibition on Buddhist art in 2001. As Jackie Menzies, head curator of Asian art, recounts: 'We decided to do a show on Buddha because Buddhism is out there in the community, everyone has heard of Buddha, it's easy and readily comprehensible. And people will know about it, and it's so basic to Asia, so fundamental to so many Asian cultures.'[10]

It is common museum practice these days to conduct focus group sessions to test new exhibition concepts before they are fully developed. The research indicated that people of Asian backgrounds would indeed be interested in an exhibition on Buddha if it were a cultural exhibition, not just art. In general, people wanted as much context as possible, such as the life story of the historical Buddha, the meaning of Buddhist symbols, how Buddhism has affected different countries, the range of different forms of Buddhism, and so on. In short, they wanted the show 'to tell a story'. In response to this research, Menzies proceeded to shape the exhibition accordingly.

Visitors to *Buddha: Radiant Awakening*, which opened in November 2001, were led through seven large, interconnected halls filled with beautiful works of art, many of which had been loaned by private collectors and some of the world's most prestigious museums, such as the Hermitage and the British Museum. So art objects remained the centrepiece of the exhibition, but their display was arranged according to a narrative. The first hall told the Life of Buddha, represented by the Eight Great Events, and the following rooms explained how Buddhism spread across time and space. As Menzies explains:

> I don't believe that you can simply exhibit the works of art. We could have just had a hundred images of Buddha. But in the surveys beforehand everyone said 'I don't think I want to come if there's a hundred sculptures of Buddha sitting in a room'. So I think if you're doing exhibitions you have to somehow work out exactly what approach you're taking, what will resonate with your audiences.[11]

Moreover, a lot of attention was paid to the potential for attracting more Asian visitors. Indeed, the genesis of the *Buddha* exhibition, according to Menzies, was a visit she made to a crowning of the stupa ceremony at a meditation centre in the Blue Mountains, an hour and a half's drive from central Sydney:

> The stupa had been donated by the Burmese community, while the images to be enshrined in niches around the base, as well as the *hti* (umbrella) for the pinnacle, had been sent out from Burma. It was a great community day with everyone relaxed and cheerful, the weather perfect, and a buffet of delicious food. It was so obvious that Buddhism was thriving and expanding throughout Australia that I resolved to investigate further this new aspect of the Asianisation of Australia.[12]

Indeed, in the past few decades, dozens of Buddhist places of worship have sprung up across the greater metropolitan area of Sydney, established with the active support of local migrant communities. From the Art Gallery's point of view, reaching out to these thriving Asian Buddhist communities and to somehow get them involved in the exhibition was an attractive idea; it would make good the social imperative of cultural democratisation that museums are now under pressure to comply with.

As a result, an important aspect of the *Buddha: Radiant Awakening* exhibition was the setting up of a so-called Wisdom Room, a spacious room in the middle of the exhibition space, where each week—for the duration of the full fourteen weeks of the show—a Sydney-based Buddhist community group would 'show their wares', as it were: to put themselves on display. People visiting the exhibition unavoidably moved into the Wisdom Room during their itinerary through the rooms full of serene and beautiful works of art, and encountered something they might not have expected: living Buddhist cultures. The participating groups included the Taiwanese Nan Tien Temple in Wollongong, the Sydney Zen Centre and the Vietnamese Phuoc Hue Buddhist Monastery in Wetherill Park. Activities included a Korean tea ceremony, the making of a mandala, chanting and meditation and calligraphy.

The Wisdom Room turned out to be a great success, receiving much positive feedback from visitors and from the participating groups. It brought large numbers of Asian and non-Asian people to the Art Gallery who were sometimes more attracted to the Wisdom Room activities than to the art displays. As Menzies reflected, one month after the opening of the exhibition:

> I think it's terrific, the way we just handed that space over, the Wisdom Room, to every group, so they can do what they like. That is involving them. It's interactive. It's empowering. I think all that's very important in terms of what Buddhism is, it is a living religion, it's important to all these communities.[13]

Buddha: Radiant Awakening attracted a huge number of visitors and it was a milestone in the gradual 'mainstreaming' of Asian art in the gallery. The timing seemed right: opening a few months after the dramatic events of 11 September, 2001, it was a time when the public mood was firmly focused on the search for spiritual values. In this sense, putting Buddha in the limelight clearly struck a chord. But what can the exhibition tell us about the art museum's efforts to respond to the demands of cultural democracy?

One could with justification argue that the *Buddha* exhibition represented a case of the art museum being turned into a cross-cultural contact zone, a space where encounters between groups with very unequal sources of power and disparate cultural identities could take place. More specifically, the Wisdom Room was a space where groups that normally exist out of sight from the dominant culture gained visibility, if only temporarily, in a very privileged site of that culture.

The Wisdom Room was indeed an innovative community participation initiative that successfully brought new groups into the Art Gallery of New South Wales, but it should be said that as a particular kind of professional activity it was itself marginal within the gallery's routines. The setting up of the program required an intense effort in building up relationships and doing the painstaking work of cultural brokerage, work that often remains invisible. As public programs director Ladd observed: 'From the experience [of the Wisdom Room] we learnt that if we really wanted minority communities involved in future gallery activities, we must first go out and engage them on their own turf'.[14] It seems clear that such venturing out of the imposing building into the vast cultural diversity of the world outside—that is, a decentring of the art museum itself—is not going to be a part of the Art Gallery's core business any time soon.

What *Buddha: Radiant Awakening*—its packaging of objects of art in a sustained narrative context topped up by the extensive community engagement program—*has* opened up is the possibility of a more pluralistic attitude towards art, a recognition of its polysemy—the different kinds of meaning and value that can be attached to it. Menzies articulates this consideration well in relation to the objects on display at the *Buddha* show: 'I think we've displayed them quite sensitively without putting them all in mock-up altars or demeaning them or whatever. So we're showing them as good works of art as well as, I hope, respecting what they do mean to people who are Buddhist.'[15]

Here, Menzies shows an astute understanding of the politics of interpretation that is inherent in exhibition display, and that a more democratic display would allow visitors to relate to the objects from their own points of view. But this new-found pluralism cannot be taken too far. The core of the Art Gallery's institutional product is and remains 'art'. Asked what an exhibition should minimally be for her as a curator, her response was resolute: 'It has to be art. I believe in the integrity of objects.' She echoes here her director, Capon, who insists that art has to be the starting point for all exhibitions at the gallery. 'Yes, absolutely, it has to be', he says. 'Otherwise you end up with conceptual exhibitions where the work of art is merely a bit of information. If the work of art is merely there to provide information there's not a great experience, and then you might as well forget the whole thing.'[16]

In the end, then, presenting 'beautiful and wonderful works of art' is and remains the Art Gallery's core business. This means that an implicit notion that one knows what is 'art' remains intact, and this sets limits to the inclusion of other, non-aesthetic discourses. This became evident during the preparation of the exhibition, including the curatorial work of selecting the objects. As Menzies recalls, it proved to be important to maintain the boundaries of museum professionalism and art-historical scholarship:

> I dropped involving the communities in the selection of objects after we had a few meetings. Professionally this is an art museum, so although at first we did talk about that idea of involving people, you soon realise that there is something specialist about knowing what the art is and having access to good collections of art. So we did drop that idea of community involvement.[17]

In other words, there was a limit to the process of democratisation and pluralisation that was set in train with the inclusion of the community groups: that limit was reached when it came to the judgement of aesthetic value—the art museum's most exalted source of cultural power. While the *Buddha* exhibition, through educational labels and narrative wall texts and through the thematic arrangement of the objects, told a story—the story of a Buddhism radiating in manifold directions—it did so, as Capon put it, 'through works of art, so that people can actually look at wonderful works of art and enjoy it'.

But not everyone was pleased with this delicate blending of the conceptual and the artistic. In reviewing the exhibition, art critic Bruce James complained bitterly about the lack of 'the language of common connoisseurship' in the presentation of the objects. He was also dismissive of the Wisdom Room, which he described as 'a Dharmic theme park in the middle of an art show'. And he concluded 'I would have thought the very purpose of *Radiant Awakening* was to awaken audiences to the glories of Buddhist art, not Buddhism—for certainly the categories are separable. They have to be, otherwise this is not an exhibition but a sacred service.'[18] James, then, adopted a purist, Western aesthetic point of view. To him, any contextualisation of the objects within their conceptual, cultural or spiritual history was an unwelcome dilution of the art museum's mission.

It is illuminating to juxtapose James's comments with those of a very different visitor, Venerable Tenzin Lektsog, a Tibetan-trained monk who came to the exhibition every day, primarily to visit the Wisdom Room. He had a very different view of the meaning and value of the objects:

> So let me ask you, when you entered the BUDDHA exhibition and saw the first image of the seated Buddha, did you see a piece of rock or did you see something else? ... What was it that you saw? Perhaps ... like me, you might have seen something inspirational and worthy of veneration, perhaps something to help you find the courage to face your own suffering and even death with a measure of equanimity. Some special people are able to see deeper than this. They know very well that a rock is just a rock irrespective of whether it stays in a quarry or later becomes a statue ... So it is not the object that I venerate, it is the feeling [it generates] that increases my sense of interconnectedness with those around me.[19]

This view makes it clear that 'becoming a work of art is not always the highest and best thing that can happen to an object'.[20] The fact that *Buddha: Radiant Awakening* could elicit such contrasting responses and experiences proves that it succeeded very well in making it possible for visitors to establish a diversity of relationships with the objects, where different, even conflicting 'regimes of value' are juxtaposed.[21] The monopoly of the bourgeois aesthetic disposition had been broken—hence, of course, James' complaint. Tellingly, one visitor, a Chinese woman, came to the show every week—thanks to the availability of a season ticket—bringing exquisite crystals with her that she lay on the feet of some of the statues and gave away to other visitors. It was, she said, a way of honouring her recently deceased mother. So the temple of art became another kind of temple; the show was both an art exhibition and a sacred site.

Thus, the art museum has become a hybrid institution. Social and cultural pressures are gradually bringing about changes in museum practice, as well as a repositioning of art, an interrogation of why and how it is of value, and for whom. As a result, art museums are becoming both more democratic and more contentious—an inevitable effect of the overall cultural pluralisation that has characterised contemporary liberal democracies. However, it is also clear that as essentially nineteenth century institutions they cannot ultimately discard the values—such as the absoluteness of aesthetic value and the civilising capacity of art—that form the very condition and legitimisation of their existence. As Nick Prior has observed, 'the potential dissolution of an autonomous high culture' would surely mean the demise of the art museum as we know it.[22] Hence, ultimately, the art museum will always operate as a monument, physically and symbolically, where cultural change is both staged and contained.

PART IV

Transforming Space into Place:

Inscribing Memory in Landscape

10 LANDSCAPES TRANSFORMED

BILL GAMMAGE

I suggest that the Tasmanians consciously transformed their landscape in planned cycles, and for rainforest areas tentatively I suggest cycles of at least 900 years. These claims sit in the shade of mighty predecessors. In 1965 Bill Jackson argued that for thousands of years Tasmania's vegetation was greatly altered by fire. He found much less rainforest and much more eucalypt forest, heath and grassland than climate alone dictated. No bushfire could produce such changes: they required 'a long history of firing by the Tasmanian natives'.[1] Jackson kept refining this argument. In 1999 he showed that rainforest was much less common in Tasmania than in comparable New Zealand climates, and that evidence of 'pre-historic' firing was invariable in Tasmania but nonexistent in New Zealand, which until recently had no people.[2] Jackson made it clear that the Tasmanians had transformed their landscape.

In 1969, acknowledging Jackson, Rhys Jones showed that throughout Australia, Aboriginal burning made a more complex vegetation mosaic than climate alone dictated. To make plains or thin forest, or to generate new growth, people lit fires varying in timing and character. Jones called this 'fire-stick farming'.[3]

Jackson and Jones opened a new world to non-Aboriginal understanding. Jackson showed for how long Tasmanians had been firing the land, Jones how widespread and controlled firing was. Both made central the importance of fire to Aboriginal land management, although what Aborigines did not burn is as important as what they did.

I follow the track Jackson and Jones blazed. Elsewhere I argue that throughout Australia, Aboriginal land management was purposeful, systematic, sustained and effective. People made habitats for each plant and animal species, and edges between habitats for animals that feed in one habitat and shelter in another. They did so to obey the Law, and to make resources abundant, convenient and predictable. They planned to produce not merely vegetation mosaics, but a landscape of plants and animals consciously balanced and distributed.[4]

Here I restate this argument briefly for Tasmania, then explore how long-term it was. See figures 10.1, 10.2, 10.3, 10.4 and captions on pages 155–8, then return to the text below.

★ ★ ★

Jackson's work implicitly raises the question of how long-standing such patterned management was. Regular firing over thousands of years does not necessarily signify patterns. Yet I suggest that it was so, and that over centuries the Tasmanians moved the patterns around. They laid on the land a vegetation template, which in part Jackson detected, then used that template to regulate resources. It was the template they moved. We can explore this both as a cycle, that is, a succession of plant communities on one location, and as a movement, that is, a sequence of plant communities crossing the countryside.

Figure 10.1: *Joseph Lycett,* Aborigines using fire to hunt kangaroos, *c. 1821*[5]

Here dense forest rises from low ground to separate grassy hills. A sharp edge divides trees from grass. Fires block kangaroos from the forest and drive them to the spears. Yet the hunters are protecting the forest: they have fired its lee edge so that the wind takes the flames into the grass. When the wind lay the other way they would burn the opposite edge—that must always have been so, otherwise those sharp forest edges would be frayed by fire. A skilful burning regime has kept the forest dense, the grass open, the game accessible.

Much Tasmanian rainforest, for example at Mount Field and the Styx,[9] has a curious feature: it is overtopped by giant eucalypts. Typically they are about 350–400 years old, and are senescent: they won't live much longer.[10] How did they get there? Eucalypts cannot grow through rainforest. Since eucalypts are there, rainforest was not. Yet rainforest is the climax vegetation in the areas I speak of. Thus where eucalypts are, rainforest was cleared off, not once by a bushfire—that

Figure 10.2: *Joseph Lycett,* View from near the top of Constitution Hill, Van Diemen's Land, *c. 1821*[6]

The view is south over Bagdad plains, showing a pattern like the last but on a much larger scale, both on and off Bagdad Creek. No single fire, no single type of fire, could create such a pattern. Its distinct but adjacent burning regimes required intimate local knowledge and great skill.

won't do it—but by deliberate, repeated fires. Under repeated fire, Bill Jackson found, rainforest gives way to a succession of plant communities, notably wet or dry eucalypt forest, then grassland.[11] To change rainforest to grassland took no small persistence.

Senescent eucalypts overtopped rainforest in pre-contact times. In July 1827 Henry Hellyer saw this south of Emu Bay on the north coast:

This is a horrid place [to] be in, neither Sun nor Moon to be seen, no part of the sky[,] being completely darkened by dripping Evergreens consisting of Myrtle, Sassafras, Ferntrees, immensely tall White Gum and Stringy-bark trees from 200 to

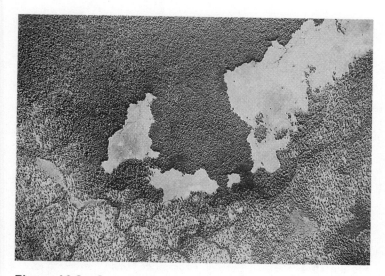

Figure 10.3: *Goderich Plain (top right) and Gatcomb Plain (bottom left), north of the Wandle River near Guildford, 12 April 1949*[7]

This land was used little by Europeans before 1949. Rainforest should be its climax, or natural, vegetation; instead, the landscape is even more diverse than in Lycett's paintings. Plains abut both rainforest and open eucalypt forest, while eucalypts fringe the Wandle River, with grass patches both on and off the flats. At least five distinct fire regimes made such diverse country.

300 feet high and heaps of those which have fallen lying rotting one over the other from 10 to 20 feet high.[12]

In November 1827 Edward Curr echoed Hellyer:

enormous Stringy Bark Trees many of them three hundred feet high and thirty feet in circumference near the roots exclude the rays of the Sun and in the gloom which their shade creates those trees flourish which affect darkness and humidity ... sassafras, dogwood, pepper trees, musk trees ... in some situations blackwood of the best quality ... fungi, mosses, lichens, [and] ferns.[13]

Figure 10.4: *Wineglass Bay on Freycinet Peninsula, from north to south, c. 2001*[8]

This land has never been farmed. Behind the beach runs a sharp edge between trees and grass. It crosses low hills, and in the south rises to a fine wallaby trap. The same soil straddles the edge. The trees are dominated by Tasmanian blue gum [E. globulus], including many dating from European times. In other words trees have germinated in the forest but not outside it. This illustrates a generalisation that eucalypts on ground recently cleared by axe or fire (in this case, fire) can generate from seed stock, but in long-cleared grassland no seed stock flourishes, and eucalypts can only generate, if at all, by edge or wind invasion.

How old was the vegetation sequence signalled here? From their size the overtopping eucalypts were 350–400 years old. In the rainforest below were giant eucalypt logs, some of them rotting, indicating an earlier eucalypt generation. To gain headway over regenerating rainforest, eucalypts would need that earlier generation: how old was it? In Victoria, where warmer and drier conditions induce wood rotting more quickly than in rainforest,[14] 350-year-old mountain ash (*E. regnans*) logs are still largely unrotted,[15] so these Tasmanian logs were at least that old. (Some may have been much older, much more rotten, but such older generations were not necessarily part of a minimum cycle.) Thus for at least 350 years, from 700 to 750 years before 1827, the country was eucalypt forest. Had it been rainforest the logs Hellyer saw lying so thickly could not have grown; had it been grassland the logs would have been burnt. Earlier the country was grassland, for young eucalypts need space to flourish, and earlier still it was rainforest, the climax vegetation. I cannot say for how long it was grassland. It might seem reasonable that if rainforest on one side and eucalypts on the other were at least 350 years old, so was the grassland between. But people sometimes advanced eucalypts onto grassland. On Paradise Plains, isolated 170–190-year-old eucalypts may have grown from branches the Tasmanians left, a practice Hellyer also saw,[16] so a grassland minimum seems closer to 200, rather than 350, years. A rainforest to rainforest cycle thus took at least 900 years (200 + 350 + 350). I caution that this is a minimum, and that pollen sequences might refine it.[17] But at least 900 years before 1827 Tasmanians burnt rainforest to make grass, kept it so for at least 200 years, then for at least 350 years burnt to let eucalypts take hold, then stopped burning and kept fire away to let rainforest return. In short, over at least 900 years they cycled different plant communities over the same ground.

Plant communities were cycled by being moved. On 4 July 1831, on the Ringarooma River just west of Derby in the north-east, George Robinson described:

> the immense quantity of fallen timber which covered the ground, the slipping and sliding off the timber ... This forest is of great extent and consists of immense gum and stringy bark trees, some of which was forty and fifty feet round, and the intermediate space filled up with lesser trees of the dogwood, stinkwood, sassafras and musk, as also the stately ferntree.[18]

Or, mature rainforest under old eucalypts. Yet four miles west, Robinson:

> passed through an extensive forest of mimosa ... Numerous [other] trees, some of them fifteen feet round, were notched to their summit where the natives had gone up in quest of opossums; and numerous ferntrees had been broken down by the natives. After travelling in this route for about ten miles came to an open and extensive plain covered with grass and fern ... This appeared the resort of the natives and my sable companions informed me that it was the native track. I was much gratified at meeting with this country after being immured in a forest for four days ... kangaroo ... were plentiful ... The fern and trees had been fresh burnt.[19]

That 'extensive forest of mimosa' was made by fire. Acacias regenerate quickly and thickly after fire: they are commonly the first recolonisers of burnt land. Without fire, in time other species overtop the wattle, and it dies out. That has not happened here, so the firing was relatively recent. Tree fern, *Dicksonia antarctica*, prefers rainforest. It resists fire and survives on grassland, but under repeated burning does not generate there.[20] Its presence indicates former rainforest. So, walking east to west, Robinson reports rainforest indicating no fire for centuries, then recently fired land carrying wattles, tree fern and numerous large trees, then a grass and tree-fern plain made by firing repeated for enough decades to clear off the trees. In other words, he reports colonising fires moving from west to east.

This fire pattern has been detected elsewhere. In 1988 Bob Ellis and Ian Thomas published a valuable account of the making of Paradise Plains, not far from the country Robinson wrote of. They concluded:

> The present area of grassland on Paradise Plains was formed during the last 200 years or so by the burning of rainforest. To

the east of the Plains is primaeval rainforest; but to the west of the Plains is closed eucalypt forest of recent origin, as is shown by the presence of old open-grown trees and occasional remains of rainforest trees, amongst the tall forest-grown younger eucalypts. As one progresses further west across the plateau, the eucalypt forest appears to have been established for longer, since it contains forest-grown veterans and fallen trees and older secondary rainforest. At the western extremity of the plateau, the remains of eucalypt logs were found on a ridge top beneath secondary rainforest more than 200 years old. It may be that, as existing grassland became impoverished or overgrown with fire-resistant vegetation, the Aborigines abandoned it and generated new grassland by burning adjacent rainforest.[21]

The plains lie west–east; the prevailing winter wind is westerly. West to east, Ellis and Thomas describe eucalypt logs under secondary rainforest, then eucalypt forest becoming progressively younger, then acacias, then grassland, then mature rainforest.[22] This can only be explained by Tasmanians using westerlies to drive grass fires into the eastern rainforest. Were this all, it might be random. But people did not want plains too big, for that would make hunting unpredictable. Nor did they want to destroy too much eucalypt forest or too much rainforest, for they too were habitats. So they took care not to burn too often the eucalypt edge behind them. This let eucalypts regenerate, then later let rainforest reclaim the ground. In short, people moved not only the plain but also a forest succession from west to east. That required varied fire regimes and skill greater than fire controllers can manage today, but Tasmanians did it consistently for centuries. Ellis and Thomas note similarly transformed landscapes nearby, at Diddleum Plain[23] and near Mt Maurice.[24]

Tasmania's fiercest burning winds are hot summer northerlies, which every few years sweep south off the mainland, bringing shrivelling heat. In the 1950s Bill Mollison noted plains made by burning rainforest from north to south. At their south edge, grass gave way abruptly to mature rainforest; at their north, an open eucalypt woodland was advancing onto grassland. There was no soil change. Tasmanians had waited for a northerly, moved clear of the eucalypt seedlings advancing from the north, then lit the plains to drive fires south into the rainforest. Thus slowly, sometimes no doubt by mere metres, they pushed the rainforest south, and regulated the eucalypts advancing from the north to match. This kept each plain a suitable hunting size, but over centuries moved it south.[25]

At Gatcomb Plain (see Figure 10.3), eucalypts overtop rainforest to the north rather than the south, so the rainforest has advanced south. But a swamp anchors the plain's northern tip, and since swamps work best in open country people apparently halted the rainforest's southward advance. Yet they had to burn to bring on green pick, so the plain extends south up a ridge, then over the ridge an open eucalypt forest straddles the Wandle River.[26] This conveniently associated the resources of rainforest, open forest, plain, swamp, river and ridge. Yet I suspect the pattern is more open in the south than the Tasmanians would prefer. Perhaps Gatcomb shows what happens if you *don't* move plains.

I do not know how long it might take to move a cycle across a single location. The time would vary, though probably not much, according to such factors as drought and bushfire, and such influences as soil, temperature, altitude and aspect. It might also have been varied, possibly a lot, to balance totems or to make different-sized plains. For such reasons I doubt that all three communities—rainforest, grass and eucalypts—were necessarily let flourish for the same length of time. This would be essential if a cycle were continually repeated over the same ground, but we have no evidence for that, nor was it necessary.

But obviously firing rainforest commenced a cycle. Ellis found charred rainforest logs in Paradise Plain's oldest grassland

and eucalypt logs in its western rainforest, both more than 200 years old.[27] This touches Jackson's 200-plus years that rainforest needs to recolonise an area,[28] but it will take more centuries for rainforest to reach and capture those charred logs, so the span must be much longer. Hellyer and Curr saw unburnt rainforest 350–400 years old, but Robinson saw burnt rainforest of similar age. That implies some burning at about 400 years, and possibly some longer. Similarly, mature rainforest today without overtopping eucalypts might indicate either a longer span, or the European termination of Tasmanian land management. So I cannot extend that minimum 900-year cycle. But given one cycle, why not more? Of course, people need a learning curve, but there is no reason to suppose that this was not thousands of years ago. Bill Jackson dated Tasmania's deliberate burning sequence at 70 000 years.[29]

Certainly, the moving was both centuries slow and, as figures 10.1 to 10.4 show, purposeful. In those purposes must lie some consistency. Eucalypts and grass need fire to prevent rainforest domination, but having made templates, why did people trouble to move them? I offer three possibilities:

- *Rainforest* To burn rainforest every 400 years or so might stop it becoming either too dense to travel or hunt or gather in, or not dense enough, not rich enough in plant and animal habitats, because of the dominance of species such as myrtle (beech), a giant which can comprise half the rainforest canopy.[30]
- *Eucalypt forest* Burning eucalypts controls leaf-eating insects and helps grass, but even under skilful firing, grass thins as trees grow and consume moisture and soil nutrients—something eucalypts are very good at. Marsupials graze forest grass but prefer green pick on open plains, and they are easier to kill there, so eucalypt forest might be let back to rainforest while fresh grassland is made nearby. In wet eucalypt forest it would also be wise to recycle seeds in

the soil before they rot, otherwise instead of eucalypt regeneration there might be edge invasion of grassland by rainforest, as at Paradise Plains, or long-term grassland, as at Wineglass Bay.

- *Plain* Grass was probably the pivot of a cycle, and I regret knowing so little about it. Even on fertile soil in time, repeated firing saps soil nutrients from fodder grasses, much as with wheat stubble, and they may give way either to buttongrass, which is edible while young but never succulent, or to fire-tolerant shrubs such as heath,[31] as at Gatcomb. People and animals liked heathland berries and tubers,[32] but plains were made with such care to promote feed that grazing animals would seek before all else: only thus could animals be made convenient and predictable. So plains were moved before the grass lost vitality. Nutrient-reduced soil also helped eucalypts regenerate.

On time scales so far detected, not all rainforest, or eucalypt forest, or grassland, was moved. So far, much of each offers no hint that it was ever anything else. But rainforest logs have been found in buttongrass moorland more than 2700 years old at Mount McCall in the south-west, and more than 5000 years old in Rumney Creek Plain just east of Hobart.[33] Given how much of Tasmania's vegetation has been moved, it is not impossible that it all was, albeit sometimes long ago. The Law that directed Tasmanian land management was, after all, universal. Indeed, it was the Law, not the cycle, that demanded memory. Just as today, one generation could see a cycle in all its stages; just as with other religions, countless generations passed on the Law.

I anticipate one question: could bushfires have caused it all? Jackson estimated that before contact less than 0.6 per cent of Tasmanian fires were bushfires.[34] Others think the percentage higher, yet in rainforest regions never above 10 per cent, including the fierce fires of European times.[35] Bushfires were too few and too hot to cause the widespread patterning I have reported.

When Bill Jackson argued that the Tasmanians burnt rainforest to favour other plants, he noted one difficulty. 'The boundaries between vegetation types at present seem remarkably stable ...', he wrote in 1999, 'because of the apparent static nature of the community boundaries at present, it is still difficult to understand how such extensive areas of disclimax vegetation could arise in even 34 k yrs'[36]—34 000 years being the 1999 European estimate of how long people had been in Tasmania. Plant community boundaries—edges—are indeed stable if left alone or subjected to a single fire regime, but my case is that Tasmania was deliberately changed by distinct and shifting regimes. The boundaries were not stable. This completes Jackson's argument that people transformed Tasmania's landscape over many thousands of years, and adds to it that they did so purposefully, skilfully and systematically.

The Australian Academy of the Humanities titled the 2004 symposium 'Memory, Monuments and Memorials'. In the landscapes Tasmanians transformed, all these are one. When you go into the bush, or into what Europeans call wilderness, the memory, monuments and memorials of the Tasmanians will be all around you.

11 'PLANTING HOPES WITH POTATOES': GARDENS, MEMORY AND PLACE MAKING

Katie Holmes

In 1936 the centenary of South Australia's founding provided an occasion for Winnifred Scott to remember 'Some Old Homes and Gardens near Adelaide' and surmise about the emotions that went into their making:

> They make a deep appeal, those early homes and gardens which were the very foundation stones of our State. If one could recall the hopes, the plans, the courage that went to the making of them—what a worth-while record it would be.
>
> Little plots planted with sweet-briar, old world herbs, and rosemary for remembrance; large gardens with great stone gate-posts, long avenues, vineyards, orchards, archery grounds, croquet grounds, and a very gardener's delirium of trees and plants from all over the world; small cottages in bungalow style; substantial houses with thick walls, and cedar fittings, built for an easy

hospitality, and furnished with treasures from old homes over the sea.

They were a home-loving garden-making folk, those first comers to the province of South Australia, but at the outset things were not easy ...

From the very outset irrepressible horticulturists were experimenting, comparing notes on results in a new land, and a climate which had the seasons the wrong way round, and condoling with each other over difficulties—particularly 'the pig nuisance,' for pigs roamed free in early Adelaide, wrecking the brave little unfenced garden patches. Still the optimists worked on, planting hopes with potatoes, and faith in the future of the province with olives, figs, and pomegranates.[1]

Winnifred Scott's evocation of the early days of settlement in South Australia reveals one of the central dynamics at work in early garden making, namely, their 'double vision': gardens looked back to the home the settlers had left but, importantly for my purposes in this chapter, looked forward to a different future; a future based on hope and faith, on the desire for a different and possibly better life. The plants chosen to symbolise this future are noteworthy: potatoes provide a dietary staple, while olives, figs and pomegranates are all of Mediterranean origin and thrive in hot summers. They are also plants commonly found in the Old and New Testaments: the faith in the future that they represent was infused with a Christian vision. 'Civilisation', in the form of gardens, was taking root.

In Simon Schama's mammoth book *Landscape and Memory*, he observes in the introduction that 'before it can ever be a repose for the senses, landscape is the work of the mind. Its scenery is built up as much from strata of memory as from layers of rock.'[2] Susan Martin, in the next chapter, looks at some of the ways in which garden*ing* acted as a spur to memory. I ask: in what ways does gardening use memory to look forward? And, closely related, what work did gardening do for colonial Australians in establishing a sense of belonging, a sense of place, and how was it gendered?

To those with even a passing knowledge of Australian colonial history, the belief that the early colonists pined for home, and that these memories often took the form of flowers and gardens, is commonplace. The 1856 lithograph by John Dicksee, 'A Primrose from England', of immigrants swooning over a pot of primroses, their faces lit up as if transfigured by the very sight of this floral memory, powerfully evokes this sentiment.[3] Significantly, it is the women in the painting who are most transfigured, their faces glowing as if illuminated by beams sent from the primrose petals. The central woman, dressed in blue and veiled, looks almost *Pieta*-like. The men, although interested, are not nearly so affected. This is not to suggest that men did not carry memories of home, or were not moved by the sight of such a tangible reminder, but the implication of the lithograph is that it was the women who were the bearers of both the memories, and indeed the meanings,

Figure 11.1: *J. R. Dicksee 'A Primrose from England', 1856, copied from the painting by Edward Hopley, A Primrose from England (c. 1855), lithographed by J. R. Dicksee.*[3]

of 'home'. Children sit at their mother's knee imbibing the meanings and memories. An engraving of the lithograph reproduced in the *Illustrated London News*, in about 1858, was accompanied by a description of the primrose's arrival:

> The announcement excited a great sensation. Upwards of three thousand people turned out in to the street to see the gentle stranger brought ashore, and the pressure of the crowd was so great that it was found necessary to call out the police to preserve order, and to make a line through which the primrose might be escorted on shore, to be seen by all her admirers.[4]

Here the primrose itself is coded female, signifying gentility and delicacy, an object of wonder and a creature at risk in colonial society. In these two representations, women, mothers, are the bearers of culture and the transmitters of memories. In colonial society, they were also often the gardeners. In particular they were the aesthetic gardeners, especially among the middling classes. In a typical division of labour, men looked after the vegetable garden—a garden that catered to the immediate needs for food and survival and was an extension of men's breadwinner role—and women tended the flower garden. Hence women's gardening was more involved with creating beauty, and, importantly, looked forward to a more established, beautiful and settled place.

Gardens are a form of expression carrying their own meanings, both collective and individual. In this, they are like language. They are also a form of what the linguist Alton Becker calls 'languaging'. He writes:

> Languaging is context shaping. Languaging both shapes and is shaped by context. It is a kind of attunement between a person and a context. Languaging can be understood as taking old texts from memory and reshaping them into present contexts. This is the basic way languaging contrasts with language. Most current theories of language have no place for memory.[5]

Importantly, Becker notes that languaging takes place at the level of particularity, that each of us has a 'repertoire of prior texts, acquired over a life time, to be reshaped and used in making sense of experience'.[6] But in the uttering and recycling of these prior texts, in the adaptation of them, we create new forms. To paraphrase Rhys Isaac: 'We speak the old, *we reach for the new*. In doing so we aspire to something ahead of us not yet realised.'[7] Becker calls this 'entelleche'; Isaac uses the word 'desire'.

From very early in the settlement of Australia, we can see in the inscribing of gardens and in the act of their creation the desire to create something new: something made in the memory of the old, which becomes transformed in its making. It is a desire or a yearning with a double vision: reaching backwards to a remembered place and past, and forward to an imagined place and future.

Gardens are part of the colonising/settling process. They were central to the success of settlement in the part they played in the creation of a sense of place, in building what Alan Atkinson has called a 'palace of memory'. Women were central to this process: to an important degree, they were the carriers of the 'prior texts', and the creators of the new ones. (They also quite literally carried texts into the new world. Georgiana Molloy wrote effusively to Mangles, thanking him for sending her Mrs Loudon's *Flower Garden*.[8] Reading English gardening texts for inspiration on how to create Australian gardens was part of this process of re-imagining the garden.) When our focus is on the garden and the intimate cultivation of space that gardening involves, we can see that the role women played was central in envisaging the new country as a place of hope and a place with a future.

Just as women were often the gardeners, they were also often the letter writers, and many of the letters we have that talk about gardens in any detail are from women. The connection between garden and home—both the memory of home and the new home being created—was so strong as to make it an obvious point of discussion and news. In families where there was a shared love of and interest in the garden, writing about it provided an important means of translating information about the new home. It was, if you like, common ground, or became so in the writing of it. Given the foreign nature of so many of the immigrants' experiences and the landscape they encountered, gardens, and what went into their making, were an important bridge. Gardens then inscribed twice: in the planting and in the telling; they became part of the story settlers told about the settlement of their new country.

One example of the creation of a garden, and the ensuing transformation of the landscape, comes from the diary of an early Port Phillip settler, Anne Drysdale. Anne arrived in Port Phillip from Scotland in 1840 at the age of forty-seven.[9] She lived first as a guest of a settler family by the name of Thomson, and Dr Thomson, assuming the land was his to give, bestowed some of his thousand acres on Anne. Seventeen months after her arrival she moved to her new home on the Bellarine Peninsula. The first thing Anne did when taking up residence at Boronggoop, in August 1841, was establish a garden. 'Garden and flower seeds' were put in the garden, '8 peach and cherry trees' planted.[10] Slowly the area surrounding the house was transformed into what one visitor described in 1846 as a 'beautiful garden filled with gay luxuriant flowers'. We learn more about this garden from another observer who, writing for intending emigrants, noted the 'wonderful change for the better' that had occurred in the garden since his visit three years previously, and described it as having 'gravelled walks dividing the different parterres', a design that reminded him strongly of 'home'. It was, in other words, a proper garden, displaying its Scottish affinities. It was also productive: her melons were 'pronounced … the finest … ever … grown in the country', and the fruits of her garden were used at her own table and as gifts. The presence of melons in this garden alerts us to the fact that this garden was an imperial garden, harbouring plants from around the world, an expression of global exchange.

Anne's garden may have carried plants and memories of 'home' (her prior texts), but in her gardening she looked beyond Scotland. Anne, able to accommodate native plants within her vision of the garden, selected flowers from the surrounding bush to plant, and she sent seeds of local flora such as 'native Indigo' to her relatives in Scotland, describing it as 'a pretty blue flower it is very hardy here but you may try some in the green house'. She requested that they return the favour: 'fine fushias or any green house plants' were among those she desired.[11] So the garden itself became part of her accommodation to her new home, and marked a system of exchange and transaction. Memories of 'home' were planted there, bringing her past into the present. But in the planting they were also reshaped, sharing the plot now with new and different growth. The geologist and ecologist John Cameron writes about the relationship formed when people begin to experience places through interaction: 'the landscape shapes experience, through which memory is generated. The memory shapes subsequent perceptions and experiences of landscape.'[12] Through particular, individual interactions, settlers' experiences of their landscape, their place, changed. 'Prior texts' were transformed and new memories generated.

In a discussion about the use of the phrase 'sense of place', Cameron opts for the ecologist Relph's description: 'The word "place" is best applied to those fragments of human environment where meanings, activities and a specific landscape are all implicated and enfolded by each other'.[13] Geographers have been particularly attentive to the ways 'place' is 'constituted and maintained through social relations of power and exclusion'.[14] For Cameron, a 'sense of place' is an individual experience, although it can be shared. From a historian's perspective, Alan Atkinson in *The Europeans in Australia* notes that:

A sense of place depends on the understanding that a sum may be more than its parts, that a geographical point, whatever its mere black-and-whiteness on a map, can house something absolute, even some immortal spirit. Such a sense crept very gradually into the collective imagination of Europeans in Australia.[15]

One of the crucial steps involved in the creation of that sense of place was an investment in it: it too needed to become Atkinson's 'palace of memory'. A place needed to be actively engaged with, a sense of belonging established.[16] Gardening was one of the ways colonists achieved this, first at an individual level and later at a collective one. We see the gradual shift from a sense of loss and mourning for the home left behind, to one of memory and transformation. The success of colonisation depended on this ability to create first a sense of individual and then collective futures. Hope was a crucial ingredient. For Indigenous people, European gardens were part of a 'hope-destroying' enterprise. As Deborah Bird Rose observes of settler societies: 'we are here not only by violence, but also by a misguided and misleading hope for the future'.[17]

Along with the narrative about immigrants pining for home, and thus planting English plants in their gardens, comes the oft-made assumption that most immigrants removed all native plants, finding no place for them in their cultivated patches. Sometimes this was the case, and Louisa Meredith, along with many other women, was scathing of its practice:

The system of 'clearing' here, by the total destruction of every native tree and shrub, gives a most bare, raw, and ugly appearance to a new place. In England we plant groves and woods, and think our country residences unfinished and incomplete without them; but here the exact contrary is the case, and unless a settler can see an expanse of bare, naked, unvaried, shadeless, dry, dusty land spread all around him, he fancies his dwelling 'wild and uncivilized.' About some of the older houses in the colony a growth of fruit-trees, and often British forest-trees, has succeeded the despised aboriginal productions, and sometimes a few of the grand Norfolk Island pines tower above the lower groups.[18]

Art historian Caroline Jordan argues that such a response from women like Louisa Meredith and Mary Allport was both classed and gendered:

> [a] protest against the direct actions of their masculine counter-parts ... While women were excluded from agency in the masculine depredations of killing, clearing and dispossession on the frontier, they were able to occupy an exemplary role as aestheticizers and civilizers, the natural champions of the picturesque and through it, of environmental and species conservation.[19]

While some publicly criticised the *tabula rasa* approach to the land, others advocated or simply implemented a different approach. We have already heard from Anne Drysdale. William Kerr instructed Victorian gardeners in 1841 on how to grow native plants:

> Make plantations of the indigenous plants and shrubs of the handsomest dwarf growing flowering kinds, such as *aster tomentosus*, *gracilis* and *longifolia* (daisy trees), *exocarpus stricta* (cherry tree), [lists of plants to try] ... The following are well adapted for trailing up sticks or against a wall; *Gylcine rubicunda*, this is the handsome rich blue flowering creeper which adorns the bush in every direction in the spring months ... There are many others of equal beauty and deserving of a place in the flower garden; but the above will suffice for a handsome plantation, mixed with plants and shrubs of English production, and other exotics. Continue digging up flower beds, being careful not to injure the roots of bulbs with the spade.

In December, readers were advised:

> Finish planting out the different kinds of hardy, half hardy and tender annuals, and other flowering plants into the border, giving

them water until they have established themselves. Continue planting native shrubs: one necessary thing to observe is to take them up with all their roots and fibres intact: plant them in loose well prepared ground, shaking the mould well about the root and afterwards give a watering, which watering may be continued until they have recovered their removal.[20]

The writer Mary Fullerton, in her autobiography *Bark House Days* (1921), recalled the establishment of her childhood garden:

Where they all came from, the simple flowers, I cannot remember; from neighbours established before us, I suspect, except such as came as seeds in letters from friends afar, who, through the blessed if infrequent post, had touch with our remoteness. There was a laburnum at the back [and] gooseberry bush ... too ... Mother had many sentiments—daisies, violets, buttercups and primroses, and, last of all, a daffodil; these gathered England about her.

So her mother planted the flowers of home, but allowed others their place as well. Fullerton and her siblings attempted to make a flower garden in the bush: 'Better success attended our efforts at transplanting bush flowers into the home garden. For years we had a flourishing variety of native plants that took gratefully and gracefully to the finer soil and more human surroundings.'[21] The story that Mary Fullerton tells about her childhood garden has her mother giving priority to her garden of memory, while allowing her children, appropriately, to seek out the new. The resulting hybrid nature of the garden conveys the bifurcated vision essential to the success of gardening and place making in colonial Australia.

One of the functions that the garden seems to play in the letters of immigrants is as a reassurance to concerned relatives that life here really is all right, and indeed has many of the trappings and comforts of life at home. Katie Fowler, who migrated to Queensland in 1866 to marry Walter Hume, always made a point of commenting on the gardens she saw, and the state of those around her own home. Shortly after her arrival and marriage, she travelled to Toowoomba by train, commenting that 'it seemed quite strange to be travelling in so <u>civilised</u> a manner thro' this primeval country!' The scenery on the way she described as 'very pretty', although she was not enamoured with the gum trees:

> They are tall grown trees but the foliage is most disappointing. It hardly deserves the name. The leaves are narrow & grey-looking & hang down so as to afford no shade—they are called Evergreens but never green [would be] more appropriate ...
>
> The great <u>want</u> in the scene, is <u>real green</u> foliage, like <u>oak, beeches</u>, etc. The universal Gumtrees produce a misty effect, something like olives.

In contrast to this picture, Katie wrote to her sister about her new home in words that would have been as reassuring to her family as the sight was to herself, even if it did still contain rather odd elements:

> I have twice ridden over to Drayton & been introduced to my new home—it is looking exceedingly pretty now the roses, honeysuckles & passion flower on the Veranda are in bloom—<u>bushes</u> of scarlet geranium, 3 or 4 inches in diameter make the garden in front look quite gay. The rest of the enclosure is paddock, with some fruit trees in it, & 2 or 3 <u>graves</u> at the farther end, for in the early days here there were no Cemeteries, & people were buried in their own domain—does it not seem strange? There are 7 weeping willows about the place, which are looking lovely now like bright green fountains.

One month later Katie qualifies her initial report on her new garden, noting that it was 'a perfect wilderness when we took possession. Weeds & flowers are grown equally rampant. Only the part around the house has any pretensions to be a garden—the rest is grass & fruit trees.' As for the activity of gardening itself, Katie notes that in November it was either too hot or too wet, and the evenings did not provide much opportunity for gardening as the twilights were so short that 'it is dark almost as soon as it is cool enough to go out'. Difficulties aside, the important thing is that she was gardening: sowing the 'Tott and Barnes' seeds she had brought with her, and reporting back on plants that were known and familiar to her family, such as the oleander: 'How I wish dear Mama could see it'. Memory and transformation were already at work.[22]

Another immigrant equally keen on gardening was Rachel Henning. During her first visit to Australia in 1855, she noted one of the important factors influencing the ways in which colonists 'saw' the native flowers that surrounded them:

> I do not care enough about the Australian flowers to take much trouble with them. I often wonder what can be the difference. I suppose it is the want of any pleasant associations connected with them. I often see very pretty flowers in the bush and just gather them to take a look at them, and then throw them away without any further interest, while at Home every wildflower seemed like a friend to me.[23]

Connection was thus made through association.

When Rachel returned permanently to Australia in 1861 she went to stay with her sister Amy and Amy's husband in Bathurst. She began to gather memories of home about her— despite evidence of ecological disruption:

> We have, also, rather too much of even such a good thing as sweetbriar … It must be lovely when in flower, but it is not exactly 'adapted to the wants' of sheep and cattle, and it is extremely difficult to extirpate. However, I have not taken warning, but have collected some seeds to sow at Marlborough. I saw it growing wild in the bush as I came up to Bathurst, and rejoiced greatly, as it is the only approach we have in this country to wild roses.[24]

Soon Rachel was planting her own garden, and making associations with the Australian flora that she had felt so lacking before.

> Amy and I walk most days, and lately we have taken to gardening
> ... [A] benevolent lady gave us a quantity of plants and cuttings,
> which we planted. By dint of a good deal of watering and
> shading, they are growing very well, and we now have a begin-
> ning of a garden ...
>
> It is quite warm now, as warm as many English summer days.
> All the gardens about us are full of peach- and willow-trees, and
> the light green of the willows and the masses of peach-blossom
> look so very pretty together. The paddocks are full of clover, and
> the flowers are beginning to come out in the bush; the yellow
> wattle is beautiful, and there are some pretty little white shrubs
> like heaths in flower.[25]

Whereas earlier Rachel did not care enough 'to take much trouble' with the wildflowers, now she can see their beauty. Her reference point is still an English one—'pretty little white shrubs like heaths in flower'—enabling her to translate what she is seeing into a language and knowledge shared by her readers. Rachel's approach to her environment is changing. As she cultivates the land around her, so her own roots become more firmly grounded and the meanings of her garden change.

Transformations in the ways in which colonists saw and experienced their landscape occurred in part because plants grew differently here, and even familiar ones looked different from those back home. Plants that in England could only be grown in a greenhouse thrived here in the outdoors. In June 1881 the Gardener's Mutual Improvement Society of South Australia observed:

> within a few miles of Adelaide we unite in producing the plants
> of England, France, Italy and Spain, and we had growing not
> merely in greenhouses and shadehouses but in the open space

and air, and in open gardens, the products of north and south of Europe, of the high lands of Asia, plants, trees and flora from America and Africa as well as our own indigenous flora.[26]

For other immigrants the Australian countryside, and the gardens that grew here, would always disappoint. Miss Oliver, writing in 1871 to the Emigration Society, which had organised her passage, noted of the country around Horsham in Victoria's Western District:

> As to the scenery, there is none. It is certainly the ugliest country I have ever seen, reminding one of the N. of France …
>
> The garden is looking nice, but nothing to equal the flowers at home. The soil is bad, & the heat with hot winds dry up every thing.[27]

The ability to overcome the sense of loss involved in leaving 'home' and creating a 'new home' in the 'new country' was something not all immigrants possessed (whether for structural or personal reasons). One of the ingredients of 'success'—if that is what we would call it—was both the desire and the ability to transform the meaning of 'home'. Gardens were crucial to this process. Through gardening, places—and the sense of attachment and relationship that word implies— were created and cultivated.[28] The gendered nature of this process raises some interesting issues. If the creation of 'home' was largely a woman's activity—and concerns about restless men wandering the goldfields looking for a woman, a home and a garden to settle them suggest that it was[29]—then women's role in the creation of a sense of attachment and loyalty was a crucial one. Their real and symbolic function in creating a 'palace of memory', and in envisaging the new country as a place of hope and a place with a future, was central.

Henry Lawson's story 'The Lost Souls' Hotel' captures something of this as a character ponders the nostalgia for a garden:

I'd dig a tank or reservoir for surface water as big as a lake, and bore for artesian water—and get it, too, if I had to bore right through to England; and I'd irrigate the ground and make it grow horse-feed and fruit, and vegetables too, if I had to cart manure from Bourke ... And I'd—no, I wouldn't have any flowers; they might remind some heart-broken, newchum black-sheep of the house where he was born, and the mother whose heart he broke—and the father whose grey hairs he brought down in sorrow to the grave—and break him up altogether ...

On second thought I think I *would* have some flowers; and maybe a bit of ivy-green. The newchum might be trying to work out his own salvation, and the sight of the roses and ivy would show him that he hadn't struck such a God-forgotten country after all, and help strengthen the hope for something better that's in the heart of every vagabond till he dies.[30]

In Lawson's story, gardens carry both the nostalgic memories of home, and also, and in the end more importantly, a sense of hope and a future, a better life. I have been suggesting that women were central to this hopeful vision of a new country, but why have the narratives placed women as the haloed bearers of the primrose—the past—and all it symbolises?

Perhaps some of the answer to this lies with Lawson himself, the radical nationalist writer who valorised men's engagement with the land as the defining experience of landscape. Within this narrative there is no place for 'prior texts', for fond memories of home. And no place for women, except as a kind of impediment ('the mother whose heart he broke'). Similarly, narratives of colonisation have often emphasised the 'clear and conquer' mentality rather than stories of accommodation and negotiation. Men's future investment might be seen to lie in transforming the landscape so as to extract what wealth they could from the soil, a practice now seen as disastrous for the future of the land. Or, when it came to gardening, creating monuments of Empire such as the Botanic Gardens we see in our capital cities, or those of stately homes around the country.

By focusing on domestic gardens, and women's role in creating them, we can see the process of place making as a gendered as well as a racial activity, involving, as Susan Martin has pointed out, sexed, gendered, raced and nationalised subjects. David Day has argued that narratives of success are crucial to the ability of a 'supplanting society' to succeed.[31] I would suggest that those narratives may begin in the smallest of places: the garden; and take us to the largest of stories: how settlers came to develop a sense of, and relationship with, the places they created.

In the conclusion to her discussion about 'some old homes and gardens near Adelaide', Winnifred Scott, she of the 'planting hopes' phrase, notes:

> To each of us, if we are fortunate, there comes the picture of some garden of memory. For me the scent of gum leaves, pine and cypress, and thyme borders under the hot sunlight call up a garden where I played ...
>
> To gather and keep such pictures before they are lost would be worthwhile, for the home life of the past gives the keynote of the time, and sympathy with our brave home builders will never be quite lost so long as we love gardens.[32]

In Winnifred's 'garden of memory', native Australian plants grow alongside introduced species, their scents mingling to create new memories of a new home. We may not share Winnifred's adulation of the past, but her sympathy for the importance of gardens in it, and the access they allow us to the 'keynote of the time', is well placed.

12 REMEMBERING THE SELF IN THE COLONIAL GARDEN: GARDENS AND SUBJECTIVITY

SUSAN K. MARTIN

Gardens are intimately associated with memory, through scent, through sight, through association. This works in two directions—gardens draw on past memory, but they might also be seen to use memory to project a future.

I want to address specifically the first aspect of this association, by asking a question about the operation of memory in colonial gardening. Do gardens or garden*ing* constitute the spur to memory, the nostalgic sign of British settlement and British colonialism, in Australia?[1] There seems little distinction, yet it is that mythical object—the 'European garden' in Australia—which is so commonly taken to constitute and mirror the European subject. Allaine Cerwonka, in *Native to* *the Nation*, dismissively calls such gardens 'homesick gardens' that register 'nostalgia for an imagined British homeland most Australians had never seen'.[2]

Rather than being such a frozen, static space as this suggests, however, gardens of whatever type and era are more like poststructuralist understandings of the self—they are always in process, they are constantly made and remade, they have no static moment, except within an imaginary space. There is no absolute end product, because gardens are endlessly mutable. They are not entirely fit objects for the unproblematic formation of a stable subject, despite implications to the contrary. For gardeners in nineteenth century Australia it may not have been the garden that most easily allowed them to remember and remake an English self and overwrite Australian space, but garden*ing*—the repetition of a set of tasks and movements brought from their origins.

The gardening European is certainly occupied in remaking space, and in memory-driven and memory-making activities that alter the intimate environment, as well as self. It is not simple to determine to what extent it is the process that is the Europeanising activity—the act of gardening that most unproblematically activates memory and transforms imaginative space, and to what extent it is the 'thing' produced—the garden. In the nineteenth century textual production of gardens, which is one of the main means of accessing these gardens, it is not the gardens that are most often narrated, but the gardening—the making, not the end product.

I am not suggesting that gardening itself is a European practice. The *Mabo* decision, after all, rests on not only the continuous holding of gardens, but also hundreds of years of continuous cultivation of garden plots.[3] If gardening can be read as a spatial practice that facilitates the growth of food and belonging to place, then Aboriginal burning practices can also be categorised as 'gardening'. The 'European gardening' I am referring to here is the specific set of understandings and spatial practices carried from a European 'home' place, and replicated, more or less, in the new space to be colonised.

In contemporary critical terms gardening might then be read as one aspect of the performance of a colonial subjectivity.[4] It has been argued that the movement of British subjects to the colonial context threatened their subjectivity in a number of senses, positive and negative.[5] Simon Ryan sees the constitution of the Explorer self in relation to the Australian landscape as one way in which that was addressed. Tanya Dalziell discusses the ways in which popular fictions at the end of the nineteenth century address the fact that the '"white race", and the privileges and powers accorded settlers under colonial conditions are neither secure nor essential'.[6] Such texts both chronicle the fragility of the white settler subject, and are part of the narrative that attempts to stabilise it. British subjectivity and subjection can be remembered and reconsolidated on a much smaller scale also, which is, arguably, where gardening comes in.[7] Gardening in the colonies may be a performance that remembers a sexed, gendered, raced, nationalised subject.

Diary material from the nineteenth and twentieth centuries, as Katie Holmes has pointed out, narrates the planting of gardens in relation to making a new place homelike.[8] The incorporation of plants and seeds, and even garden designs and shapes from 'home', creates echoes. Diaries and fiction also narrate *gardening* as a practice that renders the self in the new space a familiar self, which remembers a British subject even when (or perhaps especially when) the garden is not recognisably British.

In the long-term farm diaries of John and Catherine Currie, working, clearing, dairying and gardening in Bacchus Marsh and then Gippsland from the 1870s onwards, plants and plantings are described, but there is no narrative, sketch or outline of garden plans or general appearance. For example, in early August 1873, John describes grafting fruit trees, and planting, among other tasks:

[Aug] 5 grafted some Green Gages and one Apple ...
Aug 10 John Wells fetched me some Grafts from the Mars [?] ...
11 Stoped [sic] at home. Grafting trees. Crooks pear. 2 trees first ... a [?] Burnips [?] Boston Russet. 8. Irish Peach "8—Cox Orange Pippon 8, Crooks Long. 4. Bon Creistan[?] L [?] Some purpule [sic] Plums. and some Cherry Plums.[9]

When the family move to a selection in Gippsland, one of the first things John does is fence a garden.[10] By August 1876 John and Catherine are gardening almost every day:

August 23 fine day = very. John gardening sowed onions Lettuce and celery. L Grant here for the Harrows
[August 30] very wet this morning. the children gone to school. John clearing = I sowed a few peas in garden ...
[September 15] not quite so rough [windy] to day John fenceing in morning sowed the Barley afternoon We sowed some melons & cucumbers yesterday = with two or three Tomatoes.

Despite this activity, no description or plan or projection is given of this garden, nor of 'the garden that is to be' which Kate is describing across the same period (e.g. Jan 6, 1877), though they clearly have a plan, in that particular plants have their designated places:

[June 15, 1877]: ... still wet. john planted the last row of apple Trees and I planted half the bed of strawberries.
[On July 12, 1879, two years later] John went to Drouin ... and the fruit trees had come. we Planted them in their Places— the necterine [sic] first near the path, then Madeline Tardive [?] Peach Comet next and Lady Palmerston.

Whatever the unspoken design, what is described is process, not product. This may be partly a class issue. Although the Curries also planted decorative plants and flowers in the home garden, their early descriptions are of a food garden in which design elements may not have been paramount as compared to some middle-class gardens of the period, where quite elaborate coloured plans of intent or achievement exist. Nevertheless I would argue that for Kate Currie, along with clearing and farming, it is the repetitious act of gardening with familiar plants, particularly those brought from her Scottish immigrant family at Bacchus Marsh, along with the establishment of networks of gift and exchange which accompany the activities,[11] that generate and reinforce her sense of herself, and particularly her self as settler. Almost every page of the diary describes activities in or around the garden.

Similar but different representations of gardens and gardening can be traced in nineteenth century fiction about gardening. I do not see these narratives as simple historical texts —although they are still among the many narratives of culture, they are artefacts that carry additional cultural investment. Just because they are highly constructed 'artistic' narratives, if for no other reason, they bear a different relation to culture, and represent that culture in different ways. Literary texts have been used quite distinctly in Australia to derive particular understandings of national identity and subjectivity.[12] One intervention in that discussion is the examination of other forms of literary and textual production in circulation in the nineteenth century.[13]

Finished gardens, when they appear in fiction, are frequently seen as, or stand for, a static colonial identity—Britain successfully remembered. Most commonly they are markers for successful settlement and colonisation—the possibility of reconstituting the old world in the new, for transforming indigenous wilderness into introduced cultivation. The ways in which this representation occurs varies. At its most conservative it is a narrative that introduces the garden fully formed, rather than the gardening involved in establishing and maintaining it. In Charles Rowcroft's *The Australian Crusoes, or the Adventures of an English Settler and his Family in the Wilds of Australia*,[14] set in Tasmania, the garden is part of a boundary that is finally successfully created between the house and the absolute other—in this case, the bush. The hero, Thornley, in his old age watches his grandchildren play on his 'plot of English grass, whose lively green, and thick, close sward, contrasted pleasingly with the brown coarse tufts of the native plains beyond'. He is among 'English' fruit trees, securely separated from those native plains, although even these are described as 'park-like'. This garden is proof of settlement, and proof against indigeneity—here, as elsewhere, narratives that exclude native vegetation frequently conflate indigenous peoples with indigenous plants, and produce a stable subjectivity by remembering themselves in the absence of (and yet implicitly against) such alien others.

Henry Kingsley's settler novel, *The Recollections of Geoffry Hamlyn*, similarly depicts completed gardens, not gardens in the process of establishment. At Garoopna Station the extent to which the garden is a memory of England, mirrored and commodified, is made explicit: 'three French windows opened on to a dark cool veranda, beyond which was a beautiful flower garden. The air was perfumed by vases of magnificent flowers [from the garden,] a hundred pounds' worth of them, I should say, if you could have taken them to Covent-garden that December morning.'[15] This garden is established, and established as English and Antipodean: its products are familiar enough to sell at the heart of empire—Covent Garden flower market—but exotic and valuable in their inversion of season.

In the evangelical Christian and temperance fiction of South Australian novelist Maud Jeanne Franc, the garden *is* a garden in process. Gardening is an ideological activity that produces appropriate feeling in the gardener. It is gardening, not the garden, that converts the gardener, and in the novels the important gardens are gardens-in-process. Here gardening is the way in which past homes and past selves are recalled and reconstituted. This may be because of Franc's gender, her evangelical agenda, or the fact that these were locally produced novels directed, at least initially, at a local audience.[16] Franc uses the garden-in-process to reconfigure a Christian middle-class British subject in the colonised landscape. As well as some form of national or colonial subjectivity, representations of the practice of gardening in her novels allow the organisation of evangelical Christianity (cultivation of the soul—personal and national); and temperance (cultivation of the body and soul—again personal and national).

In Franc's first novel, *Marian, or the Light of Someone's Home*, the eponymous heroine emigrates to Australia and starts planting seeds of Christianity and contentment wherever she goes. The novel is overtly about appropriate and inappropriate settlement. Appropriate settlement includes gardening as a way of remembering and remaking English values in the colonies. In the planning and working of a garden, proper subjects are made. The bush homestead to which Marian travels as governess is prosperous, but the sign that higher things of the mind and spirit are not valued is indicated by the neglect of the garden and of anything non-commercial. Unlike *The Recollections of Geoffry Hamlyn*, the novel *Marian* explicitly praises gardening as a pursuit that is separate from a bad Australian subjectivity seen as exemplified by commodification and greed. The values placed on the garden are ethical and spiritual, not the monetary values of Covent Garden.

In this novel the making of the garden, not the *made* garden, signifies the appropriate advancement of the hero Allen to a point where the enlightened Marian can marry him. It is the constitution of Allen as settler gardener, not settler with a garden, or proven settler because he has a garden, that reconfigures him. Allen builds a garden around the house, ostensibly for his ailing sister Julie, but actually as part of his attempts to woo the angelic Marian and prove himself worthy of her. In a pivotal scene in the novel he shows Marian and his sister Julie the results:

> The paths had been left of a pleasant breadth; four might have walked comfortably abreast, for there was no deficiency of ground inclosed [sic], and the purpose of all was pleasure, a very unusual one in Australia. Utility was here put entirely out of the question.
>
> ... they turned into a path evidently winding round the whole of the enclosure. 'Do you see what I have done?' and he pointed to either side of the path, along which were newly-planted vines, rapidly putting forth buds and leaves.
>
> 'Grape-vines!' said Marian. 'Well, but I thought you intended to have no fruit here.'
>
> 'So I did, but you see, Miss Herbert, in planting these, I was thinking of something almost as agreeable in summer as fruit, I mean shade!
>
> ... —stoop down, if you please, ladies, and you will discover something else. Do you see those little unmeaning twigs, all putting out buds and leaves?'
>
> 'Yes—why, they are rose slips!'
>
> 'Every variety that I could lay hands upon,' laughed Allen ...
>
> 'How beautiful!' said Marian, with admiration. 'How much I admire the idea! Can you not fancy, Julie, that you see the roses in bloom, and the vine-leaves and tendrils interlacing above?'[17]

This is a garden in process, and an idea of a garden—and primarily it is proof of Allen's *gardening*. Marian's gardening skills, the planting of her seeds from 'home', install memories of proper British subjectivity into colonial space endangered by greed and avarice (and this greed and avarice are thus conveniently figured as having nothing to do with the British or empire). By gardening, Allen practises (in both senses) proper British subjecthood. The same manoeuvres occur in other Franc novels. Men and women who garden (not just men and women *with* gardens) remember a previous life and self through practice and repetition.[18]

Franc's gardens are not just 'English gardens' or 'Homesick gardens'. Although they remember Britain, they invariably incorporate native and indigenous plants. The garden in *Beatrice Melton's Discipline* includes 'whispering shea-oaks and golden wattles [that] bloom among green almonds, towering poplars, and shady willows ... [with] [f]ruits and flowers ... and vegetables in abundance'.[19] These gardens, which invoke English gardens but incorporate the native (whether plants, landscape or wilful forgetting of indigenous inhabitation) in some sense, cannot unproblematically offer a memory of Englishness or, indeed, whiteness. Gardening—weeding, watering, hoeing, planting, lifting—the bodily experience of it and the narration of it, more clearly reiterates or performs this certain type of self—for the white gardener.

I want to close by looking at the Tasmanian gardener Mary Morton Allport, who was also a flower and portrait painter, and in one striking photograph, a harpist in the garden. Ian Henderson has discussed the importance of Allport's painting skills in the production of herself as middle-class subject.[20] Her paintings of her own garden might be seen to reproduce the static image of the 'homesick garden'. However, Allport also narrates herself, in her diaries and letters, as a garden*er* and her classed settler identity is partly produced through the act of gardening.

In the journal she kept for her absent son Morton, she comments at one point, 'Just as Hill had clipped all the hedges and made the garden look like paradise in Queen Anne's time, the Kay's drove up' [*sic*] (22 January 1853).[21] Servant help assists in presenting the garden (and the class status of the family with the garden), while Allport also uses her own gardening to modify and engineer her position. The garden is a place where the genteel classes come to stroll. For instance, on 16 January 1853, 'The Powers came and walked through the garden'. On 24 April, 'The Pitcairns and Mr. Martin called and walked in the garden', and such visits are a regular occurrence. The garden is also admired for its superior produce, and this is positioned in Allport's discussion of it not as a commercial feature, but more as if it were the garden of an English estate: 'I took the Butterworth's [*sic*] down to the garden, where like every one else, they exalted our fruit above all the island, especially a new seedling peach' (5 March 1853). The garden is presented as a sight and a site for visits and viewing: 'Went to-day with Minnie and Mrs. Beck to take Mrs. Compton some Nectarines and Peaches, and to ask them to come and see the garden on Wednesday' (28 March 1853).

Allport constantly gives gifts—'I sent some asparagus up the street on Friday' (7 January 1853); 'I found eight more strawberries for old Doctor Bedford' (19 January 1853); 'Wrote to Mrs. Dawson by the *Rodney*. Sent "Dennis" the cat on board with some vegetables for Captn. Maclean, some fruit for Mr. Lee and tulip roots for Mr. Cooper' (11 March 1853).[22] She also uses gardening to avoid some social contacts: 'Mr. Fraser came just as I was going to gather parsley, but I was too busy to ask him in' (25 January 1853); 'Mrs. and the Misses Rogers called, but I was in the upper orchard, topping and tailing young onions for soup' (7 January 1853). Some of the gifts of fruit both assert superior social position, and evade undesirable social contacts and acquaintances, as when daughter Minnie is invited to stay the night with the unsuitable Mrs King, and Papa decides that Minnie will be sick: 'sent a basket of fruit and a note to Mrs. Compton to say that Minnie was not well enough to accept their invitation. NB. Her nose *did* bleed this morning very much' (4 April 1853).

Allport's garden affirms her genteel British settler status. Her paintings help to install the space of her garden as an appropriate site in which that active subject may be performed and remembered. Her gardening activities position her in part as a genteel English gardener—the summer months, in particular, enable her to perform the Lady Bountiful dispensing produce. As well as distributing generously among her social equals and superiors, and patronising middle-class inferiors, she bestows largesse on the poor: 'Gave apples and grapes to the herd of urchins at the gate' (9 April 1853). However, the image of her topping and tailing onions, gathering and drying walnuts, and packing apples is more complicated—it does suggest that the performance of the gendered gardening settler subject was a more flexible one than I have been indicating, and that the making of the genteel white settler gardener required continual repetition and reiteration to sustain it.[23] The main focus of Mary Allport's journal is on the garden as a space for genteel strolls, and for the gathering of fruit, nuts and vegetables as leisure activity and for use as gifts. She does make it clear, however, that some of the produce is intended for sale, as when she describes the walnut drying and apple and pear packing on 16 April 1853, finishing by commenting, 'Five hundred bushels are stowed away which we expect to fetch a pound a bushel'.

The tension between commerce and gentility is evident when some visitors see the garden not in terms of gentility or aesthetic space, but in terms of commercial gain, as when Allport 'had to go round the garden' with Mr and Mrs Douglas Kilburn and 'He said there was a very good living to be made out of it, and supposed there were thousands of bushels of fruit' (30 March 1853). The garden as commercial space helps sustain Allport's class status in that it provides the necessary money to position her, but it also threatens that status, which is dependent on her self-production as a particular type of leisured, genteel gardener, disconnected from the public and commercial. The journal works to separate the potentially commodified garden from the elevated, domestic, genteel gardener and mostly this works very effectively, but there are fractures. Allport's reiterations of herself as gardener, like the concentration on gardening in Franc's novels, work to resist such fractures and represent a homelike (English, settler) gardener, rather than a 'homesick' garden. In a different but parallel way Kate Currie uses her role as gardener to place herself, and elevate herself as much as possible, within her community, and in her own self-representation in her diaries.

13 TASMANIAN LANDSCAPES IN PAINTING, POETRY AND PRINT

ROSLYNN HAYNES

What turns land into landscape and creates place from mere space? Place is space that has meaning and hence identity. It is a site of collective memory that we can access and sometimes retrieve from other people's memories (as Sally Morgan famously did in *My Place*). Simon Schama's seminal book *Landscape and Memory* was one monolithic attempt to deconstruct the dense fabric of associations that make up some categories of landscape. I am not about to Schamarise Tasmania, but only to outline some of the ways in which people have tried to engrave meaningful associations on the space known to the Tasmanian Aborigines, the traditional *Palawa*, as *Trowenner*, to the early settlers as Van Diemen's Land, and now as Tasmania.

How do *we* relate to the land? We pass through it, live on it, manipulate it, exploit it, photograph it, engage with it—

commercially, pragmatically, artistically and perhaps spiritually. But compared with many cultures, modern Western societies are impoverished in the ways they relate to the land. Almost certainly, though we cannot know for sure, the *Palawa* had a rich culture linking them to the land in story, song, dance, ritual and religion. What do we have instead?

To the early European invaders of *Trowenner* the land was characterised by a succession of absences. Not only were there so few people, but also there was no history, no cultural context within which the land could be understood, no basis for interaction with it except in terms of hostility and brute conquest. For them the land was without form, and void: it could not be imagined.

As late as 1860 the very experienced surveyor James Calder wrote that it is 'as yet without a history, without traditions, and indeed almost without any association—Its past is a veritable blank and we look back into it only to discover that it has nothing to reveal'.[1] Even the loquacious Scottish playwright David Burn, who lived in Van Diemen's Land for almost twenty years, felt inadequate to describe place without an accepted history:

> It is a difficult task effectively to paint the scenery of a tenantless wilderness, where no land-marks, no spot of terror or renown … is to be found to give an impress to the features, or give tangible hold, whereby succeeding tourists may call identical localities to immediate recognition.[2]

The notion that the land had no identity before the arrival of the Europeans, that it was pristine, straight from the hand of the Creator, a Sleeping Beauty waiting to be awakened with the kiss of progress, was not, of course, politically innocent. Consciously or not, those who voiced it were contributing to the doctrine of *terra nullius*. If it was a land of nothing it must also be a land of no one—or no one deserving of it. John Dunmore Lang, Presbyterian minister, historian and controversial New South Wales politician, visited Van Diemen's Land in 1835. Sailing up the Derwent on board the *Medway*, he was moved to philosophise upon the scene in a sonnet:

> *'Tis a most beauteous Strait! ...*
> *And as the good ship glides before the breeze*
> *Broad bays and isles appear and steep cliffs hoar,*
> *With groves on either hand of ancient trees*
> *Planted by Nature in the days of yore;*

Despite the impact of this natural beauty on the eye, Lang felt a disturbing absence to the ear. The poem's structure turns on the 'But' of the next line:

> *But all is still as death! Nor voice of man*
> *Is heard, nor forest warbler's tuneful song.*
> *It seems as if this beauteous world began*
> *To be but yesterday, and th'earth still young*
> *And unpossessed ...*
> *... Wild solitude*
> *Reigns undisturbed along the voiceless shore,*
> *And every tree seems standing as it stood*
> *Five thousand years ago.*[3]

The 'five thousand years' carries a special significance. In Lang's day it was widely believed that the Creation had occurred in 4004 BC, a date calculated by James Ussher, Archbishop of Armagh,[4] so 'five thousand years ago' is code for 'at the Creation'. We find a similar assumption of an untouched landscape underlying the enthusiastic response of the Austrian Baron von Hügel to his first experience of rainforest in 1833:

> Here in this primeval forest, in this realm of Creation locked away for so long from any man's tread, and surely one of the secret corners of Nature, there is an indescribable stillness and solitude. It is as if one were under a bell-jar, cut off from the outside world, not a single sound of which can penetrate this silence.[5]

Implicit in such references to the Creation is the assertion that since the land had remained unchanged, it belonged, as of moral right, to those who were about to change and 'develop' it.

The process of relating to Tasmania imaginatively required a context and the inscription of 'stories' to provide it with unique cultural resonances. What could these stories be?

For nineteenth century immigrants the inevitable comparison was with 'home'. If the new land supplied similarities it was applauded; if not it was, in most cases, found wanting. In this regard, Tasmania had a clear advantage over the other Australian colonies in terms of landforms, climate and consequently vegetation. English novelist Anthony Trollope, who visited Tasmania in 1872, declared that if he had to live anywhere in the world other than England it would be Tasmania, where he would not be averse to being offered the post of governor in the most attractive Government House in the empire. His reasons depended wholly on the island's similarities to 'home':

> Everything in Tasmania is more English than is England herself. She is full of English fruits, which grow certainly more plentifully and, as regards some, with greater excellence than they do in England. Tasmanian cherries beat those of Kent,—or, as I believe, of all the world,—and have become so common that it is often not worth the owner's while to pull them.[6]

In a similar vein, Louisa Anne Meredith, English-born writer and artist who migrated to Tasmania in 1840, produced several illustrated books including *Our Island Home*, in which she writes:

> The little gardens ... with their great bushes of geraniums in bloom, were all full of sweet English spring flowers, looking happy and healthy, like the stout rosy children that everywhere reminded me of HOME ... many will be the pallid cheeks and wasted forms which ... will find their fairest sanatorium in these glorious scenes.[7]

Ransacking Europe for geographical similes, Meredith finally found them inadequate and took refuge in the language of the Romantic Sublime, with a particular debt to Byron:

> I have heard the view of Hobart from the water compared to that of Genoa from the gulf; but ... I must candidly confess that the natural beauties of the capital of Tasmania are superior to those of its Italian rival ... the irregular outline of the estuary of the Derwent, with its jutting promontories, and background of swelling hills and mountains is, I imagine, perfectly unique; while the undulating surface of the city conduces immensely to its picturesqueness. And over all there looms the gigantic figure of the mountain, with its head in the clouds, and its feet in the sea, filling the eye with its vast proportions, and impressing the mind by its awful majesty.[8]

In convict times, the most self-conscious and complex exploration of the desire for a cultural context, and the need for literary associationism to provide it, was that of John Mitchel, political activist of the Young Ireland Movement. Transported to Van Diemen's Land in 1850, Mitchel was an international celebrity and hence was not incarcerated in a detention centre but treated with all the diplomatic niceties. He was permitted to bring out his family and his library, and allowed considerable liberty of person as long as he remained within his designated parole area, around Lake Sorell in central Tasmania. Mitchel arrived determined to hate his prison but found himself unable to hold out against its natural beauty:

> as we float here at our ease, we are willing to believe that no lake on earth is more beauteous than Sorell. Not so berhymed as Windermere is this Antarctic lake ... not so famous in story as Regillus or Thrasymere; in literature as Como or Geneva ... neither do its echoes ring with a weird minstrelsy, as ring, and will ring for ever, the mountain echoes of Loch Katrine and Loch Achray ... Why should not Lake Sorel [sic] also be famous?

... Some sweet singer shall berhyme thee yet, beautiful lake of the woods ... and the glancing of thy sun-lit, moon-beloved ripples shall flash through the dreams of poets yet unborn.[9]

This lack of reference to events in European history and to standard literary texts relegated Tasmania, along with the rest of Australia, to inferior cultural status. The sense of malaise and isolation that haunted Tasmanian writers of the 1960s and 1970s was largely attributable to this failure to acknowledge an alternate history, an alternate sense of place.

Not all immigrants, and especially not short-term visitors, were obsessed with the need for similarity and recognition. On the contrary, their stories of place focus on difference. In April 1792 Admiral Bruni d'Entrecasteaux, anchored for five and a half weeks in Recherche Bay, was captivated by the paradoxical qualities of wilderness. His description was the first to define the unique features of old-growth forests:

> With each step one encounters the beauties of unspoilt nature, with signs of decrepitude ... Nature, in all its vigour, and at the same time in decline, offers to the imagination something more imposing and picturesque than the sight of this same nature embellished by civilised man's industry. In wishing to conserve only its beauty, man has managed to destroy its charm, and ruin its exclusive character—the one of being always old, and always new.[10]

At first the fascination with the new focused on the endemic flora of Van Diemen's Land, especially its tree ferns (*Dicksonia antarctica*), since ferns were becoming a fashionable adjunct to Victorian homes in Britain. In 1834, just before he found himself in a bell jar of silence, von Hügel was extolling the immensity and the diversity of the rainforest as a 'new world':

> Mighty trees rise to a height that I do not care to record, for my estimate would smack of exaggeration. Between and beneath these tall trees there is a second stratum of vegetation, an

understorey of trees perhaps fifty or sixty feet high and beneath these again ... stand the majestic tree-ferns. Their trunks are covered with innumerable different varieties of small ferns and their fronds, from 10 to 12 feet long, stretch out horizontally like those of a palm.[11]

Mainly, however, it was the artists who alerted their contemporaries to facets of landscape that could be only partially understood in terms of the prevailing artistic fashions of Europe —the Picturesque, and the Romantic Sublime. John Skinner Prout, Simpkinson de Wesselow, John Glover, Knud Bull and, later, William Charles Piguenit struggled with, and delighted in, the differences from their own artistic traditions. Glover was perhaps the most remarkable of colonial artists in his ability to observe, record and delight in the new land that he had come to settle in at the advanced (for those days) age of sixty-four. In 1830, before leaving the scene of his artistic success in London, he wrote to his patron, Sir Thomas Phillipps: 'I have at length determined to go to the Swan River New South Wales [*sic*] ... the expectation of finding a new, beautiful world— new landscapes, new trees, new flowers, new animals, new birds etc, etc, is delightful to me'.[12] Glover's geography underwent revision, but not his sentiments.

It should not be surprising that Glover inscribed many of his own cultural assumptions on the landscape in the paintings of his gardens, of rural landscapes in the style of Claude, and the celebration of his harvest. What *is* surprising is that he also engaged in a dialogue with it, allowing the land to write its own unique signature on his painting. This is particularly true of his landscapes with Aboriginal figures. Several critics have branded Glover the arch-colonialist land-taker, claiming that he insensitively painted Aborigines on land from which they had just been removed to serve the benefit of colonists such as himself. I read these paintings differently, more in line with

Glover's own letters about his contact with the Indigenous people. We know he was fascinated by aspects of their culture in a way that few if any of his contemporaries were. In the 1835 catalogue notes to *A Corroboree of Natives in Van Diemen's Land* (1840), he wrote: 'One seldom sees such gaiety in a Ball Room as amongst these untaught Savages', and he made similar comments in relation to other paintings of Aborigines.[13] Perhaps he idealised their way of life, certainly in view of their contemporary suffering, but he was also open to its possibilities, its value, and especially to what he perceived as the Aborigines' close and joyful relationship with their land, a relationship that he would have liked to emulate and, in his own very different way, did.

The master narrative of colonial cultures is the celebration of explorer heroes who subdue the land and domesticate it for the benefit of the grateful settlers huddled round the coast. The American frontier epitomised such legendary heroes and Britain had its champions in Sir Richard Burton, David Livingstone and Cecil Rhodes. The deserts of Central Australia produced a new anti-hero figure in the succession of failed explorers who were lionised far beyond the few successful ones. 'Lost Leichhardt', Sturt, Burke and Wills became the celebrities of Australian primary school history books. But who were Tasmania's heroic explorers? Few Tasmanians know of them and even fewer from other states, because they were not public explorers, leaders of great expeditions, but government surveyors, employees of the Van Diemen's Land Company or solitary prospectors. They include the highly coloured and self-inventing Dane, Jorgen Jorgenson, self-styled King of Iceland, Henry Hellyer, George Frankland, William Sharland, James Calder and James 'Philosopher' Smith. The courage required to explore and map the central highlands region of Tasmania may be imagined from Jorgenson's account of the treacherous terrain he and his party had to traverse:

The place just under the mountain appeared to be perfectly clear, but we soon discovered our mistake in our descent, the Scrub even in the clearest places reached over our heads ... I now saw that we should have to cut our way through many miles of country. To do this would in common computation occupy 11 days at least, and then it is not certain whether between the two ranges we might not meet with similar or even greater obstacles.[14]

Henry Hellyer, foremost explorer of the VDL Company, had a similar experience to report as he and his men found themselves on a narrow ridge at the junction of the Arthur and Hellyer rivers:

A highly dangerous, serpentine, strong and rocky ridge, so narrow at the top, that a single large tree would often occupy the whole width of it; and we were obliged to creep along its almost perpendicular sides to get past such a tree. It resembled the top of a wall of a large castle; and on either side below us was a rocky ravine many hundred yards deep.[15]

Government surveyor James Calder's experience in 1849 of the area around the Franklin River, now one of our most revered sacred sites, is conspicuously lacking in appreciation of the Romantic Sublime:

This locality [the Deception Range] presents no other view but that of a sterile wilderness, and scenes of frightful desolation. The great ravine, which borders Deception Range to the westward ... is a hideous defile ... A large and furious torrent flows through it, which collecting all the water that falls on a wide extent of mountainous country, emerges from the glen a large and beautiful river. I called it the Franklin ... The valley of the Acheron opens on a miserable plain ... producing neither a blade of grass, nor a particle of any useful herbage ... [and] bare, white-looking hills of unsurpassed sterility ... the picture is inconceivably forbidding and gloomy.[16]

This was the picture the nineteenth century explorers inscribed on the land—and it stuck, long after their names were forgotten.

The lone prospectors who roamed the west coast in search of gold eventually initiated the belated mineral boom of the 1890s and a new attempt to overlay a culture of success and progress on the dismal reputation of the area. Certainly the mining companies had better publicists then than they do now: John Watt Beattie, the photographer, and Marie Bjelke-Petersen, whose Tasmanian-set novels of the early 1900s were international best-sellers. Bjelke-Petersen was heroic, too, in her way. As part of the research for her novels she went to Queenstown and lived it rough, riding the perilous mine haulage up to Lake Margaret, 600 metres above Queenstown, and travelling by horseback through dense forest to the aptly named Savage River. For her the rainforest around Queenstown and the Gordon River represented the power of nature to subvert socially sanctioned norms. Kerrigan, the hero of her novel *Dusk* (1921), modelled on Robert Sticht, manager of the Mount Lyell Mining Company at the time, finds in these wild places an exhilarating psycho-sexual energy and a fearful fascination at not being in control. Bjelke-Petersen's D. H. Lawrence–style prose is given full scope in describing scenes that we would now call wilderness:

> a riotous confusion of strong growing things, which clung savagely together and almost strangled each other in their fierce passionate embraces!
>
> Cable-thick lianas wound around rotting tree-trunks, succulent vines sprawled insolently over grass, trees and ferns. There was a reckless profusion of green everywhere!
>
> Kerrigan did not speak, he glanced out on the lawless loveliness of the landscape.[17]

Similarly, Dusk Harleth, the heroine, is both attracted and repelled by the Gordon River:

below its satin-smooth gorgeously coloured surface there lurked abyssmal [sic] deeps, which stirred with forces that were as fierce, wild, and treacherous as the mighty powers lurking in the deep impenetrable jungle ... she stood watching the untamed loveliness of the scene, a loveliness which was not ethereal, vague, spiritual, but profuse, exotic and tropically sensuous.[18]

Bjelke-Petersen had her explorer-heroes too, even if they were heroines in disguise. In *Jewelled Nights*, society girl Elaine Fleetwood disguises herself as a handsome young osmiridium miner, Dick, and toils on the Savage River with a rough gang to repair the family fortunes, rather than marry a rich suitor.[19] The novel was filmed in 1925 with Tasmanian actress Louise Lovely in the role of Elaine–Dick.

The next wave of heroic explorers were the 'piners' of the west coast, who collected Huon pine from the river banks—as the convicts at Macquarie Harbour had done. Barnes Able and Charlie Docherty were the first white people known to have followed the Gordon River, and then its tributary the Serpentine, up to Lake Pedder, while the Morrison brothers, Keith, Reg and Ron, rowed and dragged their wooden punt and boxes and sacks of provisions up through the gorges of the Franklin to the point where the Lyell Highway now crosses it. Almost forgotten for decades, these heroic figures have recently been reclaimed in literature and film. The story of the piners was retold by Richard Flanagan in *A Terrible Beauty*, and Simon Cubit has publicised the stories of the highland cattlemen. Roger Scholes based his Gothic film *The Tale of Ruby Rose* (1987) on the life of isolated fur trappers in the central highlands, and Nic Haygarth has recently published *Baron Bischoff*, a biography of prospector James 'Philosopher' Smith.[20]

What do these frontier tales say about the land? Usually they are not about outright conquest but about endurance and qualified failure, as in the west coast poems of Marie Pitt who was married to a miner at Mount Magnet near Waratah and later at Mount Read:

> ... *a black Sou'wester screaming without,*
> *Hard through the 'horizontal' scrub ...*
> *While the pine hut rocked like a ship at sea,*
> *And the wall plates plucked at the ten-inch spikes*
> *Bedded deep in the myrtle logs— ...*
> *I hear the thresh of the spiteful hail,*
> *And I feel the life of the wind beneath,*
> *The forward heave and the lightning lurch*
> *And the shuddering gap like a living thing,*
> *As we crouched in the heel of the tempest's grip*
> *High on the shoulder of Hamilton ...*[21]

On the other hand, the strong swinging rhythm and rousing chorus of Pitt's ballad 'The West Coasters' reflected the contemporary triumphalism associated with clearing the forests and suggested a victory song over the slain pine, sassafras and myrtle that accurately revives nineteenth century values, celebrating the heroism of men pitting themselves against the forest:

> *From Emu Bay to Williamsford,*
> *From Strahan to Dundas,*
> *Through horizontal scrub they bored,*
> *And quaking black morass.*
> *Old Bischoff saw their camp-fires pass,*
> *Mount Lyell saw them grow;*
> *Tramping through the button-grass ...*
> *Forty years ago!*
> *... They slew the pine and sassafras,*
> *The myrtle host laid low,*
> *Tramping through the button-grass ...*
> *Forty years ago!*[22]

Despite these small conquests, overall, the land is victorious—usually because it is treacherous and malign. We still see the reiteration of this deeply incised story in modern writings about Tasmania's west coast. In Richard Flanagan's *Death of a River Guide* the river triumphs, Aljaz drowns.[23] He achieves apotheosis only by losing his identity in the layered history of place, of family, of ancestors, all the way back to the *Palawa* legends of the sea eagle. Similarly, in Carmel Bird's Gothic novel *Blue Bird Café*, the rainforest buries the fictional mining town of Copperfield, just as it had absorbed the symbolic lost child, Lovelygod Mean, seemingly without trace.[24]

Because these nineteenth century heroes are associated so closely with conquest, they are ambivalent heroes for today. For conservationists they have been replaced by the new breed of frontiersmen—the nature photographers, whose exploratory journeys are perceived as being in the service of the land, not in domination. Instead of subduing the frontier, our new heroes have 'discovered' it, even, in a sense, 'created' it, for our generation, by teaching us to see it in a new way.

Modern Tasmanian literature has been overwhelmingly preoccupied with the past—a highly selective past that focuses almost exclusively on the convict period and perpetuates the malaise that haunted Tasmania for a century and a half. Both convicts and the penal system that imprisoned them have provided a ready source of stories invoking and perpetuating shame and blame. In these stories the land itself is complicit in the iniquitous social structure to persecute the relatively innocent. The involvement of the land in this saga of ongoing evil was the joint invention of two middle-class, nineteenth century gentlemen who had never set foot on the west coast but felt fully qualified to elaborate on the kiss of death that Nature had bestowed there: (i) the Reverend John West, esteemed historian and passionate opponent of transportation;

and (ii) Marcus Clarke, journalist-turned-novelist and self-perceived convict of sorts, dispossessed of his expected family inheritance and packed off to Australia, like his hero Rufus Dawes. For unacknowledged purposes each propounded a theory of a haunted, terrible land. 'Sacred to the genius of torture, nature concurred with the objects of its separation from the rest of the world, to exhibit some notion of perfect misery,' thundered John West in 1852. 'The torrents which pour down the mountains mingle with decayed vegetable matter, and impregnated with its acids discolour the water of the harbour; and the fish that approach the coast often rise on the waves and float poisoned to its shores.'[25]

West's trenchant phraseology was accepted as fact by later writers: James Bonwick used this passage almost verbatim in *The Bushrangers* (1856), Marcus Clarke dramatically embellished it in *His Natural Life* (1874), Richard Butler quoted it in *The Men that God Forgot* (1975) and Robert Hughes in turn adopted Clarke's style in *The Fatal Shore* (1987).[26] Clarke pulls out all the stops to describe the west coast—the first convict prison at Macquarie Harbour for those violent recidivists who could not be trusted within striking distance of settler society:

> Upon that dreary beach the rollers of the southern sea complete their circuit of the globe, and the storm that has devastated the Cape, and united in its eastern course with the icy blasts that sweep northward from the unknown terrors of the southern pole, crashes unchecked upon the Huon pine forests, and lashes with rain the grim front of Mount Direction ... The sea line is marked with wrecks. The sunken rocks are dismally named after the vessels they have destroyed ... All around breathes desolation; on the face of nature is stamped a perpetual frown.[27]

Clarke did not scruple to transfer this atmosphere, along with the prisoners, to the climatically benign east coast, to Port Arthur. Wherever the penal system was in operation, the land that supported it was, *ipso facto*, equally tainted: 'The south-east coast of Van Diemen's Land ... resembles a biscuit at which rats have been nibbling'.[28]

With a vigorous Gothic tradition like Clarke's in place, what novelist wants to bother with facts? The misanthropic Hal Porter clearly enjoyed reincarnating Rufus Dawes in the person of Judas Griffin Vaneleigh in his 1960s novel, *The Tilted Cross*. The land is still unfailingly malign, still in collusion with social and political corruption. For Porter, Van Diemen's Land has shrunk to the sleazy district of Wapping and the polluted Hobart Rivulet on which he lavishes considerable detailed description. Vaneleigh is gazing into the foul water where rats are 'furrowing the Rivulet's junket of maggots and putrescence':

> It stank of the slaughter-house and its turbulent mane of blow-flies; it stank of the Rivulet and its throbbing nap of maggots. The muzzled gruffness of blowflies and cockchafers was the tamest note in a festival of uproar ... from every gin-crib, rum-shack and grog-shop in Hobart Town gushed the bawlings and whinnyings, the obscenities vile to the point of innocence, the punctilious blasphemies.[29]

Some forty years later in *Out of Ireland*, Christopher Koch appropriated and amplified Porter's images of the Hobart Rivulet: 'Here, it seemed, was Hobart Town's cloaca. The black, oily water was stagnant and almost motionless, and every sort of filth floated in it ... I struggled against the idea that the foul miasma of the place was settling on my flesh.'[30]

In the latter half of the twentieth century the treatment of the *Palawa* was belatedly co-opted to supplement the convict horrors. Scarcely a novel of the last forty years set in Tasmania refrains from invoking the treatment of convicts and/or the nineteenth century Tasmanian Aborigines; and of these scarcely any fail to incorporate, on the flimsiest pretext, escapee Alexander Pearce, self-confessed cannibal, or Truganini's be-trothed, with his hands chopped off by European woodcutters and thrown overboard to drown. Why this now-tedious recurrence? Horror has always been fashionable in fiction, believed to add that special depth of tragedy necessary to a 'great novel', but it is particularly seductive in a world of unsatisfying materialism and rationality. The appeal to historic horror has also become an unacknowledged accomplice in reviving a form of environmental determinism, discredited by most geographers since the 1930s. When Martin Bryant massacred thirty-five people at Port Arthur in April 1996 there were many voices ready to 'explain' the event in essentialist terms as an inevitable working out of the inherent evil of place. It seemed to them a satisfying explanation.

Over the last thirty years wilderness has been constructed as a unique and complete cultural tradition, providing a new aesthetic, a morality, a religion, a political ideology, with new heroes and new icons. It is offered as the comprehensive land rights issue for all Australians, present and future. Visual images of Tasmanian 'wilderness' (itself a word that has been recycled and redesigned) have impacted so strongly on our conceptions of Tasmania that we now privilege wild places in a way that would have been considered eccentric, if not insane, even half a century ago. As in the case of the Central Australian deserts, the despised and rejected place has come to be revered, even iconic, a national symbol perpetuated for economic or political advantage or just for the purpose of establishing difference. Why does wilderness now have so much kudos? What has caused us to reassess wilderness—or even to notice it?

Contrary to the impression given by Scott Millwood's evocative film *Wildness* (2003), Olegas Truchanas and Peter Dombrovskis were not the first to appreciate and 'discover' Tasmania's wilderness. Apart from the original *Palawa*, whose response we can only surmise, there were nineteenth century Europeans who admired, and even sought out, what we now designate wilderness. George Frankland, surveyor-general of Van Diemen's Land, amazed himself, one feels, by his passionate, Wordsworthian response to Lake St Clair. Here are extracts from his official report in 1835:

> I will not dilate on the extreme beauty of the scenery as it might be considered out of place in an official Report, but I must confess that while narrating the circumstances of the journey, I feel inspired by the first discovery of such romantic Country, impressions which revive even in cold narrative.
>
> I believe that every man in the party felt more [or] less the calm influence of this scenery and to all, this day's journey was a matter of recreation.[31]

This is certainly not the usual language of surveyors' reports. Frankland's sketches of Lake St Clair captivated the artist John Skinner Prout, who took some of his *plein air* painting group there to see for themselves; they were not disappointed by the reality. Rowing up the lake, Prout was moved to write in his extravagant, jocular way:

> Here, then ... we have at last reached a land of beauty such as the painter sees in his dreams and the poet sings in his verse. Of what need to go further my friends? Here let us cast anchor, and set up our tent. Let us send for our wives and our children, and relatives. Let us spend the rest of our days on this blissful shore.[32]

In 1863 Morton Allport, an adventurous Hobart solicitor, took his new camera and a party of friends to Lake St Clair where he produced twenty-four amazing stereoscopic photographs of the area, probably the earliest examples of Australian wilderness photography. From the 1890s professional photographers John Watt Beattie and Stephen Spurling III recorded areas we now label wilderness (Beattie's photos were used for the first landscape stamps issued anywhere in the world). William Piguenit, the first Australian-born professional artist, also saw Frankland's drawings and determined to inveigle himself into a surveying expedition to make his own recordings.

Piguenit's large canvases, purchased by the Tasmanian and other state galleries, became public property with far-reaching effects. They reclaimed these western regions from their reputation of infamy and situated them within the tradition of the Romantic Sublime. Tasmanians could be proud of their state's magnificence, even if they did not contemplate going there. But soon they did contemplate it. By the 1940s bushwalking had become the élite sport of Tasmania and it was out of that tradition that Olegas Truchanas and, later, Peter Dombrovskis emerged.

Never has wilderness been so beloved, so beleaguered—and so politicised. The morality, religion and idealisation of wilderness are new stories with new images being inscribed on the land—now. But they are problematic. By analogy with land rights and with Aboriginal traditions of the Dreaming, who owns these stories? Who has the right to tell them? What is the appropriate way to engage with them?

Wilderness, however we now define it, is the most contested place on earth. It epitomises the human desire to preserve the sacred in a secular age. There is an interesting analogy with those medieval and Renaissance paintings of the Annunciation that depict the Virgin being visited by the Angel in her enclosed garden, with its cultivated and highly stylised flowers. This *hortus conclusus* was understood as a reference to Paradise as a walled garden, from the Greek *paradeisos* meaning a royal (enclosed) park. Mary, the new Eve, is secure in her garden of purity, but beyond the wall we glimpse the wilderness, the unregenerate landscape where evil flourishes. Today wilderness has been constructed as the new garden, walled in by World Heritage listing and legislation to protect it from exploitation and destruction. But we know how shaky that wall can be. Legislation is unreliable; political alliances change; and the forces of 'evil' invade the garden. And what does the purity of the new wilderness-garden actually mean? Like Eden, and like Mary's garden, it is still conceptually defined by opposition—in this case, opposition to cultivation, industrialisation, and centres of habitation, which are often, in environmental discourse, relegated to the morally besmirched category.

Why *is* it sacred? And what does that now mean? From whom, and for whom, should it be protected? Who should be kept out and who, if anyone, should be allowed in? These are complex and difficult philosophical questions that we cannot consider in a vacuum, or without our own prejudices and proclivities. However much we try, we can never really edit ourselves out of our stories of place. As anthropologist Allesandro Duranti says, 'We do indeed keep meeting ourselves in our voyages'.[33]

PART V

Memorialising Tasmania:

Shame, Sorrow and Self-Respect

14   DISPOSSESSION

JIM EVERETT

My discussion of dispossession in the context of the broader theme of 'Memory, Monuments and Museums' is not an academic one. To write anything meaningful about dispossession as a Tasmanian Aborigine requires me to write a story that is about my own experience and about events that have happened in my lifetime.

I was born on Flinders Island on the 22 October 1942 to Keith Everett and Ena Gwendoline Everett (née Maynard). My brother Eric is six years older than me and my sister Barbara was a year and five months younger than me. She died at the age of fifty-two. My parents' families originally lived on Cape Barren Island, survivors of colonisation. Their clanspeople were from north-east Tasmania, the clans of the Greater Cape Portland nation. My mother's family descends from four Aboriginal women who lived with white sealers: Wottecowidyer from the Cape Portland people, Wyerlooberer of the Pipers River people, and Plangerperener and Ploorernelle who are believed to be of the Cape Portland people. Ploorernelle was Fanny Cochrane's mother; Fanny was born at Wybalenna. There is little known about their pre-colonial family histories, as such knowledge was obviously of little concern to white sealers who were only interested in exploiting them to make money from the seals they hunted. My nearest tribal ancestor on my father's side is Wapperty, daughter of Manalargenna, a well-known leader in the Cape Portland nation. White sealers took Wapperty, like many Aboriginal women, to islands in the Furneaux Group off north-east Tasmania. Wapperty had a daughter to Miti, a Maori who spent some time in Tasmanian waters on board an American whaling boat. Miti was a son of Te Pahi, a Maori chief in the Bay of Islands of Aotearoa, now New Zealand.

I can remember my grandfather, Edgar Leopold Maynard, my mother's father, telling me stories about when he was a boy growing up on Cape Barren Island and how he loved being out bush when he was about thirteen years old, trapping possums for their skins. He told me of a time when a ship was wrecked on the island's coast, and how the island's school was used as the mortuary for the dead who were washed ashore. He told me the story about how his father and uncles sat around on a log discussing what to do with the dead. Grandfather Maynard was born around 1886 and would tell me story after story about his life on the islands. He told me things about his life and although he was simply telling me a yarn without regret, it was clear that many white people had treated him and his family with little respect. His wife, my grandmother Maria, had grown up on the islands too and I remember her as a loving grandmother, who died in Melbourne when I was in my early teens.

Remembering my family, parents, grandparents, uncles and aunties who have since died, it is apparent that they were all conditioned in their thinking and seemingly silenced by an inner fear of their Aboriginal history. I can remember 'Uncle' Geoff Everett lending me a book of research by Tindale about Cape Barren Islanders. He told me not to let anyone know I had it, because he believed that he could be jailed for possessing it. It was rare to hear any of my family talk about being 'coloured', much less discuss their Aboriginality. When these rare occasions occurred, our mature-aged family members were self-identifying as 'quarter-caste', or 'half-caste'. Other terminology used was 'part-Aboriginal', or simply 'islanders'. I grew up not knowing who I was, along with my brother and sister. My cousins fared no better, and even today there are members of my family who do not identify as being Aboriginal. This sort of thing was widespread in Tasmania through the conditioning that white people imposed on our families.

My parents moved us to East Gippsland in south-east Victoria in 1946. They did this to get away from the feeling of low self-esteem from being Aboriginal in Tasmania. We had quite an extended family in Victoria by 1950, with uncles, aunties, and family members from the islands living in the towns where we were going to school. Racism was always there, but it lacked the sting of what my family had felt in Tasmania. Our family moved around Victoria quite a lot because dad was a bush-cutter, who worked wherever the contracts took him. It was a wonderful time, and my memories of it all are the happiest of my childhood. We were poor, but all the more rich for having a family that considered itself independent and capable of looking after family, no matter what. The men in my extended family were proud workers, and would work as hard as any man to prove to the wider world that 'islanders' were good workers.

At age sixteen, I joined my father on fishing boats at Phillip Island on the south coast of Victoria. Fishing or working on island trading boats was a common work experience for 'island' men. Dad was sick of city life in Melbourne, and I feel too that he wanted to return to the islands. This took dad, my brother Eric and me back to the islands from where we came. Eventually our whole family returned to Flinders Island, including grandfather Edgar Maynard. It was a new experience of racism in Tasmania that we felt, one that was cruelly covert. It was certainly something that influenced my life at the time. This covert racism made me try my hardest to present myself as being a white person as much as was humanly possible. It couldn't work and took me through a very confusing time in my life. In fact, trying to be white brought a measure of not being welcome by white people nor the Aboriginal community. The fishing boats I worked on were from San Remo and Melbourne, allowing me visits to the islands, but kept me away for much of each year.

My life seemed to take a turn in 1961, a time when work was still a bit hard to find and my lack of education and my slight build didn't make it any easier. Most of the work I might be employed in was labouring, anyway, and I had dreams of being more than a labourer. It appeared to me that to be accepted and liked, one had to have a 'good' job, more money than labourers get and the trappings of a car and a house. Having been a 'loner' for most of my life made it easy for me to go off and do my own thing. I was nineteen years of age, mum and dad were living on Flinders Island, as was my sister, and my brother was employed on building Monash University. The army had everything I needed at that time: a uniform, accommodation, mateship and regular pay. I joined up for three years, but before leaving the training camp at Kapooka, I had signed up for six years.

My memories of being in Signals Corp are still clear, as if it were only yesterday: my mates, the camp, the booze sessions in Sydney; they were great fun. Racism was not around all that much, though there would always be a corporal or a bombardier who would pick on black fellas. It didn't bother me all that much because I didn't really consider myself to be 'black' at the time. I was the only black fella in 1st Division Signals Regiment. Anyway, when I got picked on I believed it was only because I wasn't up to scratch. In 1963, I transferred to the Small Ships Squadron in Engineers Corp, meeting new mates and learning new skills. There was a mate in Engineers that I remember, Peter from Thursday Island. Again, there was little racism in our platoon. We were learning road building, bridge building, explosives and demolition and I had a whole lot of other experiences. My nickname was Nugget and Peter was called Blackie.

It wasn't until my mother was diagnosed with angina and given only three years to live, that I encountered the harshness of racism in the army. No matter how much I tried to get a discharge, or special leave so as to be with my mum while she had failing health and expected death sometime soon, the brass wouldn't give an inch. I went AWOL ('absent without leave') at least once each month, finally making it home to Flinders Island in 1965. My discharge was finally granted later that year and my mother lived until 1983.

During this time I worked on the Soldier Resettlement Scheme, clearing land for ex-servicemen. Many of the men who were to get farms worked with us, building houses and sheds, and spreading lime-sand on the newly created paddocks. Most of these 'new' farmers were from other parts of Australia; only a few were from Tasmania. Many of the men who worked on clearing land, building and driving tractors and trucks were from Cape Barren Island. Many of these 'island' men were ex-servicemen who had served in the war. Not one of them was offered a farm. It was another form of dispossession; they were treated as black fellas, and most certainly not as Australian citizens. There are too many stories to tell about the racism on the islands and too much to tell about how it was always made to look like it wasn't racism. But it was there and it was oppressive and belittling.

After spending four years in the Australian Army, I returned to sea life on fishing boats, island traders, and a short few months on a Norwegian oil tanker. Eventually, a government grant for Aboriginal enterprise assisted me to buy my own crayfish boat in 1970, raising a dilemma of who I really was. By 1979, my focus had changed enough to determine that I was at least a Tasmanian Aboriginal 'descendant', influencing me to join in the Aboriginal Struggle that was developing in Tasmania. At this time the word 'descendant' was used by white Tasmanians to mean 'not really Aboriginal'.

By 1980 I had a better understanding of what had happened to my people during the early colonisation of our country. With experience of living on Flinders Island at this time, I was able to see covert racism at its worst. Many white people pretended to respect 'islanders', when underneath it all, I could see a paternalism shown by many white people that served to enhance their self-image. It was clear that most white people did not want us to be acknowledged as Tasmanian Aborigines, nor acknowledge any rights that might endorse Aboriginal identity. There was little equal treatment during these years, and our people could feel it.

My brother and I worked my fishing boat, the *Christine Carol*, and I can remember having to fist-fight a local fisherman in the Flinders Island pub, because he didn't take kindly to my challenge that I could catch more fish than he could by Christmas. This was because he told me that black fellas couldn't catch as many fish as white fellas. I was the first to get an Aboriginal Loans Commission loan to buy the boat and the way many fishermen treated me was as if I had been gifted the boat because I was a 'half-caste'. There were great white people around at the time, but there were more who felt that we shouldn't be assisted with anything more than being employed as cheap labour on the mutton-bird islands. My life was simply enjoying being a fisherman, and writing poetry and writing a few songs with a couple of white island mates. There was always a friendly banter going on between us and my name had changed from Nugget to Tracker and my mates had their nicknames too.

In 1978 I met a young black fella called Michael Mansell, who was talking up big in the media about how we were

Tasmanian Aborigines, challenging racism and calling for land rights. Mansell was challenging his own people too: either stand up or continue to be trampled on was his message. It was 1979, though, when he became more publicly present in my mind. He had stirred the bull ants' nest and the media were feeding like crazy on his challenges to white Tasmania. The radio talk-back programs were full of white Tasmanians' views, telling the world that we were not Aboriginal because we had white blood in our veins. It was a terrible time to hear racist discussions about us on the radio. Most views were that we should feel humble and appreciative for what white people had done for us. I can still hear the radio publicly bludgeoning us into shutting up and accepting the place allowed us in white society. This so-called 'place' was what my grandparents and parents had lived through, a situation that younger generations were not about to tolerate any longer.

During the whirlwind years of the 1980s, the Tasmanian Aboriginal community was prepared to do whatever it took to achieve a new freedom from being controlled. We would march the streets of Hobart and Launceston; we would take over government offices, including the Premier's office. We were prepared to go to Libya to seek freedom from white Australia and we were prepared to apply to the International Court of Justice, seeking a ruling on Australia's illegal occupation of our lands. This has not yet been achieved. The national Aboriginal Movement was organising these sorts of actions both in Australia and overseas.

All the while, the assimilation agenda rolled on, with governments finding new ways to hide it in policies and programs. These are recent memories that recall our political struggle for freedom and reminders that cultural genocide continues as a covert desire in much of the white Australian psyche. So much so, that the Australian government, fearing proposals for an Aboriginal treaty, changed its propaganda language to cut us off at the pass. Our designation changed from being Australian Aborigines, albeit Aborigines of Australia, to Aboriginal Australians, meaning Australian citizens albeit Aborigine. We were being dispossessed of our identity to prevent us from gaining ground on winning a treaty with Australia.

But the Struggle continued on through the 1980s with a focus and a will to be free of racism and to see justice done in such matters as land, economy and identity. At the end of the 1980s, we felt that we had achieved our goal. It seemed that the Tasmanian government, and most Tasmanian people, now acknowledged us as being a living Aboriginal community with inherent rights. It seemed that now we might be able to get on with the job of community development and cultural restitution. But no, things would change yet again. And although we had battled against hard Australian prime ministers, we were not ready for the under-handed way that Prime Minister Bob Hawke and his several ministers of Aboriginal Affairs were to treat us. They used deceit and lies to overcome the Aboriginal Movement and the power of money to buy off the more prominent Aborigines, who would leave the Struggle for promises of high status in the white Australian political pyramid.

The Hawke regime established the Aboriginal and Torres Strait Islander Commission (ATSIC) in 1990 to provide the structure that would change the Aboriginal Movement. He succeeded in luring many Aboriginal activists into highly paid, high-status jobs, effectively taking control of the Aboriginal affairs agenda. In this way, Hawke changed the nature of major Aboriginal organisations over the following years, breaking down the National Aboriginal Movement altogether. The Aboriginal Struggle changed from community politics to playing the government game. Hawke killed the lot, bought off the Movement with dollars and presented ATSIC Aborigines in the media as 'The Aboriginal Leaders'.

Hawke coupled his ATSIC plan with another political strategy in the form of the Aboriginal Reconciliation program.

This has been seen by most Australian Aborigines as a 'feel-good for white people' program. Hawke gave the Minister for Reconciliation the power to select the Reconciliation Council, ensuring that the more radical Aborigines were not empowered in the process. Moreover, the minister set the agenda, ensuring that there would be no discussion on a treaty. However, there was a positive twist to the Reconciliation program's final report, with a recommendation for ongoing discussion on a treaty between the Australian government and Aborigines. And, of course, there has been absolutely no action taken on discussing a treaty by the Howard government, or any of the state and territory governments.

But what has really come to be? At the turn of the century ATSIC remained a group who looked after their self-interest. Many of the ATSIC commissioners and regional councillors in Tasmania had been elected on a very small number of votes and were quite unknown by the established Aboriginal community. How could this be, one might ask, for it would be expected that the better known Aboriginal political activists would receive strong Aboriginal community support to out-vote less well-known people. But it happened mainly because most Tasmanian Aboriginal activists do not identify as Australian citizens. They were not entitled to participate in ATSIC elections unless they enrolled on the Australian Electoral Roll. The dilemma was that to join in the ATSIC system was to accept the status of Australian citizenship and undermine the very principles that justify a treaty with white Australia.

Dispossession of land, culture, identity and history is current for Australian Aborigines. If changes have happened at all, they are not for the better. Of course it can be said that today's Aborigines do have better opportunities than our parents did, but these opportunities are subject to doing things within the conformity of white Australia. To create a situation where life's circumstances are based on Aboriginal culture and heritage, in a workplace, for example, requires long-term argument by

Aborigines against white Australian views that we should not be given 'special privileges'. For instance, the Australian government spends billions of dollars on educating Aborigines in mainstream education, yet provides inadequate resources to enable Aboriginal communities to develop local cultural education systems. The poverty that most Aborigines experience should not exist, with high imprisonment rates, high unemployment, third-world health circumstances and broken communities. A feeling of being excluded from the economy by the mob that stole our lands is current in most Aboriginal communities across Australia.

I have travelled Australia to a great many remote Aboriginal communities and know well my own Tasmanian Aboriginal community. I saw five-year-olds sniffing petrol in 1986, saw police assaulting Aborigines for nothing more than being black. I have seen young Tasmanian Aborigines treated badly in schools, to a point where a girl in secondary school was failed in her exams because she insisted on writing her exam paper on being Aboriginal. In my lifetime, the Housing Department in Tasmania has persistently worked away with a policy to change our extended family structure to that of a nuclear one, and therefore changing our culture in the process.

My memories of the Struggle are that we were together in challenging white Australia, right up until ATSIC. From that point on, we were undermined by the selfishness of a few Aborigines taking leadership roles in the corporate process with government. The governments of Australia warmed to the ATSIC game and used it to great advantage in changing the way Aboriginal communities were to be 'reconstructed'. In Tasmania, not once did the leaders in ATSIC come out to Aboriginal communities to sit and talk and to ask how they could best represent the needs, aspirations and dreams of their people. The ATSIC commissioners and councillors have made decisions that impacted on their own people without first taking direction from their community elders and leaders.

They were well paid to attend meetings, provided with trips overseas, lauded in the Australian media and granted higher status than the people they supposedly represented. The 1990s were the years that changed the Aboriginal Struggle from being community-based political action to being a corporate process owned by the Australian government. The ATSIC leaders were promoted as new role models, with images of being the kind of Aborigines that white Australia wanted. And yet there were no changes to higher imprisonment rates, terrible health circumstances, high unemployment and increasing assimilation. Today we see Aborigines less empowered than during the post–World War II years and being driven by ever-increasing pressure into a 'bugger-you-Jack-I'm-okay' mentality.

But what about Aborigines in Tasmania today? We seem to live with a whole system that talks a lot about doing good things, yet still have the same basic problems that we had twenty years ago. High unemployment in itself is a big cause of Aboriginal problems. Long-term planning for community development, with Aboriginal leaders facilitating the process of community discussion, would go a long way to finding solutions. Government resources that centred around Aboriginal community development, with real jobs such as those available in the public service, would go a long way to solving problems. Land rights and water rights are central to the survival of Tasmanian Aboriginal culture. It's our heritage and we have rights that are legal under our clan laws. These laws need to be acknowledged as a part of Australian law, or as separate laws for Aborigines on their own lands. My traditional grandfathers, Manalargenna and Edgar Maynard, were proud men who wanted nothing more from life than freedom and a fairly level lifestyle.

There are a great many Aborigines around Australia who are dedicated to achieving better things for their own people. These are not necessarily those well-known public figures, or those who hold high education qualifications; many are cultural leaders in their communities. The human resources are already in place, in urban areas and the country, Aborigines who are valuable to Aboriginal community development. It is crucial now for Aboriginal community leaders in Tasmania to bring their communities closer together and develop plans for our children and grandchildren to have a future as free Aborigines. This may never happen, but if were to be possible, there are a great many people, black and white, who would chip in to support these ideas.

Things change so quickly and situations of the past are lost in a new world of politics and bureaucracy. ATSIC failed because the Aborigines who claimed positions in its structure were shortsighted. They lacked real vision, without which there were no planned objectives. These people could not see that it was their obligation to their people that should direct their roles when so close to government. By not coming out of the ivory-tower white parliaments and government agencies and not acknowledging their communities' rights as major stakeholders and as owners of ATSIC's role, they failed. Instead of bringing pride and vision with cohesion, they brought subordination to the government corporate process. There are no ceremonies for our heroes, no memory of our wars in the history taught to our younger generations, and no cultural cohesion in it all. Of course there are survivors, but not many have cohesion of presence.

We still have extremely high rates of Aborigines in custody; we have paid little if any attention to the final report and recommendations of the Royal Commission into Aboriginal Deaths in Custody. We still have a higher rate of unemployment than other groups in our own country and are still expected to undergo white fella education, with no support from governments to develop Aboriginal community cultural education systems. We are still being expected to assimilate. Television has all but dropped any pretence of having Aborigines in the soaps, or dramas, or advertising, because we are the living reminders of colonisation. We are reminders to white Australia that we have been robbed, murdered and totally dispossessed, all under an orchestrated dismissal of Aborigines as a people. Australian Aborigines are Australia's 'mill-stone' in demanding compassion for those who suffer from what white Australia's founders did to us. We are the manifestation of Australia's living hell, with no expectations of human rights or fairness.

But Aborigines don't have time to moan and groan forever. It's time now to develop our social structures so we may be safe and free. It's time for Aborigines to develop memory and commemoration of our dead from the colonial wars. It's time for us to embrace a freedom that only we can choose. Today's Aboriginal 'leadership' has lost itself and new leaders are now required to stand up and be counted. The cultural leaders, our Aboriginal teachers and educators, must make a stand and bring a new hope to Aboriginal communities. These new leaders are everywhere: in communities, government jobs, private enterprise and commerce, and in all walks of life. These people are the backbone of Aboriginal strength and aspirations, and they must bring life into Aboriginal people as a people. Aborigines must do this for themselves or forever be subordinate to the colonial construct called Australia. It must be freedom first, for without freedom we are slaves to white society.

15 COMMEMORATION: TASMANIAN SLICES

MICHAEL ROE

I have always inclined to the view—rather like Pollyanna's, or even John Howard's, although one could say too in the spirit of Whiggism—that the historian should be more lenient than severe in treating his subjects, and make the most of whatever story is before him. That attitude prevails in what I am now about to write, with perhaps greater risk than usual of consequent distortion. The kind of popular enthusiasm that goes along with commemorative activity is not a strong Tasmanian trait. The dominant Tasmanian temper is individualist rather than communal, sceptical rather than laudatory, pragmatic rather than idealist. This syndrome makes against enthusiasm for commemoration.[1]

Interacting with these dispositions, and surely to an important if indefinable degree a major cause in their shaping, was the nature of the island's post-settlement history. In accord with my Pollyannish Whiggery, I am not one for stressing the grim and gothic elements of the Tasmanian story, but of course they existed and the historian must recognise them. But there lies an abrasive rub. Whereas the historian '*must*' engage in that recognition, a large part of the island's population over many years often did not do so. That avoidance applied most obviously to convictism, most of all in terms of personal descent, and to Aboriginal matters. One of the many values of Jim Everett's previous chapter, is to show that avoidance on the second point applied across the races, with some Tasmanians denying their descent from Aboriginal ancestors as did others from convicts.

Arguably, it is part of human nature's survival mechanism to minimise the terrible by as far as possible ignoring it. If so, what has happened in Tasmania can be read as proof of one of my oft-floated fantasies: that one of the values of studying the history of this society is to gain remarkable insight into the nature of human nature. Whatever, the Tasmanian grim and gothic were managed by being minimised. Some might well find this response to have been wrong, in terms of both ethics and effect: however great the effort, this critique can go, the grim and gothic could not be dissolved and even gained greater potency from being avoided rather than confronted. These arguments have some force, but my own stronger reaction is less to emphasise that than to affirm that the historian's task is more to understand why people acted as they did rather than condemn them for so doing. Such is the necessary corollary to my tendency to lenience.

That is a side issue for our present purposes. What matters is the symbiosis between the Tasmanian coolness towards celebratory enthusiasm in general and the traditional minimising of key aspects of post-settlement history. It will be obvious whither my argument is pointing. What I have to tell does not comprise a story of powerful excitement, in any absolute terms. What is remarkable is that there be a story at all to tell—a story moreover that at times did recognise the gothic and grim.

While materials apropos of commemoration do not add up to 'powerful excitement', their mass is considerable. History in various forms: reminiscence and autobiography; fiction that invokes history; festivals and reunions—all are substantially there. I am going to dip into this reservoir by looking first at a series of events of the late 1830s that I see as comprising the first commemorative surge, and then at the recognition of the successive fifty-year periods after 1803. That September John Bowen established a tiny settlement just upriver from present-day Hobart, at Risdon Cove. The next February David Collins came over from Port Phillip and shifted the focus to the continuing site of Hobart, and eight months later came northern settlement on the upper Tamar estuary.

The first episode of the later 1830s was the least remarkable.[2] David Collins died in office as Lieutenant-Governor in 1810, to be buried in what is now St David's Park. Not even his tomb escaped the neglect that the graveyard suffered. In 1836–37 there was a stir, importantly from the Executive Council, and so arose a monument. Around this same time, May 1837, the Executive Council received a plea from 112 Hobartians that 'four likenesses of Aborigines ... painted by Mr Duterrau may be purchased ... to be preserved in some public place as a Memorial in future times of the original inhabitants of Van Diemen's Land'. This duly happened, the paintings hung in the council chamber. Benjamin Duterrau has particular fame as creator of a painting that depicts G. A. Robinson as the grand conciliator of European–Aboriginal relations. It seems almost certain that the extant painting is but a scaled-down version of an immense canvas—'the National Picture'—to the same effect. Duterrau did have his vision, unreal though it might appear to posterity. The extant Robinson painting, and the four portraits, all grace the Tasmanian Museum and Art Gallery.

December 1838 saw the first official Hobart Regatta. The date remembered Abel Tasman's voyaging around the island's southern coast, and also the formal establishment in 1825 of Van Diemen's Land as a colony virtually independent of New South Wales. Lieutenant-Governor Sir John Franklin, and still more his Lady Jane, inspired the proceeding, as part of their hope to foster a benign and proud spirit among their subjects. All that is told in some splendid pages of Kathleen Fitzpatrick's study of *Sir John Franklin in Tasmania*. Fitzpatrick, an Academician, published in 1949, the very year my freshman self did 'British History B'—her subject. I take the opportunity to commemorate my teachers.

At the end of that summer of 1838–39 occurred the commemorative event that interests me most of all. I refer to the raising of a monument at Southport, some 75 kilometres downriver from Hobart, marking the nearby wreck in April 1835 of a convict transport, *George The Third*. There died 127 convicts and six others. Foremost in raising the memorial was Major Thomas Ryan, commander of the guard on the ship; his men had shot dead two convicts who led a charge from below-deck after the ship struck. Ryan strove for the memorial's erection, so he repeatedly affirmed, at the instigation of George Arthur —the man who as Lieutenant-Governor 1824–36 shaped the fortunes of this island as no other person has done. That story has been incomparably told by Alan Shaw, another of my teachers of 1949.[3] Arthur is especially known for his rigorous system of convict administration, including tough punishment. Yet the same man played a major part in raising what is in effect a monument to Vandiemonian convicts, and as such unique. That all presents mighty scope for deconstruction.

The wreck has had further commemoration—in art, ballad, folklore and literature. The last component had its chief expression in a short story extolling the heroism of one of the soldier's wives in saving the life of her own and another child. The author was Mary Leman Grimstone, who lived in Hobart in 1826–29, and retained interest in the island after she went back to Britain. There Grimstone moved among the radical intelligentsia, much like her friend Elizabeth Gaskell. Grimstone's radicalism embraced both feminism, in the mode of Wollstonecraft, and nationalism, in the mode of Mazzini. Her story of the heroine infused such nationalism into a Tasmanian context. In the Hobart of the later 1820s, affirmed Grimstone, 'all were exiles'. By 1846–47, when she wrote, 'it is now far otherwise. Van Diemen's Land, like other lands, has grown national.'

Now to move from Van Diemen's Land towards Tasmania. The name-change did not come until the advent of self-government in 1855–56, but had long been advocated, for example by John and Jane Franklin, so as to 'minimise' grim images. In this van in subsequent years were leaders of the movement against the continued transportation of convicts. They took credit—in part deserved, although, embellished by their own propaganda—in the imperial government's decision of mid-1853 indeed to stop that policy. This timing, just about fifty years after the first colonial settlement, seemed providential. Anti-transportationists took their opportunity, and linked the 'jubilee'—the term they used—of that event with their celebration of transportation's end. They affirmed—and no one contradicted them—that foundation day was 10 August, and so 10 August 1853 was chosen for this triumphal event. 'Jubilee' was the word, jubilation the theme. The organising committee in Launceston—crux of the anti-transportation movement—asserted its belief 'that the respectability and love of order which mark this community, will ensure the utmost harmony, and they invite the cheerful co-operation of all classes in giving full effect to the arrangements for this joyous occasion'. Of course, politics suffused all this, which is to say the occasion was characteristically Tasmanian. The anti-transportationists' supreme foe was Lieutenant-Governor W. T. Denison, as firm as Arthur in his defence of the benefits of convict transportation. Denison refused to grant a public holiday for the jubilee, and otherwise discountenanced it.[4]

One feature of the celebrations was to hold massive parties for children, in both Launceston and Hobart. Nicholas Shakespeare's Anthony Fenn Kemp, 'the father of Tasmania' (and discussed earlier in this volume), brought hither some of his eighteen children for the occasion. In Launceston the key speaker was Richard Dry, *his* father transported for being a United Irishman. The son was to be an early Premier of 'Tasmania', formally so-called, and Australia's first native-born knight of the realm. Another deconstruction site lies here.

The jubilee organisers' call for '*all classes*' to celebrate was aimed at ex-convicts. An ex-convict voice, strongest in Hobart, had been ready to accuse the anti-transportationists of hypocrisy and prejudice, especially in scarifying the moral impact of 'the system'. Yet there were also ex-convicts who had acted against transportation, in particular because they abhorred the cheap competition of workers still under bond. Interestingly, 'jubilee' festivities occurred in such places as Oatlands and Richmond, bastions of penalism. The dissident ex-convict interest in Hobart was not altogether won over, but in October its supporting journal changed name from *Guardian* to *Mercury*, accepting that the battle over transportation had finished. This is one of several indicators that there then prevailed greater confidence than posterity would endorse, that Van Diemenism could be transcended and erased.

Certainly the centenary commemoration of 1903–04 had some fraught touches. The state government of the day showed little enthusiasm. Its leader was one W. B. Propsting. He, I think alone, joined Richard Dry as a convict's child to hold office as Premier. Propsting did not boast such facts: rather, one of the very few blatant mutilations of the convict archive is of his father's record. The Hobart corporation now did more for commemoration than did the government; outside Hobart, activity was scant.[5]

Yet the centenary saw some readiness to acknowledge history's grim and gothic. The *Mercury* by now was the island's dominant newspaper, under the direction of the sons of John Davies, the paper's founder and erstwhile advocate for his fellow ex-convicts. That heritage rarely echoed in the *Mercury* of these years but one editorial of centenary time did proclaim:

Civilisation has its own problems to overcome, and its own safety to secure. There is savagery, and the worst of savagery within the bounds, as in the wilds … The centenary of Tasmania sees a great work done, done we hardly know how, a fair and prosperous community evolved out of what might have been a veritable human chaos.

Hobart's other daily likewise acknowledged that 'the human spirit within us grieves for those whether of the aboriginal race or our own in the struggle for what we have gained'. The chief scholarly recognition of the centenary was a series of lectures given in Hobart by J. W. Beattie, competent historian as well as superlative photographer. Beattie attended much to the Aborigines, 'for me an interest paramount'. He deplored the Risdon settlement, especially as the site of the first killing of Aborigines (in May 1804) by settlers. 'For about thirty years the ancient people held their ground bravely against the invaders of their beautiful country' ran Beattie's further theme.

Several commentators of the later nineteenth century had offered similar views. Arguably the more revealing centenary talk on this subject came via one of the government's few initiatives—publishing a brief school text on Tasmanian history. Its author was Samuel Lovell, an altogether high-minded man —his estate has endowed an annual lecture in honour of James Martineau—but he summed pre-settlement history as 'long, long ages [when] the land was being prepared under the eye of its Creator alone, to become the home of a civilized people'. Here showed the pertinent temper of early twentieth century liberalism. 'New', 'evolutionary', 'Progressive', 'Deakinite': whatever its label this ideology cared less for the first people than did the older liberal-humanist tradition personified by Beattie. It was the earlier part of the twentieth century that saw the intellectuals' minimising of the Aboriginal story, in Tasmania as nationwide.

Lovell's virtually sole reference to convict transportation noted its cessation. Beattie said a little more, some of it sympathetic to those under duress but also blaming 'convict vagabonds' for the worst brutality against Aborigines. The *Mercury's* reference to forces threatening 'a veritable human chaos' pointed to the penal past, and its weekly associate spoke of 'the convict system with all its attendant horrors and brutalities'. But the latter journal also said that while the centenary would prompt much talk of the past, no less would remain silent: 'oblivion rates among human blessings'. Both Anglican bishop J. E. Mercer and Roman coadjutor Patrick Delaney invoked shadows of the past when calling for social change in terms bespeaking their shared and forthright radicalism.

I am in danger of exaggerating gloom. Chief among positive and optimistic themes to sound in centenary rhetoric was Tasmania's membership of the Commonwealth of Australia. That, for example, was the climax of Lovell's school history; in 1908 it was he who gave the eulogy at the funeral of Andrew Inglis Clark, crucial figure in the shaping of the Australian Constitution and, as discussed earlier by Marilyn Lake, more firmly committed to nationalist ideology than any Australian public figure of the day. The Launceston *Examiner's* gloss on the centenary stressed that Tasmanians had been more emphatic 'yes' voters in pre-Federation plebiscites than any mainlanders. Tasmania's part in the national rally to empire against the Boers had its place in this story.

In late 1903 had come to completion Hobart's new Customs House, perhaps the first major Australian building intended for Commonwealth purposes to be completed after 1901. Before settling into its role, the House was used was for a centenary-celebrating art exhibition. Helping make that notable was craftwork in that art nouveau style so distinctive of the period and in which Tasmanians, especially Tasmanian women, proved skilful. Among them was Florence Parker, grand-daughter of John Davies of the *Mercury*; another member of this remarkable clan, J. F. McComas, was I think the only Australian exhibitor at New York's Armory art show of 1913, a key event in that shift of European cultural consciousness that was proceeding in these years.[6] Meanwhile Hobart had a second centenary exhibition, a prize event. The judges—Arthur and Minnie Boyd—themselves had much talent, and were to become grandparents of *the* Arthur Boyd. Minnie had as her grandfathers on one side a chief justice of Victoria, on the other an ex-convict of Van Diemen's Land.

Centenary celebrations peaked on 23 February 1904. In the morning Governor A. E. Havelock set the foundation stone of a building that for almost sixty years was to house the city's public library and still plays in our cultural life. It is just beyond the Customs House: a generally acceptable structure, most distinguished for fittings in that art nouveau style of which the architect was another gifted exponent. Later that 23 February Havelock unveiled a plinth at Risdon, commemorating Bowen's settlement. The Governor told the Colonial Office of 'a large attendance of the Public, whose demonstrations of joy and congratulations have been most loyal and hearty'. Havelock was shrewd, not given to sentimentalise his Tasmanian subjects.

Talk about the sesquicentenary began as early as 1944, the protagonist drawing on ideas he had formed years earlier still, anticipating the tercentenary of Tasman's voyaging. They envisaged a grand international festival of almost anything you might name. Premier of the day Robert Cosgrove was markedly readier than Lieutenant-Governor Denison and Premier Propsting to foster such plans. In 1941 Cosgrove had written a preface to a pioneering local analysis of convictism, *Shadow over Tasmania* (Walch & Sons), by journalist B. C. Smith. Cosgrove praised Smith's 'bright common-sense' in arguing that Tasmanians should feel pride rather than shame for their penal history: the island saw many an old-world wrongdoer achieve redemption. The government appointed sesquicentenary committees from

1946, and in 1949 carried an enabling statute. Its preamble declared: 'Whereas by the blessing of Almighty God ... through the work and courage of the founders and pioneers of Tasmania the people of Tasmania have received a heritage for which they are thankful and which they are proud to pass on to future generations ...'

The ambitions of 1944 whittled down. The directing committee's first major task was to act as the local arm for national recognition of the jubilee of Federation, a nice complement to the emphasis of 1903–04 upon achievement of that goal. Then attention shifted to more directly pertinent matters. Considerable effort went into reclaiming the Risdon monument and its curtilage, a park being established and duly opened by Governor Sir Ronald Cross on 12 September 1953. Premier Cosgrove issued a statement: 'There was much about the beginning of colonisation in this State that is not a proud memory. It is best forgotten because it cannot be undone.' Cosgrove urged that 'these commemorative months be bright and joyous'.[7]

I do not see Cosgrove's words as altogether platitudinous, but the Governor's speech and various others surely were. Nor can it be denied that the 'brightness' invoked by the Premier led to superficiality. Even I, a barracker for the 1950s in various regards, see that the sesquicentenary story gives force to criticism of those times as bland and narrow. There was little probing of darker themes. Virtually all such came in September, from two churchmen, one Anglican, one Presbyterian. Both urged that there prevail some sense of humanity's sin—specifically for the suffering imposed on Aborigines and convicts.

Matters became brighter than bright in the New Year. For many previous months had proceeded plans for a tour by the Queen and the Duke of Edinburgh. Through serendipity, it appears, the schedule determined that the royals would arrive in Hobart on 20 February, the very day that conventional wisdom and the 1949 statute had said was the 150th anniversary of David Collins stepping ashore at this place. Authority determined that the central feature of the royal visit would be the unveiling of a memorial to Collins, also prescribed by that statute. Its site was to be on the Hobart wharves, near Collins' likely landfall.

Perhaps today's consciousness can respect the memorial only for being absolute in fidelity to 1950s provincial monumentalism. From the first release of its design, others have used sterner language. Most vehement in the original field was W. L. Clennett, Launceston's city architect. He declared the design 'vicious'. So developed the most contested passage in sesquicentenary affairs. There resulted no change in the design.

The monument provoked issues beyond the aesthetic. When Buckingham Palace heard of the Hobart program, the rejoinder came that the sovereign never unveiled memorials to particular subjects, dead or alive. Accordingly, the monument had to be rejigged so as to celebrate Collins' landing and its consequence, rather than the man himself. Then there was some rumpus when research showed that Collins had landed on the *nineteenth* of February 1804, not next day. Characteristic 1950s stuff, critics might say—but still, the inscription did uphold scholarship and speak true.

'Historically, February 20 1954 will be the most joyous, most important day ever to dawn on Tasmania', wrote the *Mercury* on 19 February. Its text stressed the memorial unveiling as the centrepiece of this epic. Next day, royal yacht *Gothic* came upriver, the naval presence strong. All went smoothly. The crowds were biggish, by those cool Tasmanian standards. At the monument the Queen voiced appropriate pleasure, and the Duke congratulated the designer. A superb *Mercury* photograph captured this epiphanous moment of empire's Indian summer (Figure 15.1). Even the Tasmania I came to in 1960 had a different spirit from that here celebrated.

The British Commonwealth's emblem falls aside as the Queen pulls the cord to reveal a memorial to Hobart's foundation 150 years ago this historic day.

Figure 15.1: *Queen Elizabeth II Unveiling the David Collins Monument on the Hobart Wharf, Mercury, 20 February 1954.*[8]

The royal tour took up so much energy and resources that probably other sesquicentenary events suffered. Still, there were a variety of moments that fulfilled Cosgrove's hopes for bright cheer. A scout jamboree; choral and drama festivals; square dancing championships; art, photographic and film competitions—so the story ran. Monuments rose too in northern Tasmania. Tree-plantings had a vogue. Of grander scale was Hobart's new Commonwealth Bank, opened in September 1954 and long intended to link with the sesquicentenary. It too was very 1950s, massive concrete making for a stern exterior. Within is different, all vibrant in the same pink granite from Coles Bay that comprised the Collins memorial. The lower chamber presents history-depicting sculpture by Lyndon Dadswell that far exceeds any other Tasmanian public art of that time. Of like quality, if smaller scale, is a bas relief in timber by Stephen Walker.[9]

The latter part of the twentieth century has seen further cultural shifts in our world. Tasmanian history bears full witness to them. There have come massive changes in relation to both convicts and Aborigines. Both have acquired new dignity and esteem, made manifest by their descendants in strikingly parallel ways. Yet the implications for historical retrospect are altogether in contrast. Whereas lifting of the convict shadow extends the bounds of possible enthusiasm, awareness of Aboriginality throws the whole European enterprise into moral quandary. Descendants of the first people make this latter point with most feeling, but they are not alone.

'What a mess the Government and the Hobart City Council have made of the bicentenary', said the *Mercury* on 9 October 2003. 'It has been characterised so far by political correctness, hand-wringing, bad planning and stunning indecision.' In particular point was the decision of the government to specify 2004 as bicentennial year, thus by-passing the Risdon settlement. The government's reason was surely to avoid distressing the Aboriginal community by any hint of celebrating that settlement, site of the first colonial killing. This was a latter-day variant of minimising the Tasmanian past in order to modify its ugliest phases. In all it did, the government sought to eschew any triumphalist strain in recognition of the bicentenary.

Yet history is not to be denied, and well intentioned though the government's attitude was, it prompted reaction. Way back the Tasmanian Historical Research Association had decided that its chief bicentennial activity would be to publish a study of *John Bowen's Hobart*, by the author Philip Tardif. That went ahead, aided, it must be stressed, by a grant from government sources. Almost 300 people crammed into the Hobart Town Hall on 12 September 2003 when Tardif launched his book, buying all the 150 copies at hand. This response was in part a grassroots protest against the government's minimising of Risdon and of the island's more general latter-day history.

Later the same week, official policy was varied by the government sponsoring a church service in St David's Cathedral. It attracted modest numbers, but they heard a surpassing address by Henry Reynolds. Since then Risdon has contributed further interest. There have been two other recent books on that settlement—one upholding a neo-imperial interpretation, the other by the leader of a group that claims Aboriginality but dissents from the mainstream Aboriginal viewpoint.[10] Indeed, Risdon saw bloody massacre, argues this book, but there ever proceeded as much interaction as conflict, and the future task is to strengthen interaction and repudiate conflict.

Withal, Risdon's supreme moment came as the mainstream Aboriginal community remembered the massacre of May 1804, two hundred years on. This was at Risdon itself, the site now being under Aboriginal care. Ceremony and speeches lamented the Europeans' coming, and affirmed Aboriginal identity in somewhat the manner affirmed in Jim Everett's chapter on 'Dispossession'. Then all attending—it was an open occasion—had opportunity to visit a memorial garden. In that vale close to the killing site, the sense of tragedy and mourning surged potent.

Other events have happened that prompt a more positive view than proposed by that *Mercury* editorial. Many have been encouraged by the government agency established for the purpose. There is far too much to detail—my own formal involvement began with the Tardif episode and continued until the end of 2004. Highlights included a commemoration of Collins' settlement that took place in February at the 1804 monument and anticipated something of the power, in European mode, of the Risdon occasion three months later. The university sponsored a series of intellectually oriented lectures, among them being Peter Conrad's marvellous fulfilment as Prodigal Son. The Tasmanian Museum mounted an exhibition of its treasures, curatorial skill and quality of exhibits merging to splendid effect. The state government funded two handsome prizes for historical writing, one restricted to Tasmaniana, the other open to work by any citizen of Australia and New Zealand: winners, respectively, were Tardif's *Bowen* and *Broken Song: T G H Strehlow and Aboriginal Possession* by Barry Hill.[11]

The list could long continue. It had some dim moments, but I do not think it is just as a Pollyanna–Whig participant that I find the bicentennial story a positive one. Broadly speaking, there prevailed remembrance of the past in a tone of self-respect, rather than triumphalism on the one hand or vituperation on the other. I remarked earlier that while overall a barracker for the 1950s I could see that the sesquicentenary displayed characteristic flaws of that time. So, too, while myself sceptical of claims for the world, Australia or Tasmania being essentially a better place then than now, I accept that the bicentenary offers counter-evidence to my scepticism.

16   TASMANIA'S BICENTENARY CELEBRATIONS: WHAT'S IN A DATE?

Henry Reynolds

When the Australian Academy of the Humanities decided to hold its annual meeting and symposium in Hobart to mark the bicentenary of European settlement in Tasmania and to focus on the related subjects of memory, memorials and museums, the idea seemed straightforward enough. The symposium was planned for 2003, two hundred years after British settlement was first established at Risdon on the east bank of the Derwent River.

Tasmanians had begun to discuss the impending bicentenary during 2001. Artists, academics and state government bureaucrats held numerous informal meetings about what might be done. There was little knowledge of, or awareness about, the three mainland states' sesquicentenary celebrations as models either to emulate or to eschew. However, there was a strong feeling that the Australian bicentenary had lacked gravity or substance and that its party-like mood should be avoided.

In July 2001 the Tasmanian cabinet approved funding of $1.1 million for the bicentenary and a small office was established the following year. Two advisory committees were appointed—one of citizens from various walks of life, to which I was appointed, the other comprised well-known Aborigines. The Bicentennial Office began its work by arranging for extensive community consultations. Public meetings were called, focus groups set up and phone polling conducted in order to ascertain people's expectations and priorities in relation to the impending anniversary and what should or, perhaps, should not be emphasised.

There was a surprising degree of agreement among those who participated in the surveys and meetings. History, it was felt, should emphasise the lives of ordinary people rather than concentrate on the achievements of prominent individuals. The Aboriginal community should be consulted and their views respected, but importantly they should feel free not to participate in bicentennial events. Tasmanian regionalism should be acknowledged and there should not be any undue concentration on the history of Hobart. There was a strong preference for programs with a lasting impact—and especially for historical education—rather than for one-off major events, parties or fireworks.

But while the Bicentennial Office was able to solicit public opinion concerning how the island's 200th birthday should be conducted, it was the government that decided when the celebrations should begin. The general, and seemingly uncontroversial, view was that the period of commemoration should begin in August 2003 and run through to November 2004. But the state cabinet suddenly decided that all official or publicly funded events should be confined to the calendar year of 2004. Indeed, all the government publicity declared that 2004 was Tasmania's bicentennial year. Numerous appeals from assorted groups and individuals to include the last five months of 2003 were ignored. Accordingly, the Academy of the Humanities decided to hold its Hobart symposium in 2004.

The choice of 2004 as the bicentennial year was almost certainly made by the Premier, Jim Bacon, who had portfolio responsibility for the event. There was never any official explanation or justification for the decision. Bacon's only public comment was that the fifteen months from August 2003 to November 2004 comprised too long a period for commemoration. Furthermore, acute north–south rivalry made certain that the settlement on the Tamar River in the north, in November 1804, would have to be accorded due recognition.

Some attempts were made to provide historical justification for the decision. The Risdon settlement of 1803 had been ephemeral. It only survived until May 1804 and most of the settlers returned to Sydney, rather than join the rival, and as it turned out, permanent settlement over the river. Some comparison was made with the temporary camps of sealers established on the Bass Strait islands from 1798, but they had never been regarded as precursors to permanent British settlement. The fact remained, as critics of the government pointed out, that the Risdon settlement was an official British venture with the serious intent of following up and consummating the prior claims of sovereignty, by Cook in 1770 and Phillip in 1788. What is more, Risdon has always been regarded as the founding settlement and has been taught to be so to generations of Tasmanian schoolchildren. Why, then, was it dropped from the official bicentennial celebrations? Why was the whole world told that 2004 was the date of Tasmania's 200th birthday?

The comments of those closest to the Premier indicated that a number of interrelated issues were involved. Bacon was, at best, a lukewarm supporter of the bicentenary, whenever it was to be celebrated. He clearly realised that something had to be done—but only as little as necessary. The funding was miserly; the staffing of the office minimal. All subsequent—and perfectly reasonable and well-argued requests—for additional funding in 2003 and 2004 were turned down, despite the obvious community interest and a massive unmet demand for the funding of projects.

The Premier, it appears, was strongly opposed to anything that celebrated the arrival of the Europeans, which he viewed as an imperial invasion. He was determined to avoid any sense of triumphalism. It was not an event that should be celebrated. There were intimations from the government that re-enactments would not be sanctioned and tentative plans for the visit of sailing ships—a 'tall ships festival'—were cancelled.

Another significant detail was that the contentious original settlement at Risdon was also the site of the first serious conflict between the Aborigines and the Europeans. On 4 May 1804, a large hunting party approached the small settlement. What actually happened has been in dispute ever since. Many people—Aborigines and non-Aborigines alike—have always believed that there was a heavy toll of dead and wounded when the cannon loaded with grapeshot was fired at the hunting party. The controversy, long latent, was spectacularly reignited with the publication of Keith Windschuttle's *The Fabrication of Aboriginal History* late in 2002, with its claim that Risdon was just one example, among many, of the gross exaggeration of Aboriginal deaths at the hands of the settlers.[1] While the evidence clearly indicated that the cannon was indeed fired, Windschuttle suggested that it was not loaded with ball or shot, but used merely to create a loud noise that might have frightened the blacks, but certainly did not kill any.

As a young man Jim Bacon was a student radical and militant official with the Builders Labourers' Federation. The most obvious surviving element of his youthful radicalism that carried through into his parliamentary career was a deeply emotional support for Aboriginal land rights. He regarded the return of parcels of land to the Tasmanian Aboriginal Land

Council as the most satisfying single achievement of his political career.

The assumption made by people who were close to the Premier was that he had reached an agreement with representatives of the Tasmanian Aboriginal Centre (TAC), the Aborigines agreeing to let the bicentenary pass without protest provided that there was no recognition of the settlement at Risdon.

Not surprisingly the official declaration that bicentennial activity was to be confined to 2004 aroused considerable criticism, sparking vigorous debate, many animated conversations and a history conference organised by the University of Tasmania. There was little support for the government and scarcely any official defence of the controversial decision. For the historically minded, the Premier had imposed an official state-inspired version of the past that seriously distorted the known record. Island history was being rewritten. Right-wing critics were even more vociferous, seeing the decision to ignore the Risdon settlement as an outrageous example of political correctness, of pandering to the sensibilities of a small minority at the expense of the feelings of the wider community. When the monument at Risdon, which, as Michael Roe explains in his chapter, was unveiled in 1904 and restored in 1953, was daubed with red paint, feeling ran even higher.

But Aboriginal politics in Tasmania is fraught and complex. The official organisation, the TAC, represents the families from the mixed-descent Bass Strait community formed by European sealers and Tasmanian Aboriginal women. However, there are many other people who identify themselves as Aborigines, claiming descent from ancestors who it is thought remained on the island after George Augustus Robinson took the remnants of the tribes to exile on Flinders Island. These 'ethnographic dissidents', who are not recognised by the TAC, outnumber the Bass Strait descendants. The leading dissident,

Kaye McPherson and her organisation, the Liapootah community, held a gathering at Risdon, in September 2003, to celebrate the landing of the Europeans. Historian Keith Windschuttle was among the invited guests who watched a smoking ceremony and Aboriginal dancing conducted to celebrate reconciliation. The event could not be held on the site of the original pioneer settlement, which is now on land owned by the TAC and closed to the public.

While the competing Aboriginal organisations contended, members of the Bicentenary Advisory Committee found themselves in a difficult situation. When they were appointed, they did not know that the government was intending to decree 2004 the bicentennial year. Many of them were unhappy with the decision. Numerous suggestions to the government that something had to be done about the Risdon settlement were ignored. It appeared that the Premier was adamant. The committee was criticised in public; members were chided in private for collaborating with a deliberate falsification of history.

As September 2003 approached, criticism intensified and the Advisory Committee concluded that it was essential to commemorate in some way the arrival of Bowen's party. Members were placed in the awkward position, as a state committee, of feeling it necessary to organise an unofficial event that ran counter to the government's stated position on the matter. It was decided to recruit support among the churches. The Anglican dean of St David's Cathedral was an enthusiastic ally and agreed to hold a commemorative service on the morning of 12 September, which would offer an invitation to 'acknowledge the impact of European settlement on the Aboriginal population' and mark the contribution of all Tasmanians to the development of the state.

The service attracted a small congregation. Invitations had been sent to the Governor, the Premier and his ministers, and to all parliamentarians. No one from the government—or the Governor—attended, although a handful of key bureaucrats mingled with a few opposition MPs. The committee members had decided that they had to address several issues during the memorial service: there had to be a clear acknowledgement of the disastrous impact of European incursion on Indigenous society, but it would be counter-productive to accentuate the sense of guilt that had created the difficulty about the bicentenary in the first place.

I spoke in St David's Cathedral on behalf of the Advisory Committee, presenting an address to the congregation that said in part:

> We have come together to remember the arrival of the British party at Risdon 200 years ago today ... Any inclination to celebrate the foundation of permanent European settlement will be tempered by what we know about the consequences for the indigenous Tasmanians—the abrupt ending of their isolation and their independence which was a prelude to the rapid destruction of a society and way of life; death from violence and disease, loss of languages, customs, wisdom and profound, irreplaceable knowledge about the Island.[2]

Having acknowledged the tragic impact of the invasion initiated by the Risdon settlement, I also insisted that it was necessary to be 'rigorous, precise and fair' in seeking to explain why things turned out in the way that they did and in endeavouring to attribute responsibility for the death and destruction. It was, I observed, the British government that made the original decision to invade the island, to ignore the sovereignty of the Tasmanians and refuse to recognise their ownership of the land. It was important too, I suggested, to draw a distinction between a free-settler colony and a convict one. In the first, 'every adult colonist made an individual decision to settle in a country wrenched from prior owners—to engage in a petty, personal invasion'. In a convict colony such as Tasmania, the situation was quite different. A large percentage of the incoming population between 1803 and 1853 were unwilling arrivals; 'conscripted, convicted colonists who had absolutely no choice as to their place of residence or their participation in the infamous work of dispossession and despoliation'.

Despite the anger and the controversy over the question of when the bicentenary should begin, the calendar year of 2004 saw an escalation of activity all over the state. There was a remarkable geographical spread of events. Fifty-two communities marked the occasion in one way or another. Many aspects of the past were displayed, remembered, celebrated. Families returned to communities where ancestors had once lived. The descendants of women convicts attended a 'muster' at the site of the Cascade Female Factory. In Campbell Town, the local council initiated a convict walk that they hope will eventually wind throughout the town, with bricks set in the pavement, each bearing the name of a convict transported between 1803 and 1853. Communities featured aspects of regional economies —old mine sites, defunct railway lines, traditional droving trails. They rebuilt old boats, restored cemeteries, churches, historic organs and clocks, established history walks, painted murals, and produced brochures and pamphlets. Twenty-seven books appeared, ranging from the large multi-authored *Companion to Tasmanian History* to studies that dealt with family and community history, botany, ornithology, cooking and cuisine, farming and land use, public health, literature and printing. Two books were published outlining the history of the Risdon settlement.

Tasmania in 2004 presented an interesting case study of the way in which a small Australian community chose to remember 200 years of history. We might also reflect on the observations of Marilyn Lake and Michael Roe about what the same community had done about these matters in the past.[3]

There seemed to be very little awareness among contemporary Tasmanians about the previous history of commemoration or about the age and provenance of existing monuments and statues. There was no apparent response to what had gone before, to either emulate or avoid earlier activities relating to the 50th, 100th or 150th birthdays of European settlement. The community showed little interest in celebrating the lives of prominent public leaders or in commemorating milestones in political history, such as the formation of the Labor Party and women's suffrage, both achievements of 1903. There was no particular emphasis on the voyages and discoveries of European explorers. They were taken as given. There was some interest in the convict legacy, but not as much as might be expected following the accumulated scholarship of professional historians and the activities of the tourist industry. In any case, many areas of the state were settled after the end of transportation in 1853 and lack even the physical reminders of the system.

The year's activities indicated that there was considerable local historical knowledge. Family and community historians abounded and so too did many amateur enthusiasts, who had extensive and detailed knowledge about a wide array of specialist and arcane subjects, sometimes supplemented by private collections of artefacts and memorabilia. Commemoration was aided by the architectural reminders of the past that had survived, partly as a consequence of decades of depression and, relatedly, slow demographic growth. Tasmanians are surrounded by historic buildings, old trees and gardens, historic patterns of land use; they are proud of their historic landscape.

The highly contentious issue of Aboriginal history was skirted around, rather than addressed. Most Tasmanians clearly felt it was a matter that should be left to the Aborigines themselves and looked on with some bemusement as competing groups exchanged claim and counter-claim. The community associated with the TAC did not express any significant opposition to the bicentenary (except, as Michael Roe notes, to criticise the Premier's literary-prize winners), nor did they participate in any events or put forward programs for funding.

When, in November 2004, the Fellows of the Academy met for their annual symposium on Hobart's historic waterfront, the controversy about the settlement on the other side of the Derwent in 1803 had ebbed away. The year chosen by the Premier for the season of commemoration was almost over. Given the lack of interest or direction and the relatively low level of funding from government, Tasmanians had chosen their own way to deal with more than 200 years of European history. What they did when left to themselves bore out the accuracy of the opinion sampling at the beginning of the commemorative process. They concentrated on their own communities, on social history and on the achievements of humble ancestors. There were no large, lavish public events and the fact that Tasmania was celebrating its bicentenary was rarely apparent to fellow Australians or guests from overseas, much to the concern of the ambitious tourist industry. It was a quiet, modest, low-key birthday and that, it would seem, was the way Tasmanians wanted it to be.

NOTES

INTRODUCTION

1 Kirk Savage, 'The Politics of Memory: Black Emancipation and the Civil War Monument', in John R. Gillis (ed.), *Commemorations: The Politics of National Identity*, Princeton University Press, New Jersey, 1994, p. 130.

2 Savage, 'Politics of Memory', pp. 130–1.

3 On the construction of national communities through heritage, see David T. Herbert (ed.), *Heritage, Tourism and Society*, Pinter, London, 1995, pp. 50–2.

4 Paul A. Pickering and Alex Tyrrell (eds), *Contested Sites: Commemoration, Memorial and Popular Politics in Nineteenth-Century Britain*, Ashgate, Aldergate, 2004, p. 7. See esp. chs 1 and 7.

5 See Pierre Nora, 'Between Memory and History: Les Lieux de Mémoire', *Representations*, vol. 26, Spring 1989; and *Realms of Memory: The Construction of the French Past*, vol. 1, Cambridge University Press, Cambridge, 1992.

6 Graeme Davison discusses some of these issues in *The Use and Abuse of Australian History*, Allen & Unwin, Sydney, 2000.

7 See Dominick LaCapra, *Writing History, Writing Trauma*, Johns Hopkins University Press, Baltimore, 2001, ch. 1.

8 LaCapra, *Writing History*, p. 22.

9 Pyrs Gruffud, 'Heritage as National Identity: Histories and Prospects of the National Pasts', in Herbert, *Heritage, Tourism and Society*.

10 Paul A. Shakel (ed.), *Myth, Memory, and the Making of the American Landscape*, University Press of Florida, Gainesville, 2001, pp. 11–12.

1 A HISTORY OF MEMORY

1 Gwen Harwood, 'An Impromptu for Ann Jennings', in Robert Gray and Geoffrey Lehmann (eds), *Australian Poetry in the Twentieth Century*, Heinemann, Melbourne, 1991, pp. 193–4.
2 Frances Yates, *The Art of Memory*, University of Chicago Press, Chicago, 1966.

2 REMEMBERING AND FORGETTING

1 Richard Rorty, *Contingency, Irony and Solidarity*, Cambridge University Press, New York, 1989.
2 Richard Rorty, *Essays on Heidegger and Others: Philosophical Papers*, vol. 2, Cambridge University Press, New York, 1991.
3 Milan Kundera, *The Art of the Novel*, Linda Asher (trans.), Harper, New York, 1986.
4 Gabriel García Márquez, *Living to Tell the Tale*, Edith Grossman (trans.), Jonathan Cape, London, 2003.
5 Robert Manne (ed.), *Whitewash: On Keith Windschuttle's Fabrication of Aboriginal History*, Black Inc., Melbourne, 2003, p. 223.
6 Charles Taylor, *Sources of the Self*, Harvard University Press, Cambridge MA, 1989.

3 MONUMENTS OF MANHOOD AND COLONIAL DEPENDENCE

1 Richard White, *Remembering Ahanagran: Storytelling in a Family's Past*, Hill & Wang, New York, 1998, p. 4.
2 Bain Attwood, '"Learning about the Truth": The Stolen Generations Narrative', in Bain Attwood and Andrew Markus (eds), *Telling Stories: Indigenous History and Memory in Australia and New Zealand*, Allen & Unwin, Sydney, 2001; John Murphy, 'The Voice of Memory: History, Autobiography and Oral Memory', *Australian Historical Studies*, vol. 22, no. 87, 1986.
3 Paula Hamilton, 'The Knife Edge: Debates about Memory and History', in Kate Darian Smith and Paula Hamilton (eds), *Memory and History in Twentieth Century Australia*, Oxford University Press, Melbourne, 1997, p. 12.

[4] See Ellen Fitzpatrick, *History's Memory: Writing America's Past 1880–1980*, Harvard University Press, Cambridge MA, 2002, esp. pp. 1–12.

[5] John Hirst, *The Sentimental Nation: The Making of the Australian Commonwealth*, Oxford University Press, Melbourne, 2000.

[6] Ken Inglis, *Sacred Places: War Memorials in the Australian Landscape*, Miegunyah Press, Melbourne, 1998.

[7] Graeme Davison, *The Use and Abuse of Australian History*, Allen & Unwin, Sydney, 2000, pp. 37–55; and Marilyn Lake, 'Monuments, Museums and Memory', in Alison Alexander (ed.), *The Companion to Tasmanian History*, Centre for Tasmanian Historical Studies, Hobart, 2005, pp. 463–5.

[8] Bean quoted in K. S. Inglis, 'The Anzac Tradition', *Meanjin*, vol. 24, no. 1, 1964; and Carmel Shute, 'Heroines and Heroes', in Joy Damousi and Marilyn Lake (eds), *Gender and War: Australians at War in the Twentieth Century*, Cambridge University Press, Melbourne, 1995, p. 38.

[9] Notes, 7 April 1908, CO papers, 418/60/106, UK National Archives. On the ongoing conflict between Deakin and the Colonial Office, see also J. A. LaNauze, *Alfred Deakin A Biography*, vol. 2, Melbourne University Press, Carlton, 1965; and Neville Meaney, *The Search for Security in the Pacific 1901–14: A History of Australian Defence and Foreign Policy*, Sydney University Press, Sydney, 1976.

[10] Deakin to Consul-General, letter included in Governor General to Colonial Office, 4 March 1908, CO 418/60/105; Charles Lucas, note, 7 April 1908, CO 418/60/105.

[11] See Charles H. Pearson, 'The Black Republic', reprinted in H. A. Strong, *Charles H Pearson Reviews and Critical Essays*, Methuen, London, 1896; Pearson to Bryce, 20 June 1892, Bryce Papers, Bodleian Library, Oxford.

[12] Pearson to Bryce, 12 March 1890, Bryce Papers, Bodleian Library, Oxford.

[13] Hirst, *Sentimental Nation*, p. 127.

[14] George Bell, US Consul in Sydney, letter of introduction, 15 March 1897, A. I. Clark Papers, University of Tasmania Archives, C4/C391 (12).

[15] Hirst, *Sentimental Nation*, pp. 11–13.

[16] 'Why I am a Democrat', in Richard Eley (ed.), *A Living Force: Andrew Inglis Clark and the Ideal of the Commonwealth*, Centre for Tasmanian Historical Studies, Hobart, 2001, pp. 29–35.

17 Clark to Wendell Holmes, 26 October 1901, Clark Papers, University of Tasmania Archives, C4/C211.

18 Roosevelt to Cecil Arthur Spring Rice, 16 March 1901, in Elting E. Morison (ed.), *The Letters of Theodore Roosevelt*, Harvard University Press, Cambridge MA, 1951, p. 15.

19 Theodore Roosevelt, *An Autobiography*, Macmillan, New York, 1913, p. 598.

20 Charles Lucas note, 18 September 1908, CO 418/61, UK National Archives.

21 Deakin's letter enclosed, Governor General telegram to Colonial Office, 14 September 1908, CO 418/61/147, UK National Archives.

22 Deakin diary, visit to the United States, 1885, NLA 1540/2/38, Canberra.

23 William Stebbing (ed.), *Charles Henry Pearson Memorials*, Longman's, Green & Co., London, 1900, p. 131.

24 Stebbing's *Memorials*, p. 131.

25 Stebbing's *Memorials*, p. 132.

26 Stebbing's *Memorials*, pp. 132, 133.

27 Stebbing's *Memorials*, p. 133.

28 Roosevelt to Pearson, 11 May 1894, Pearson Papers, MS English letters, folio 190, Bodleian Library, Oxford.

29 Stebbing's *Memorials*, p. 132.

30 Deakin's travel diaries, Deakin Papers, NLA, 1540/2/38.

31 Deakin's travel diaries, Deakin Papers, NLA 1540/2/38.

32 Deakin's travel diaries, Deakin Papers, NLA 1540/2/38.

33 Deakin's travel diaries, Deakin Papers, NLA 1540/2/38.

34 Deakin's travel diaries, Deakin Papers, NLA 1540/2/38.

35 Deakin's notebooks, Deakin Papers, 1540/3/22.

36 Lawrence Buell, *Emerson*, Belknap Press of Harvard University Press, Cambridge MA, 2003, pp. 44–60.

37 Deakin's travel diaries, Deakin Papers, NLA 1540/2/38.

38 Deakin's travel diaries, Deakin Papers, NLA 1540/2/38.

39 Deakin's travel diaries, Deakin Papers, NLA 1540/2/38.

40 *Commonwealth Parliamentary Debates*, House of Representatives, 14 January 1902.

41 Inglis, *Sacred Places*, p. 103.

42 Shute, 'Heroines and Heroes', p. 37.

43 Inglis, *Sacred Places*, pp. 378–9, 429.

44 Inglis, *Sacred Places*, p. 379.

4 TEDDY ROOSEVELT'S TROPHY

1 Copyright David McCalman. Reproduced with permission.

2 Robert A. Tarlton to [Sophie Tarlton?], 21 April 1895, private family possession; 'Robert A. Tarlton', *Adelaide Advertiser*, 8 February 1919, p. 1; David McCalman, 'A Full Life and its Memories, 1916–65: Part One: Home is Africa', unpublished memoir, Melbourne, 2003, pp. 5–6.

3 Brian Herne, *White Hunters: The Golden Age of African Safaris*, Henry Holt, New York, 1999, pp. 60–1.

4 Herne, *White Hunters*, pp. 61–2.

5 Cited in Herne, *White Hunters*, p. 61; see also Bartle Bull, *Safari: A Chronicle of Adventure*, Penguin, Harmondsworth, 1992, p. 172.

6 Bull, *Safari*, p. 172.

7 Herne, *White Hunters*, p. 6.

8 Theodore Roosevelt, *African Game Trails*, St Martins Press, New York, 1988 [1910], pp. 9, 38, 40, 49.

9 Cited in Herne, *White Hunters*, p. 188.

10 The term is discussed, though not specifically in connection with Kenya, in David Lowenthal, *The Past is a Foreign Country*, Cambridge University Press, Cambridge, 1985, p. 22.

11 Evelyn Waugh, *Remote People*, Penguin, Harmondsworth, 1985, esp. pp. 135–63; Evelyn Waugh, *A Tourist in Africa*, Mandarin, London, 1989, pp. 36–57.

12 McCalman, 'A Full Life', p. 7.

13 Karen Blixen, *Out of Africa*, Penguin, Harmondsworth, 1954; Isak Dinesen [Karen Blixen], *Letters from Africa, 1914–31*, Frans Larson (ed.), Anne Born (trans.), University of Chicago Press, Chicago, 1981.

14 Herne, *White Hunters*, p. 39.

15 McCalman, 'A Full Life', p. 18.

16 Roosevelt, *African Game Trails*, p. 337.

17 Herne, *White Hunters*, pp. 11–46.

18 McCalman, 'A Full Life', p. 13.

19 Herne, *White Hunters*, p. 22.

20 Gail Bederman, *Manliness and Civilization: A Cultural History of Gender and Race in the United States, 1880–1917*, University of Chicago Press, Chicago and London, 1996, pp. 170–215. I am indebted to Marilyn Lake for alerting me to this reference.

21 Michael Kammen, *Mystic Chords of Memory: The Transformation of Tradition in American Culture*, Knopf, New York, 1991, pp. 275–7.

22 Paul Russell Cutright, *Theodore Roosevelt, The Naturalist*, Harpers, New York, 1956, pp. 98–179.

23 Copyright David McCalman. Reproduced with permission.

24 Bull, *Safari*, p. 164.

25 Roosevelt, *African Game Trails*, p. 38; Bull, *Safari*, pp. 164–5.

26 Bull, *Safari*, pp. 166–9.

27 Roosevelt, *African Game Trails*, p. 384.

28 Roosevelt, *African Game Trails*, ch. 1, *passim*.

29 Roosevelt, *African Game Trails*, pp. 38–42, 47–9.

30 Roosevelt, *African Game Trails*, p. 457; Herne, *White Hunters*, p. 67. On the ethos of the Lado enclave, see John Boyes, *King of the Wa-Kikyu: A True Story of Travel and Adventure in Africa, Written by Himself*, Methuen, London, 1912. It is dedicated to his friend William Northrop Macmillan.

31 Roosevelt, *African Game Trails*, pp. 381–2; Bull, *Safari*, pp. 130–6.

32 Roosevelt, *African Game Trails*, esp. pp. 194–223, 381–3; Bull, *Safari*, pp. 172–3.

33 Roosevelt, *African Game Trails*, p. 119.

34 Roosevelt, *African Game Trails*, pp. 464–503; Bull, *Safari*, p. 179.

35 Herne, *White Hunters*, pp. 104–8.

36 Leslie Tarlton to Theodore Roosevelt, 5 July 1910; Theodore Roosevelt to Leslie Tarlton, 18 July 1910 (letters in family possession).

37 Bull, *Safari*, p. 163.

38 Arthur Conan Doyle, *Our African Winter*, Duckworth, London, (1929) 1999, pp. 212–14.

39 McCalman, 'A Full Life', pp. 17–23.

40 George Orwell, 'Shooting an Elephant', in *Inside the Whale and Other Essays*, Penguin, Harmondsworth, 1962, pp. 91–9.

41 Robin Wallace-Crabbe, *A Man's Childhood*, Imprint, Sydney, 1997, pp. 85–90.

42 McCalman, 'A Full Life', pp. 33–8.

43 T. C. Bridges and H. Hessel Tiltman, *Heroes of Modern Adventure*, Harrap, London, 1927; Cherry Kearton, *Photographing Wild Life across the World*, Arrowsmith, London, n.d. The book is dedicated to Kearton's 'dear friend' Theodore Roosevelt.

44 McCalman, 'A Full Life', p. 21.

45 Copyright David McCalman. Reproduced with permission.

46 McCalman, 'A Full Life', p. 43.

47 Herne, *White Hunters*, pp. 180–93.

48 McCalman, 'A Full Life', pp. 54–86.

[49] Laurens Van Der Post, *Venture into the Interior*, Penguin, Harmondsworth, 1957.

[50] McCalman, 'A Full Life', p. 90.

[51] Jean Starobinski, 'The Idea of Nostalgia', *Diogenes*, vol. 54, 1966, pp. 81–103.

[52] George Rosen, 'Nostalgia: A "Forgotten" Psychological Disorder', *Clio Medica*, vol. 10, 1975, pp. 28–51.

[53] Lowenthal, *The Past*, pp. 7–8; Fred Davis, *Yearning for Yesterday: A Sociology of Nostalgia*, Free Press, New York and London, 1979, pp. 14–39; Svetland Boym, *The Future of Nostalgia*, New York, 2001, pp. xiii–xv. I am indebted to Marilyn Lake for this last reference.

[54] Lowenthal, *The Past*, pp. 8–10.

[55] Davis, *Yearning*, pp. 49–69; Willis H. McCann, 'Nostalgia: A Descriptive and Comparative Study', *Journal of Genetic Psychology*, vol. 62, 1943, pp. 97–104.

[56] Boym, *Future of Nostalgia*, pp. xvi–xviii.

[57] Davis, *Yearning*, p. 47.

5 THE HERITAGE OF 'OLD ENGLAND'

[1] *Some Private Correspondence of the Rev. Samuel Marsden and Family, 1794–1824*, G. Mackaness (ed.), privately printed by D. S. Ford, Sydney, 1942, p. 14.

[2] M. Staples, 'Sunshine and Shadow: The John Glover Sketchbooks', in D. Hansen, *John Glover and the Colonial Picturesque*, Tasmanian Museum and Art Gallery and Art Exhibitions Australia, Hobart, 2003, pp. 248–67.

[3] Alan Atkinson has gone furthest in addressing such issues. See 'The Free-Born Englishman Transported: Convict Rights as a Measure of Eighteenth-Century Empire', *Past and Present*, no. 144, 1994, pp. 88–115; *The Europeans in Australia: A History, Vol. 1. The Beginning*, Oxford University Press, Melbourne, 1997; *History and the Love of Places*, University of New England, Armidale, 1998; and *The Europeans in Australia: A History, Vol. 2. Democracy*, Oxford University Press, Melbourne, 2004.

[4] D. Lowenthal, *The Past is a Foreign Country*, Cambridge University Press, New York, 1985, esp. pp. 96–105; P. Mandler, *History and National Life*, Profile Books, London, 2002; P. Readman, 'The Place of the Past in English Culture c. 1890–1914', *Past and Present*, no. 186, 2005, pp. 147–99.

5 P. Mandler, '"In the Olden Time": Romantic History and English National Identity, 1820–1850', in L. Brockliss and D. Eastwood (eds), *A Union of Multiple Identities: The British Isles*, Manchester University Press, Manchester, 1997.

6 By 1832 it was believed that the convict past would be lost to the collective memory. In a futurist fantasy, an Australian of the year 2032, when asked by an Englishman about the beginnings of British settlement, admitted that 'some of the old people are rather touchy when asked about the first settlers, but I never heard the reason': J. Molony, *The Native-born: The First White Australians*, Melbourne University Press, Carlton, 2000, p. 157.

7 Apart from America, Australia has 'the highest per capita population of genealogists in the world': G. Davison, *The Use and Abuse of Australian History*, Allen & Unwin, Sydney, 2000, p. 80.

8 Atkinson, *The Europeans in Australia*, vol. 1, p. 245.

9 The earliest family records were often inserted retrospectively: E. Lea-Scarlett, *Roots and Branches: Ancestry for Australians*, Collins, Sydney, 1979.

10 Atkinson, *Europeans in Australia*, vol. 1, p. 247.

11 P. Clarke and D. Spender (eds), *Life Lines; Australian Women's Letters and Diaries 1788–1840*, Allen & Unwin, Sydney, 1996, p. 107.

12 'The children born in these colonies, and now grown up, speak a better language, purer, and more harmonious, than is generally the case in most parts of England. The amalgamation of such various dialects assembled together, seems to improve the mode of articulating words': Molony, *The Native-born*, p. 63.

13 For example, the dances that have been evidenced in colonial Australia were not regionally derived folk dances but 'either those country dances popular in upper-class circles or else those dances widely known in different areas of the British Isles': S. Andrews. 'Dance', in G. B. Davey and G. Seal (eds), *The Oxford Companion to Australian Folklore*, Oxford University Press, Melbourne, 1993, pp. 93–104, at p. 94.

14 L. Colley, *Britons: Forging the Nation 1707–1837*, Yale University Press, London, 1992.

15 Atkinson, *Europeans in Australia*, vol. 1, pp. 121–3.

16 See J. Walvin, *Fruits of Empire: Exotic Produce and British Taste, 1660–1800*, New York University Press, London, 1997, chs 2, 5, 8.

17 Atkinson, *Europeans in Australia*, vol. 1, pp. 40–1.

[18] J. Brewer, *The Pleasures of the Imagination: English Culture in the Eighteenth Century*, HarperCollins, London, 1997; J. Gascoigne, *The Enlightenment and the Origins of European Australia*, Cambridge University Press, Port Melbourne, 2002.

[19] Atkinson, 'The Free-Born Englishman Transported'.

[20] See, in general, Colley, *Britons*.

[21] D. Cressy, *Bonfires and Bells: National Memory and the Protestant Calendar in Elizabethan and Stuart England*, Weidenfeld & Nicolson, London, 1989.

[22] D. Cressy, 'The Fifth of November Remembered', in R. Porter (ed.), *Myths of the English*, Cambridge University Press, MA, 1992, pp. 73–4.

[23] Curiously, November has loomed large too in the calendar of Australian nation formation: Ned Kelly, Armistice Day and the dismissal of the Whitlam government.

[24] Cressy, *Bonfires and Bells*, p. 185.

[25] L. Colley, 'The Apotheosis of George III: Loyalty, Royalty and the British Nation 1760–1820', *Past and Present*, no. 102, 1984, pp. 94–129.

[26] M. J. Bennett, 'Van Diemen, Tasman and the Dutch Reconnaissance', *Tasmanian Historical Research Association: Papers and Proceedings*, vol. 39, no. 2, 1992, pp. 74–80.

[27] C. Deelman, *The Great Shakespeare Jubilee*, Joseph, London, 1964. Interestingly enough, the jubilee followed at some remove the bicentenary of Shakespeare's birth in 1764. The germ of the idea may have come from Samuel Johnson's reflection in the following year that Shakespeare had 'long outlived his century', the test commonly fixed as a test of literary merit: R. Quinault, 'The Cult of the Centenary, c. 1784–1914', *Historical Research*, vol. 71, 1998, p. 304. Another inspiration may have been the Luther jubilee of 1767.

[28] Quinault, 'The Cult of the Centenary', pp. 304–5.

[29] D. Jarrett, *Three Faces of Revolution: Paris, London and New York in 1789*, George Philip, London, 1989, pp. 40–4.

[30] S. Porter, *The Great Fire of London*, Stroud, Sutton, 1996, pp. 132–4; J. E. Moore, 'The Monument, or, Christopher Wren's Roman accent', *Art Bulletin*, vol. 80, 1998, pp. 498–533.

[31] Porter, *The Great Fire of London*, p. 173; Moore, 'The Monument', p. 525. For a time it was a contested site. This diatribe was finally removed in 1831: C. Welch, *History of the Monument*, Corporation of the City of London, 1893, pp. 40–1.

32 Statues of William III were erected at Bristol and Hull in the 1730s: H. Smith, 'The Idea of a Protestant Monarchy in Britain 1714–1760', *Past and Present*, no. 185, 2004, p. 109.

33 There was even a suggestion that the Bill of Rights be inscribed on it in 'Saxon English': Quinault, 'The Cult of the Centenary', p. 305.

34 N. B. Penny, 'The Whig Cult of Fox in Early Nineteenth Century Sculpture', *Past and Present*, no. 70, 1976, pp. 94–105.

35 Colley, *Britons*, pp. 217–19. The jubilee was hurriedly arranged to mark, not the fiftieth anniversary of George III's accession, but the beginning of the fiftieth year of his reign.

36 A. Atkinson, 'Past and Present', in A. Atkinson and M. Aveling (eds), *Australians 1838*, Fairfax, Syme & Weldon Associates, Sydney, 1987, pp. 8–9.

37 D. Young, 'Early Hobart Regattas', *Tasmanian Historical Research Association: Papers and Proceedings*, vol. 52, 2005, p. 71. Young does not posit a connection with the jubilee of British settlement.

38 Davison, *The Use and Abuse of Australian History*, p. 38.

39 M. S. Rivière, 'In Honour of a Fellow-explorer: Flinders' and Bougainville's Monuments to Lapérouse in Mauritius and at Botany Bay', *Humanities Research*, vol. 10, no. 2, 2003, pp. 9–20.

40 Davison, *The Use and Abuse of Australian History*, p. 38.

41 For the commemoration of more radical heroes in mid-Victorian Britain, see A. Pickering and A. Tyrell (eds), *Contested Sites: Commemoration, Memorial and Popular Politics in Nineteenth-century Britain*, Ashgate, Aldershot, 2004, esp. chs 2 and 5.

42 P. Mandler, *The Fall and Rise of the Stately Home*, Yale University Press, New Haven, 1997, pp. 22–5.

43 Mandler, *History and National Life*, p. 25.

44 Mandler, *The Fall and Rise of the Stately Home*, p. 25. Especially important in the Australian context was Murray's *Home and Colonial Library*, the earliest purchase of the subscription library founded in Evandale, Tasmania, in 1847: K. Adkins, 'Orger and Meryon: Booksellers to the Colony', in P. Eggert and E. Webby (eds), *Books and Empire: Textual Production, Distribution and Consumption in Colonial and Postcolonial Cultures*, special issue of *Bulletin of the Bibliographical Society of Australia and New Zealand*, vol. 28, nos. 1 & 2, 2004, p. 11.

45 Adkins, 'Orger and Meryon', p. 12.

46 For example, *The History of the Norman Conquest of England: Its Causes and Its Results*, 6 vols, Clarendon, Oxford, 1867–79, and *The Growth*

of the English Constitution from the Earliest Times, Macmillan, London, 1872.

[47] Mandler, *History and National Life*, pp. 34–40.

[48] M. J. Bennett, 'Clark's "Commonwealth versus Cromwell"': Clark, Cromwell and the English Republic', in R. G. Ely (ed.), *A Living Force: Andrew Inglis Clark and the Ideal of the Commonwealth*, Centre for Tasmanian Historical Studies, Hobart, 2001, pp. 211–14.

[49] P. Nora, 'General Introduction; Between Memory and History', in P. Nora (ed.), *Realms of Memory: The Construction of the French Past. Vol. 1. Conflicts and Divisions*, Columbia University Press, New York, 1997.

[50] D. M. Wilson, *The British Museum: A History*, British Museum Press, London, 2000.

[51] It was garrisoned during the Gordon riots in 1780: Wilson, *The British Museum*, pp. 49–50. It provided a haven during the riots over the corn laws in 1814: A. L. J. Lincoln and R. L. McEwen (eds), *Lord Eldon's Anecdote Book*, Stevens & Sons, London, 1960, pp. 124–6.

[52] Wilson, *The British Museum*, pp. 67–8, 74.

[53] Wilson, *The British Museum*, p. 100.

[54] T. Bennett, *The Birth of the Museum: History, Theory, Politics*, Routledge, London, 1995, p. 28.

[55] C. M. H. Clark, *A History of Australia: Vol. II. New South Wales and Van Diemen's Land 1822–1838*, Melbourne University Press, Carlton, 1968, p. 148.

[56] Lowenthal, *The Past is a Foreign Country*, p. 102.

[57] See E. Hobsbawm and T. Ranger (eds), *The Invention of Tradition*, Cambridge University Press, Cambridge, 1983, and many other studies in a similar vein.

6 WHAT SHOULD A NATIONAL MUSEUM DO?

[1] I have reviewed some of these developments in 'Museums and the Burden of National Identity', *Public History Review*, no. 10, 2003, pp. 8–20; for other recent discussions, see Timothy W. Luke, *Museum Politics: Power Plays at the Exhibition*, University of Minnesota Press, Minneapolis, 2002; S. A. Crane, 'Memory, Distortion and History in the Museum', *History and Theory*, vol. 36, no. 4, December 1997, pp. 44–63; Sharon Macdonald, 'Museums, National, Postnational and Transcultural Identities', *Museum & Society*, vol. 1, no. 1. March 2003,

pp. 1–16; David Boswell and Jessica Evans (eds), *Representing the Nation: Histories, Heritage and Museums*, Routledge, London 1999.

2 Roy Rosenzweig and David Thelen, *The Presence of the Past: Popular Uses of History in American Life*, Columbia University Press, New York, 1998, p. 91; Paula Hamilton and Paul Ashton, 'At Home with the Past: Background and Initial Findings from the National Survey', *Australian Cultural History*, no. 22, 2003, p. 16.

3 *Review of the National Museum of Australia, Its Exhibitions and Public Programs: A Report to the Council of the National Museum of Australia*, Department of Communications, Information, Technology and the Arts, Canberra, July 2003.

4 National Museum of Australia, accessed 18 December 2004, www.nma.gov.au/about_us

5 I reflect on this episode in 'A Historian in the Museum: The Ethics of Public History', in Stuart Macintyre (ed.), *The Historian's Conscience*, Melbourne University Press, Carlton, 2004, pp. 49–63; Stuart Macintyre relates this episode in *The History Wars*, Melbourne University Press, Carlton, 2004, pp. 191–215.

6 Lionel Carmichael and J. C. Long, *James Smithson and the Smithsonian Story*, G. P. Putnam's & Sons, New York, 1965, p. 16; Nina Burleigh, *The Stranger and the Statesman: James Smithson, John Quincy Adams, and the Making of America's Greatest Museum: The Smithsonian*, HarperCollins, New York, 2003, p. 168.

7 Smithsonian Institution, *Annual Report*, 2000, pp. 9–10.

8 Davison, 'Museums and the Burden of National Identity', pp. 15–17.

9 For a useful gateway to national museum websites, see http://www.civnet.org/index.php?page=Museum_Links

10 Smithsonian National Museum of American History, accessed 20 December 2004, http://americanhistory.si.edu/youmus/welcome.htm

11 Canadian Museum of Civilization Corporation, accessed 20 December 2004 (my italics), http://www.civilization.ca/societe/principe.html

12 Deutsches Historisches Museum, accessed 20 December 2004 (my italics), http://www.dhm.de/ENGLISH/dhm_konzeption.html

13 National Museum of Ireland, accessed 20 December 2004 (my italics), http://www.museum.ie/history.asp?site_id=0

14 National Museum of Scotland, accessed 20 December 2004 (my italics), http://www.nms.ac.uk/home/index.asp?m=1&s=2

15 National Museum of Denmark, accessed 20 December 2004 (my italics), http://www2.natmus.dk/sw1413.asp

16 Museum of New Zealand: Te Papa, accessed 20 December 2004
    (my italics), http://www.tepapa.govt.nz/TePapa/English/
    AboutTePapa/
17 Compare Martin Prösler, 'Museums and Globalisation', in Sharon
    Macdonald and Gordon Fyfe (eds), *Theorizing Museums*, Sociological
    Review Monographs, Blackwell, Oxford, 1996, pp. 21–44.
18 Graeme Davison, 'National Identity', in Davison, John Hirst and
    Stuart Macintyre (eds), *The Oxford Companion to Australian History*,
    Oxford University Press, Melbourne, 1998, pp. 453–5.
19 As quoted in Mette Bligaard, 'The Image of Denmark: Museums as
    Sanctuaries of Identity', in J. M. Fladmark (ed.), *Heritage and
    Museums: Shaping National Identity*, Donhead Publishing, Shaftesbury,
    2000, p. 287; also compare Stefan Bohman, 'Nationalism and
    Museology: Reflections on the Swedish Experience', in Fladmark,
    Heritage and Museums, pp. 275–85.
20 Benedict Anderson, *Imagined Communities: Reflections on the Origin and
    Spread of Nationalism*, rev. edn, Verso, London, 1991, p. 178.
21 Charles McKean, 'A House Built for Identity', in Fladmark, *Heritage
    and Museums*, pp. 123–46; Charles McKean, *The Making of the Museum
    of Scotland*, National Museum of Scotland Publishing Ltd, Edinburgh,
    2000, esp. pp. 101–16.
22 National Museum of Scotland, accessed 19 December 2004,
    http://www.nms.ac.uk/scotland/index.asp
23 I draw here on Annie Coombes' illuminating discussion in *History
    after Apartheid: Visual Culture and Public Memory in a Democratic South
    Africa*, Duke University Press, Durham, 2003, pp. 28–67.
24 African National Congress, accessed 20 December 2004,
    http://www.anc.org.za/ancdocs/history/mandela/1996/sp0516a.html
25 'Monument to Afrikaners' triumph forced to change with the times
    in new South Africa', *Associated Press*, 10 May 2003.
26 Robben Island Museum, accessed 19 December 2004,
    http://www.robben-island.org.za/news/view.asp
27 Apartheid Museum, accessed 23 December 2004,
    http://www.apartheidmuseum.org/start.html
28 For background on this exhibition, see Reinhard Rürup (ed.),
    *Topography of Terror: Gestapo, SS and Reichssicherheitshauptamt on the
    'Prinz-Albrecht-Terrain': A Documentation*, Verlag Wilmuth Arenhovel,
    13th edn, 2003 [1989].
29 See reviews of Berlin museums by Bertrand Benoit, *Financial Times*,
    8 December 2004, and Serge Schmemann, *New York Times*,
    10 November 2004.

30 Stephen Weil, 'The Museum and the Public', in his *Making Museums Matter*, Smithsonian Books, Washington, DC, 2002, pp. 195–213.

31 *Discovering the Jewish Museum in Berlin*, Jewish Museum, Berlin, 2001; Libeskind outlines his philosophical approach to the museum in 'Between the Lines', accessed 18 December 2004, at www.jmberlin. de/pdf_en/between_the_lines.pdf; also see James E. Young, 'Daniel Libeskind's Jewish Museum in Berlin: The Uncanny Arts of Memorial Architecture', *Jewish Social Studies*, vol. 6, no. 2, 2000, pp. 1–23.

32 Deutsches Historisches Museum, accessed 18 December 2004, http://www.dhm.de/ENGLISH/zeu_hist.html

33 For a discussion of debates concerning the reopening of the Deutsches Historisches Museum, see S. A. Crane, 'Memory, Distortion and History', pp. 54–56, and a review of the *Myths of the Nations* exhibition, *New York Herald Tribune*, accessed 18 December 2004, http://www.dhm.de/ausstellungen/mythen-der-nationen/eng/ausstellung.htm See also exhibition catalogue *Mythen der Nationen 1945: Arena der Erinnerungen*, Deutsches Historisches Museum, Berlin, 2004, and interpretative essays in Monika Flacke (ed.), *Mythen der Nationen. 1945–Arena der Erinnerungen*, Deutsches Historisches Museum, Berlin, 2004.

7 REFLECTIONS OF A NATIONAL MUSEUM DIRECTOR

1 James Gardner, 'Should the Parts Add Up to a Whole? Planning the Future at the National Museum of American History', speaking notes for presentation to Organisation of American Historians meeting, 2002, p. 4.

2 Dawn Casey, 'The National Museum of the 21st Century: The National Museum of Australia', National Museums: Negotiating Histories conference, Canberra, 1999.

3 *Museums in Australia 1975: Report of the Committee of Inquiry on Museums and National Collections including the Report of the Planning Committee on the Gallery of Aboriginal Australia* [Pigott Report], Australian Government Publishing Service, Canberra, 1975, p. 70.

4 *Museums in Australia 1975*.

5 Roland Arpin, 'Going Boldly into the 21st Century', *Muse*, Spring 1994, http://www.museums.ca/publications/muse/1994/spring94/drache.htm

6   Graeme Davison, 'National Museums in a Global Age: Observations
    Abroad and Reflections at Home', in Darryl McIntyre and Kirsten
    Wehner (eds), *National Museums: Negotiating Histories—Conference
    Proceedings*, National Museum of Australia, Canberra, 2001,
    pp. 18–19.
7   *Report by the Advisory Committee on New Facilities for the National
    Museum of Australia and the Australian Institute of Aboriginal and Torres
    Strait Islander Studies* [Service Report], 1996.
8   *Report by the Advisory Committee*, p. 4.
9   'Transcript of the Prime Minister The Hon John Howard MP
    Address at the Opening of the National Museum of Australia,
    Canberra', 11 March 2001, www.pm.gov.au/news/speeches/2001/
    speech810.htm
10 'Transcript of the Prime Minister The Hon John Howard MP
    Closing Address at the Liberal Party's National Convention in
    Adelaide', 8 June 2003, www.pm.au/news/speeches/2003/
    speech2331.htm
11 Robert Manne, 'Introduction', in Robert Manne (ed.), *Whitewash:
    On Keith Windschuttle's Fabrication of Aboriginal History*, Black Inc.,
    Melbourne, 2003, p. 5.
12 John Mulvaney, 'Aboriginal Heritage', in *Prehistory and Heritage:
    The Writings of John Mulvaney*, Department of Prehistory,
    Research School of Pacific Studies, Australian National University,
    Canberra, 1990, p. 279, quoting William Dampier, *A New Voyage
    around the World*, A Gray (ed.), Argonaut Press, London, 1927 [1697],
    p. 312.
13 Constitution of Australia, Section 116: 'The Commonwealth shall
    not make any law for establishing any religion, or for imposing any
    religious observance, or for prohibiting the free exercise of any
    religion, and no religious test shall be required as a qualification
    for any office or public trust under the Commonwealth'.
14 Dawn Casey, 'Can Our Myths Redeem Us?', after-dinner keynote
    speech, Australian Centre for Christianity and Culture, Canberra,
    6 March 2003.
15 Stuart Macintyre and Anna Clark, *The History Wars*, Melbourne
    University Press, Carlton, 2003, pp. 193–4.
16 Graeme Davison, 'A Historian in the Museum: The Ethics of Public
    History', in Stuart Macintyre (ed.), *The Historian's Conscience:
    Australian Historians on the Ethics of History*, Melbourne University
    Press, Carlton, 2004, p. 54.
17 Davison, 'A Historian in the Museum'.

8 THE ARCHIVE UNDER THREAT

1 Carolyn Steedman, *Dust: The Archive and Cultural History*, Manchester University Press, Manchester, 2001; Nicholas Dirk, *Castes of Mind: Colonialism and the Making of Modern India*, Princeton University Press, Princeton, 2001.

2 Francis X. Blouin, 'History and Memory: The Problem of the Archive', *PMLA*, vol. 119, no. 2, 2004, p. 296.

3 The following paragraphs draw on an argument made in my *Time and Commodity Culture*, Clarendon Press, Oxford, 1997, pp. 188ff.

4 Thomas Jefferson, letter of 13/8/1813 to Isaac McPherson, in *Writings*, The Library of America, New York, 1984, pp. 1291–2.

5 I take the concept of a 'library model' from Gareth Locksley, 'Information Technology and Capitalist Development', *Capital and Class*, vol. 27, Winter 1986, p. 89.

6 Marcel Mauss, *The Gift: Forms and Functions of Exchange in Archaic Societies*, Ian Cunnison (trans.), Norton, New York, 1966, pp. 25–6.

7 Geoff Mulgan, *The 'Public Service Ethos' and Public Libraries*, Comedia Research Working Papers, no. 6, Institute for Cultural Policy Studies, Brisbane, 1993, p. 2.

8 Liz Greenhalgh, *The Place of the Library*, Comedia Research Working Papers, no. 2, Institute for Cultural Policy Studies, Brisbane, 1993, p. 5.

9 *Public Sector/Private Sector Interaction in Providing Information Services*, Government Printing Office, Washington, DC, 1982; discussed in Herbert and Anita Schiller, 'Libraries, Public Access to Information, and Commerce', in V. Mosco and J. Wasko (eds), *The Political Economy of Information*, University of Wisconsin Press, Madison, 1988, pp. 159–60.

10 Schiller and Schiller, 'Libraries', p. 160.

11 This argument is made in the Comedia Research Paper *Borrowed Time: The Future of Public Libraries in the U.K.*, Institute for Cultural Policy Studies, Brisbane, 1993, p. iv.

12 Schiller and Schiller, 'Libraries', p. 160.

13 Carol Henderson, 'Libraries as Creatures of Copyright: Why Librarians Care about Intellectual Property Law and Policy', accessed 29 November 2005, http://www.ala.org/ala/washoff/WOissues/copyrightb/copyrightarticle/librariescreatures.htm

14 Declan Butler, 'The Writing is on the Web for Science Journals in Print', *Nature*, vol. 397, January 1999, p. 195.

15 Butler, 'The Writing is on the Web', p. 197.

[16] Budapest Open Access Initiative, accessed 29 November 2005, http://www.soros.org/openaccess/index.shtml

[17] John Sutherland, 'Who Owns John Sutherland?', *London Review of Books*, vol. 21, no. 1, January 1999, reprinted at http://www.lrb.co.uk/v21/n01/suth01_html

9 THE ART MUSEUM AS MONUMENT

This paper is an outcome of the project 'Realms of the Buddha: Museums, Cultural Diversity and Audience Development', funded by an Australian Research Council SPIRT grant, with Ien Ang and Judith Snodgrass as chief investigators and the Art Gallery of New South Wales and the NSW Migration Heritage Centre as industry partners. Interviews with Art Gallery staff before and after the opening of *Buddha: Radiant Awakening* took place in the context of this project. I wish to thank Edmund Capon, Jackie Menzies, Brian Ladd, Ann MacArthur and Belinda Hanrahan for their kind sharing of their professional views, and Megan Parnell for her dedicated research assistance.

1 Sharon Macdonald and Gordon Fyfe (eds), *Theorizing Museums: Representing Identity and Diversity in a Changing World*, Blackwell, Oxford, 1996.

2 Pierre Bourdieu, *Distinction: A Social Critique of the Judgement of Taste*, Richard Nice (trans.), Routledge, London, 1994.

3 Hilde Hein, *The Museum in Transition*, Smithsonian Books, Washington, DC, 2000, p. 132.

4 *Museums Australia Incorporated Cultural Diversity Policy*, Museums Australia, Canberra, 2000.

5 Ivan Karp and Stephen Lavine (eds), *Exhibiting Cultures: The Poetics and Politics of Museum Display*, Smithsonian Institution Press, Washington, DC, 1991.

6 James Clifford, 'Museums as Contact Zones', in *Routes: Travel and Translation in the Late Twentieth Century*, Harvard University Press, Cambridge MA, 1999.

7 Interview, 9 April 2001.

8 Interview, 12 April 2001.

9 Interview, 15 May 2001.

10 Interview, 9 April 2001.

11 Interview, December 2002.

12 Jackie Menzies, 'Organising Buddha: Some Thoughts on the Exhibition', *TAASA Review* (Journal of the Asian Arts Society of Australia), vol. 11, no. 2, 2002, p. 12.

[13] Interview with Jackie Menzies, December 2001.

[14] Interview, September 2002.

[15] Interview, December 2002.

[16] Interview, 9 April 2001.

[17] Interview, December 2001.

[18] Bruce James, 'Buddha is lost on the way to the gift shop', *Sydney Morning Herald*, 21 November 2001, p. 16.

[19] Venerable Tenzin Lektsog, 'Gaining Wisdom in the Buddha Exhibition', *TAASA Review*, vol. 11, no. 2, 2002, p. 15.

[20] Stephen Weil, *Making Museums Matter*, Smithsonian Books, Washington, DC, 2002, p. 186.

[21] John Frow, *Cultural Studies and Cultural Value*, Clarendon Press, Oxford, 1995.

[22] Nick Prior, *Museums and Modernity: Art Galleries and the Making of Modern Culture*, Berg, Oxford, 2002, p. 213.

10 LANDSCAPES TRANSFORMED

[1] W. D. Jackson, 'Vegetation', in J. L. Davies (ed.), *Atlas of Tasmania*, Lands and Survey Department, Hobart, 1965, pp. 30–5.

[2] W. D. Jackson, 'The Tasmanian Legacy of Man and Fire', *P&P Royal Society of Tasmania*, vol. 133, 1999, pp. 1–14. See also W. D. Jackson, 'Fire, Air, Water and Earth—An Elemental Ecology of Tasmania', *Proceedings of the Ecological Society of Australia*, vol. 3, 1968, pp. 9–16; 'Vegetation of the Central Plateau', in M. R. Banks (ed.), *The Lake Country of Tasmania*, Royal Society of Tasmania, Hobart, 1973, pp. 61–86; 'Vegetation Types', in J. B. Reid et al., *The Vegetation of Tasmania*, Australian Biological Resources Study, Hobart, 1999, pp. 1–10.

[3] R. Jones, 'Fire-stick Farming', *Australian Natural History*, vol. 16, 1969, pp. 224–48.

[4] For example, B. Gammage, 'Australia under Aboriginal Management', 15th Barry Andrews Memorial Lecture (2002), University College, ADFA, Canberra, 2003.

[5] Joseph Lycett, 'Aborigines Using Fire to Hunt Kangaroos' c. 1821, from his *Drawings of the Natives and Scenery of Van Diemens Land*, London 1830, PIC R5689, nla.pic-an2962715-s20, National Library of Australia (NLA). Reproduced with permission. Lycett says this scene is Tasmanian. Tom Gunn points out that the Tasmanians did not use woomeras, shown here. Lycett never visited Tasmania, and most of his scenes are of around Newcastle in New South Wales, but

several of his Tasmanian views, including that from Constitution Hill (see Figure 10.2), are on Macquarie's 1821 route. Perhaps he copied drawings by George Evans or James Taylor, who accompanied Macquarie—after all, he was a forger. See J. Hoorn, 'Joseph Lycett: The Pastoral Landscape in Early Colonial Australia', *Art Bulletin of Victoria*, vol. 26, 1986, pp. 4–14 esp. p. 6; J. Hoorn, *The Lycett Album*, National Library, Canberra, 1990, pp. 1–3, 19.

6   Joseph Lycett, 'View from near the Top of Constitution Hill, Van Diemen's Land', c. 1821, from his *Views of Australia*, London, 1825, PIC U658 NK380/40, nla.pic-an7692946, NLA. Reproduced with permission.

7   Goderich Plain (top right) and Gatcomb Plain (bottom left), north of the Wandle River, 6 km NNE of Fingerport near Guildford, 12 April 1949: Valentines Run 6/22139, courtesy of Bill Tewson, Forestry Tasmania, Hobart. Reproduced with permission. See map 3841 Guildford 1:25 000.

8   Wineglass Bay, looking from north to south, c. 2001, from *A Steve Parish Souvenir of Tasmania*, Brisbane, c. 2001, p. 14. Copyright Steve Parish Publishing Pty Ltd. Reproduced with permission.

9   For example, at Mt Field National Park, opened in 1916 on land reportedly never logged, gullies and lower slopes support swamp gum (*E. regnans*) up to eighty-five metres high, many scarred by fire, and logs up to six metres across. The understorey includes rainforest species such as myrtle, sassafras and tree fern, but no eucalypts. Ridges have a more open understorey with young *regnans*, bracken and rainforest, while wattles edge open ground. All this suggests a *regnans* forest once controlled by fire giving way to rainforest in the gullies, and in time on the higher ground unless a fire comes. Visit to Mt Field, 18 February 2003.

10   For a summary, see P. Kostoglou, 'A Survey of Ultra Tall Eucalypts in Southern Tasmania', Forestry Tasmania report, June 2000, esp. pp. 17–27, 38. Elsewhere eucalypts about 200 years old overtop secondary rainforest.

11   Jackson, 'Vegetation'. See also M. Barker, 'Effects of Fire on the Floristic Composition, Structure and Flammability of Rainforest Vegetation', *Tasforests*, vol. 2, 1990, pp. 117–20.

12   Diary, Cascade Creek, 9 July 1827, in J. Dargavel et al. (ed.), *Australia's Ever-changing Forests V*, Centre for Resource and Environmental Studies, Australian National University, Canberra, 2002, pp. 152–3.

13   Report on land south of Emu Bay, 10 November 1827, in Dargavel et al., *Australia's Ever-changing Forests V*, p. 148.

[14] Talk with Jamie Kirkpatrick, 7 January 2005. Based on the results of extensive and detailed modelling, Jamie's belief is that Aborigines did not significantly affect Tasmania's vegetation distribution.

[15] D. B. Lindenmayer et al., 'Attributes of Logs ...', *Forest Ecology and Management*, vol. 123, 1999, p. 197.

[16] R. C. Ellis, 'The Relationships among Eucalypt Forest, Grassland and Rainforest in a Highland Area in North-eastern Tasmania', *Australian Journal of Ecology*, vol. 10, 1985, pp. 300–1.

[17] I thank Geoff Hope, Jamie Kirkpatrick and Ian Thomas for guidance in searching for pollen analyses, but I could find none specific enough.

[18] 4 July 1831, in N. J. B. Plomley (ed.), *Friendly Mission*, Tasmanian Historical Research Association, Hobart, 1966, p. 371.

[19] 7 July 1831, in Plomley, *Friendly Mission*, p. 372.

[20] M. A. Hunt et al., 'Ecophysiology of the Soft Tree Fern, Dicksonia Antarctica Labill', *Austral Ecology*, vol. 27, 2002, pp. 360–8.

[21] R. C. Ellis and I. Thomas, 'Pre-settlement and Post-settlement Change and Probable Aboriginal Influences in a Highland Forested Area in Tasmania', in K. Frawley and N. Semple (eds), *Australia's Ever Changing Forests*, Centre for Resource and Environmental Studies, Australian National University, Canberra, 1988, p. 211. See also R. C. Ellis, 'Aboriginal Influences on Vegetation in the Northeast Highlands', *Tasmanian Naturalist*, vol. 76, January 1984, pp. 7–8; Ellis, 'The Relationships among Eucalypt Forest', pp. 297–314; I. Thomas, 'The Holocene Archaeology and Palaeoecology of Northeastern Tasmania, Australia', PhD thesis, University of Tasmania, 1991; 'Late Pleistocene Environments and Aboriginal Settlement Patterns in Tasmania', *Australian Archaeology*, vol. 36, 1993, pp. 1–11; 'Ethnohistoric Sources for the Use of Fire by Tasmanian Aborigines', Occasional Paper 2, University of Melbourne, 1994; B. Craven, 'The Subalpine Grasslands of Paradise Plains, Northeast Tasmania', BA Hons thesis, University of Tasmania, 1997.

[22] The sequence at Paradise Plains has been disturbed but not disguised by post-contact fires, notably in 1908. Ellis, 'The Relationships among Eucalypt Forest', p. 305.

[23] Ellis, 'Aboriginal Influences on Vegetation', pp. 7–8.

[24] Ellis, 'The Relationships among Eucalypt Forest', pp. 302–5; Ellis and Thomas, 'Pre-settlement and Post-settlement Change and Probable Aboriginal Influences in a Highland Forested Area in Tasmania', pp. 202–5.

[25] Talk with Bill Mollison, Sister's Creek, 12 February 2002.

[26] Visit to Gatcomb Plain, 14 February 2002.

[27] Ellis, 'Aboriginal Influences on Vegetation', pp. 7–8; Ellis, 'The Relationships among Eucalypt Forest', pp. 305–7. Although most of that 200 years was in European times, the progression began before contact, and self-evidently has been let continue since.

[28] Jackson, 'Vegetation', p. 33.

[29] Jackson, 'The Tasmanian Legacy', p. 12; 'Nutrient Stocks in Tasmanian Vegetation and Approximate Losses due to Fire', *P&P Royal Society of Tasmania*, vol. 134, 2000, p. 1.

[30] Information from a Forestry Tasmania officer, Strahan, 15 February 2002.

[31] See Ellis and Thomas quote in the text (p. 161); Thomas, 'The Holocene Archaeology', p. 295.

[32] Thomas, 'The Holocene Archaeology', p. 257.

[33] 2700 years: M. J. Brown note to D. M. J. S. Bowman, n.d. 5000 years: B. M. Buckley in G. Lehman, 'Turning Back the Clock: Fire, Biodiversity and Indigenous Community Development in Tasmania', manuscript courtesy Greg Lehman, 2000, p. 9.

[34] Talk with Bill Jackson, 8 February 2001.

[35] Talk with Jon Marsden-Smedley, 13 February 2001. For fires, see J. B. Marsden-Smedley, 'Changes in Southwestern Tasmanian Fire Regimes since the Early 1800s', *P&P Royal Society of Tasmania*, vol. 132, 1998, pp. 15–29.

[36] Jackson, 'The Tasmanian Legacy', p. 7. Jackson, 'Fire, Air, Water and Earth', outlines his theory of Ecological Drift to explain Tasmania's disclimax vegetation.

11 'PLANTING HOPES WITH POTATOES'

My special thanks to Rhys Isaac, Susan Martin, Angus McGillivery, and Kylie Mirmohamadi for discussing various aspects of this chapter with me, and alerting me to material I would otherwise have missed.

[1] Louise Brown et al., *A Book of South Australia: Women in the First Hundred Years*, Rigby for the Women's Centenary Council of SA, 1936, p. 119.

[2] Simon Schama, *Landscape and Memory*, Fontana Press, London, 1996, pp. 6–7.

[3] Dicksee's lithograph is copied from the Edward Hopley painting *A Primrose from England* (c. 1855) which was then reproduced as an engraving in a newspaper in about 1858. Hopley's painting is based

on an incident in Melbourne and reported in England, when thousands of people reportedly turned out to see the arrival of the first flowering primrose from England. J. R. Dicksee, 'A Primrose from England', painted by Edward Hopley, lithographed by J. R. Dicksee, Henry Graves & Co., London, 1856, Rex Nan Kivell Collection NK833, National Library of Australia PIC U2579, nla.pic-an5577434. Reproduced with permission.

4 *Illustrated London News*, date unknown, c. 1858.

5 Alton Becker, *Beyond Translation: Essays toward a Modern Philology*, University of Michigan Press, Ann Arbor, 1995, p. 9.

6 Becker, *Beyond Translation*, p. 15.

7 This is a paraphrased version of Becker's thoughts on what he calls 'entelleche'. The paraphrasing is from Rhys Isaac, personal communication.

8 See G. M. to Mangles (August): re. boxes: 'Mrs Loudon's Flower Garden is beauteous and elegant beyond description. I feel highly indebted not only to you but to that superior-gifted Lady for the exertions made to strike off an immediate copy'.: in Alexandra Hasluck, *Georgiana Molloy: Portrait with Background*, Fremantle Arts Centre Press, Fremantle, 2002 [1955], p. 263.

9 This discussion of Anne Drysdale draws on the work of Anne Hoban, 'Anne Drysdale: A Sense of Place', Honours thesis, La Trobe University, 1987, esp. pp. 50–5.

10 Anne Drysdale, Diary, 14 August 1841, Drysdale Family Papers, State Library of Victoria, Manuscripts Collection, MS 9249.

11 Anne Drysdale, December 1841, Drysdale Family Papers.

12 John Cameron, 'Dwelling in Place, Dwelling on Earth', in John Cameron (ed.), *Changing Places: Re-imagining Australia*, Longueville Books, Double Bay, 2003, p. 35.

13 Cameron, 'Introduction', in Cameron, *Changing Places*, p. 3.

14 Linda McDowell, *Gender, Identity and Place: Understanding Feminist Geographies*, Polity Press, Cambridge, 1994, p. 4.

15 Alan Atkinson, *The Europeans in Australia*, vol. 1, Oxford University Press, Melbourne, 1997, p. 197.

16 See Peter Read, *Belonging: Australians, Place and Aboriginal Ownership*, Cambridge University Press, Oakleigh, 2000. In a recent paper, Gretchen Poiner makes a very useful distinction between 'place' and a 'sense of belonging' ('Sentiments of Place', delivered at 'Generations of Feminist Studies Conference', Adelaide, 30 June 2005).

17 Deborah Bird Rose, *Reports from a Wild Country: Ethics for Decolonisation*, University of New South Wales Press, Sydney, 2004, p. 5.

18 Mrs Charles Meredith, *Notes and Sketches of New South Wales during a Residence in that Colony from 1839 to 1844*, Penguin Colonial Facsimiles, Harmondsworth and Ringwood, 1973 [1844], pp. 56–7.

19 Caroline Jordan, 'Progress versus the Picturesque: White Women and the Aesthetics of Environmentalism in Colonial Australia 1820–1860', *Art History*, vol. 6, no. 1, 1983, p. 343.

20 William Kerr, *Kerr's Melbourne Almanac, and Port Phillip Directory for 1841*, Kerr and Holmes, Collins Street, Melbourne, 1841, pp. 135–6, 140.

21 Mary Fullerton, *Bark House Days*, Melbourne University Press, Carlton, 1964 [1921], pp. 6, 65.

22 Nancy Bonnin (ed.), *Katie Hume on the Darling Downs: A Colonial Marriage*, Darling Downs Institute Press, Toowoomba, 1985, pp. 14–15, 19, 34.

23 Rachel Henning to Mr Boyce, 29 March 1855, Elladale Cottage, Appin, in David Adams (ed.), *The Letters of Rachel Henning*, Penguin, Harmondsworth, 1969, p. 26.

24 Rachel to Etta, 20 July 1861, in Adams, *The Letters*, pp. 70–1.

25 Rachel to Etta, 10 September 1861, in Adams, *The Letters*, p. 75.

26 'Fair minute book, June 1881', Gardener's Mutual Improvement Society SA. Clipping from unnamed and undated source, re: Chief Justice's toast at 'The Gardeners Society Annual Dinner'. Held in Mortlock Library of State Library of South Australia.

27 M. A. Oliver to Miss Lewin, 2 October 1871, in Lucy Frost, *No Place for a Nervous Lady*, University of Queensland Press, St Lucia, 1984, p. 158.

28 See Barry Curtis, 'That Place Where: Some Thoughts on Memory and the City', in Iain Borden, Joe Kerr, Jane Rendell, with Alicia Pivaro (eds), *The Unknown City: Contesting Architecture and Social Space*, MIT Press, Cambridge, MA and London, 2002, p. 55.

29 See David Goodman, 'The Politics of Horticulture', *Meanjin*, vol. 47, no. 3, 1988, pp. 403–12.

30 Henry Lawson, 'The Lost Souls' Hotel', in *Children of the Bush*, Methuen, London, 1902, pp. 110–11.

31 David Day, *Conquest: A New History of the Modern World*, HarperCollins, Sydney, 2005, esp. ch. 7.

32 In Brown et al., *A Book of South Australia*, p. 122.

12 REMEMBERING THE SELF IN THE COLONIAL GARDEN

1 I use the term 'British' here to refer to an imagined nationality invested in the United Kingdom. I take Englishness to be fairly unproblematically a part of this—certainly figures mentioned, such as Mary Morton Allport, identified as both English and British. However, I have used the term 'English garden' because it was a circulating term that carried meanings not quite covered by 'British garden', and occasionally I have used 'English' where Englishness is clearly being invoked in the texts discussed. The Currie family quite clearly identified with their Scottish heritage. However, their patterns of settlement, the forms of their garden are consistent with the colonial practices of the British Empire.

2 Allaine Cerwonka, *Native to the Nation: Disciplining Landscapes and Bodies in Australia*, University of Minnesota Press, Minneapolis, 2004, p. 1. Cerwonka goes on to say, 'Mundane activities such as weeding and planting, represent one way in which nations are legitimated and people "root" themselves in the face of increased deterritorialisation' (p. 2), but it appears that this is only legitimate national activity when it is weeding out the introduced and planting the native.

3 Cerwonka, *Native to the Nation*, p. 11; S. E. K. Hulme, 'Chapter Six: The High Court in Mabo', in *Upholding the Australian Constitution*, Volume 2 Proceedings of the Second Conference of the Samuel Griffith Society, Windsor Hotel, Melbourne, 30 July–1 August 1993. The Samuel Griffith Society, http://www.samuelgriffith.org.au/papers/html/volume2/v2chap6.htm consulted 13 November 2004. It should be noted that this article confirms the importance of gardening in *Mabo* only as part of an argument that the decision is irrelevant to mainland Aboriginal peoples who, Hulme dubiously claims, did not garden or 'cultivate the land'.

4 See Judith Butler, *The Psychic Life of Power: Theories of Subjection*, Stanford University Press, Stanford, 1997, pp. 1–30.

5 Simon Ryan, *The Cartographic Eye: How Explorers Saw Australia*, Cambridge University Press, Melbourne, 1996; Susan K. Martin, 'Ladies and Grocers' Wives: The Crisis of Middle-class Female Subjectivity in 1890s Australian Women's Fictions', *Westerly*, Spring 1999, pp. 1–13.

6 Tanya Dalziell, *Settler Romances and the Australian Girl*, University of Western Australia Press, Perth, 2004, p. 6.

[7] Identity 'may be less a function of knowledge than performance, or … less a matter of final discovery than perpetual reinvention': Diana Fuss, commenting on sexual identity, in 'Introduction', *Inside/Out: Lesbian Theories, Gay Theories*, Routledge, New York, 1991, pp. 6–7.

[8] See, for instance, Katie Holmes, '"I Have Built Up a Little Garden": The Vernacular Garden, National Identity and a Sense of Place', *Studies in the History of Gardens and Designed Landscapes*, vol. 21, no. 2, April–June 2001, pp. 115–21.

[9] Catherine Currie, Diary, State Library of Victoria, SLV MS 10886. The diary is handwritten and idiosyncratic in spelling and punctuation. I have attempted a literal transcription here.

[10] Actually what Catherine or Kate describes is 'John fencing at the garden' (Currie, 1 Dec 1875).

[11] Susan K. Martin, 'The Gender of Gardens: The Space of the Garden in Nineteenth-century Australia', in Ruth Barcan and Ian Buchanan (eds), *Imagining Australian Space: Cultural Studies and Spatial Inquiry*, Centre for the Study of Australian Literature, University of Western Australia Press, Perth, 1999, pp. 115–25.

[12] The reiteration of national types in the realist fiction of the *Bulletin* school has been claimed as the source and/or proof of an influential bush myth by literary critics from the early twentieth century through to Russel Ward in 1958, and widely disputed ever since. Richard Nile, 'Tell Them that Henry Lawson is Dead', in Nile (ed.), *The Australian Legend and Its Discontents: Australian Studies Reader*, University of Queensland Press, St Lucia, 2000, pp. 95–103; Russel Ward, *The Australian Legend*, Oxford University Press, Melbourne, 1958; Vance Palmer, *The Legend of the Nineties*, Melbourne University Press, [1954].

[13] A less used intervention, but see Susan Sheridan, *Along the Faultlines: Sex, Race and Nation in Australian Women's Writing 1880s–1930s*, Allen & Unwin, Sydney, 1995; Susan K. Martin, 'National Dress or National Trousers', in *The Oxford Literary History of Australia*, Bruce Bennett and Jennifer Strauss (eds), Chris Wallace-Crabbe (associate ed.), Oxford University Press, Melbourne, 1998; David Carter, 'Critics, Writers, Intellectuals: Australian Literature and Its Criticism', in *The Cambridge Companion to Australian Literature*, Elizabeth Webby (ed.), Cambridge University Press, Melbourne, 2000.

[14] Charles Rowcroft, *The Australian Crusoes, or the Adventures of an English Settler and his Family in the Wilds of Australia*, 6th London edn, Willis

P. Hazard, Philadelphia, 1856, pp. 497–8 (first published in London as *Tales of the Colonies; or, the Adventures of an Emigrant*, 1843).

15 Henry Kingsley, *The Recollections of Geoffry Hamlyn*, Imprint Classics, Angus & Robertson (HarperCollins), Sydney, 1993 [1859], p. 244.

16 Barbara Wall, *Our Own Matilda: Matilda Jane Evans 1827–1886 Pioneer Woman and Novelist*, Wakefield Press, Adelaide, 1994, pp. 34–7.

17 Maud Jeanne Franc, *Marian; or, the Light of Someone's Home*, Sampson Low, London, 1861, pp. 136–7 (serialised in Mt Barker, South Australia, 1859).

18 The immigrant orphaned family of *Golden Gifts* mix the produce from their market garden venture: 'rows of raspberry cuttings, healthy young strawberry plants', with '[t]iny dwarf rose-bushes, two or three inches high, [bearing] buds and blossom of surpassing loveliness': Maud Jeanne Franc, *Golden Gifts: An Australian Tale*, Sampson Low, Marston, Searle and Rivington, London, 1888, p. 17.

19 Maud Jeanne Franc, *Beatrice Melton's Discipline*, Sampson Low, London, 1880, p. 11.

20 Ian Henderson, 'Eyeing the Lady's Hand: The Concealed Politics of Mary Morton Allport's Colonial Vision', *Journal of Australian Studies*, vol. 66, 2000, pp. 104–115.

21 Journal of Mary Morton Allport for her Son Morton, Allport Library and Museum of Fine Art, State Library of Tasmania [not catalogued]. Transcription by Ian Henderson. Transcription used by kind permission of Ian Henderson.

22 Captain Maclean had earlier given her some flower seeds (4 March 1853), presumably from Britain, but generally she was the giver.

23 Whereas Henderson suggests that the production of herself as ideal middle-class domestic woman 'affirmed her own confinement to a genteel, domestic "feminine" activity' (p. 114).

13 TASMANIAN LANDSCAPES IN PAINTING, POETRY AND PRINT

An earlier version of this paper was presented to the Imaging Nature: Environment, Media and Tourism conference, hosted by the Faculty of Arts, University of Tasmania, June 2004.

1 James Calder, 'Topographical Sketches of Tasmania, No. 1', *Mercury*, 21 January 1860, p. 6.

2 David Burn, *Narrative of the Overland Journey of Sir John and Lady Franklin and Party from Hobart Town to Macquarie Harbour, 1842*, George Mackaness (ed.), Historical Monographs, Sydney, 1955 [1843], p. 38.

3 John Dunmore Lang, 'D'Entrecasteaux Channel, Van Diemen's Land' [1835], in Brian Elliott and Adrian Mitchell (eds), *Bards in the Wilderness*, Thomas Nelson, Melbourne, 1970, pp. 31–2.

4 Ussher's chronological summary of the history of the world from the Creation to the dispersion of the Jews under Vespasian was published as *Annales Veteris et Novi Testamenti*. This work furnished the material for the dates that were later inserted in the margins of the Authorised Version of the Bible. Among these was the date of Creation, set at 23 October 4004 BC.

5 Baron Charles von Hügel, *New Holland Journal, November 1833–October 1834*, Dymphna Clark (trans. and ed.), Melbourne University Press, Carlton, in association with State Library of New South Wales, 1994, pp. 109–10.

6 Anthony Trollope, *Australia and New Zealand*, 2 vols, Chapman & Hall, London, 1873, vol. II, p. 37.

7 Louisa Meredith, *Our Island Home: A Tasmanian Sketchbook*, J. Walch & Sons, Hobart Town, 1879, pp. 22, 39.

8 Meredith, *Our Island Home*, p. 9.

9 John Mitchel, *The Gardens of Hell: John Mitchel in Van Diemen's Land 1850–1853*, Peter O'Shaughnessy (ed.), Kangaroo Press, Sydney, 1988, pp. 71–2.

10 Admiral Bruni d'Entrecasteaux, *Voyage to Australia and the Pacific 1791–1793*, Edward Duyker and Maryse Duyker (trans.), Miegunyah Press, Carlton, 2001, p. 32.

11 von Hügel, *New Holland Journal*, p. 109.

12 John Glover, letter to Sir Thomas Phillipps, 15 January 1830, in Phillipps Papers, quoted in David Hansen, 'The Life and Work of John Glover', in D. Hansen (ed.), *John Glover and the Colonial Picturesque*, Tasmanian Museum and Art Gallery, Hobart, 2003, p. 86.

13 Quoted in David Hansen, 'Catalogue of Paintings and Drawings', in Hansen, *John Glover and the Colonial Picturesque*, p. 218.

14 C. J. Binks, *Explorers of Western Tasmania*, Taswegia, Devonport, 1989, pp. 75–6.

15 Binks, *Explorers of Western Tasmania*, p. 68.

16 J. E. Calder, 'Some Account of the Country Lying between Lake St Clair and Macquarie Harbour', *Tasmanian Journal of Natural Science*, vol. 3, no. 6, 1849, p. 424.

17 Marie Bjelke-Petersen, *Dusk*, Hutchinson & Co., London, 1921, pp. 12–13.

18 Bjelke-Petersen, *Dusk*, p. 182.

19 Marie Bjelke-Petersen, *Jewelled Nights*, Hutchinson & Co., London, n.d. [1923].
20 Richard Flanagan, *A Terrible Beauty: History of the Gordon River Country*, Greenhouse, Melbourne, 1985; Simon Cubit, 'Squatters and Opportunists: Occupation of Lands to the Westward to 1830', *Tasmanian Historical Research Association, Papers and Proceedings*, vol. 34, no. 1, 1987, pp. 7–13; Nic Haygarth, *Baron Bischoff: Philosopher Smith and the Birth of Tasmanian Mining*, Nic Haygarth, Hobart, 2004.
21 Marie Pitt, *Selected Poems of Marie E. Pitt*, Lothian Publishing Co., Melbourne & Sydney, 1944, pp. 13–15.
22 Pitt, *Selected Poems*, pp. 99–100.
23 Richard Flanagan, *Death of a River Guide*, McPhee Gribble, Ringwood, Vic., 1994.
24 Carmel Bird, *The Bluebird Café*, McPhee Gribble, Ringwood, Vic., 1990.
25 John West, *A History of Tasmania*, 2 vols, Henry Dowling, Launceston, vol. I, 1852, pp. 181–2.
26 James Bonwick, *The Bushrangers, Illustrating the Early Days of Van Diemen's Land* [1856], facsimile edn, Cox Kay, Hobart, 1967; Marcus Clarke, *His Natural Life*, George Robertson, Melbourne, 1874; Richard Butler, *The Men that God Forgot* [1975], Mary Fisher Bookshop, Launceston, 1986, p. 8; Robert Hughes, *The Fatal Shore*, Collins, London, 1987.
27 Clarke, *His Natural Life*, pp. 83–4.
28 Clarke, *His Natural Life*, p. 81.
29 Hal Porter, *The Tilted Cross*, Faber & Faber, London, 1961, pp. 24–5, repeated p. 263.
30 Christopher Koch, *Out of Ireland*, Doubleday, London, 1999, pp. 374–6.
31 George Frankland, 'A Narrative of an Expedition to the Head of the Derwent, and to the Countries bordering the Huon, performed February and March, 1835 by George Frankland', extracted by Miss Cecily Travers, *Tasmanian Education*, vol. 9, no. 4, August 1954, p. 214.
32 Tony Brown, 'John Skinner Prout—a Colonial Artist', in Elwyn Lynn and Laura Murray (eds), *Considering Art in Tasmania*, Fine Arts Press, Sydney, 1985, p. 521.
33 Allesandro Duranti, 'Mediated Encounters with Pacific Cultures', in David Philip Miller and Peter Hanns Reill (eds), *Visions of Empire*, Cambridge University Press, 1996, p. 333.

15 COMMEMORATION

[1] Participants in the Academy symposium had been offered some introduction to this chapter through my essay, 'Our Hobart Site: Memories and Memorials', in *Symposium*, Australian Academy of the Humanities, Canberra, no. 28, October 2004, pp. 3–4. The latter tells a trifle more about the Collins-1804 memorial than does this chapter itself. Pertinent too is that essay's reference to the two conjoint structures in which the Academy symposium proceeded: one (much the smaller) built in 1903, the other of reinforced concrete in 1911. 'Virginia Woolf perhaps was not right in saying that human nature changed in those interim years', went the essay, 'but certainly there was a switch in European consciousness. The contrast between these two buildings makes the point.'

[2] Michael Roe, 'Remembrance of *George The Third*', *Tasmanian Historical Research Association Papers and Proceedings*, vol. 51, December 2004, pp. 177–93, gives appropriate detail for all four episodes of the later 1830s. Readers will find further enlightenment in Kathleen Fitzpatrick's *Sir John Franklin in Tasmania*, Melbourne University Press, Melbourne, 1949, and (for Duterrau's work) S. Scheding, *The National Portrait*, Random House Australia, Sydney, 2002.

[3] A. G. L. Shaw's oeuvre includes *Convicts and the Colonies: A Study of Penal Transportation from Great Britain and Ireland to Australia and Other Parts of the British Empire*, Faber & Faber, London, 1966, and *Sir George Arthur, Bart. 1784–1854*, Melbourne University Press, Carlton, 1980.

[4] Lloyd Robson makes interesting reference to the anti-transportationists' jubilee in his *History of Tasmania … from the Earliest Times to 1855*, Oxford University Press, Melbourne, 1983, ch. 23; however, I relied much on contemporary Hobart newspapers, especially *Colonial Times*, 9, 11, 13 & 16 August 1853, and *Guardian*, 5 October 1853.

[5] For 1903–04 I drew from my *State of Tasmania: Identity at Federation Time*, Tasmanian Historical Research Association, 2001, pp. 237–46; also informative (by no means only for this issue) is David Young, *Making Crime Pay: The Evolution of Convict Tourism in Tasmania*, Tasmanian Historical Research Association, Hobart, 1996, pp. 64–5.

[6] See Note 1.

[7] The pre-history of the sesquicentenary is best documented by the Rait Papers at the Archives Office of Tasmania, NS344/87. (Basil

Rait was 'the protagonist' of my text.) A great mass of official sesquicentenary materials—reports, committee minutes, newspaper clippings, and so forth—is held by the AOT at CB17/1-5; supplementing these, and crucial for communication between Australia and Buckingham Palace, is material held by the National Archives of Australia (Canberra) at A9709:RV/A/4. Since speaking at the symposium I have published 'Sesquicentenary', *Tasmanian Historical Research Association Papers and Proceedings*, vol. 52, June 2005, pp. 107–18.

8 Photo courtesy of the *Mercury*. Reproduced with permission.

9 I received most generous help from the archives office of the Commonwealth Bank, the story of the Hobart building being further documented in a *Mercury* supplement, 25 September 1954.

10 R. A. Watson, *John Bowen and the Founding of Tasmania*, Anglo-Keltic Society, Lindisfarne, 2003; Kaye McPherson (Tereetee Lore), *Risdon Cove: From the Dreamtime and the First Hundred Years*, Manuta Tunapee Pugguluggalia, Lindisfarne, 2001.

11 Both awards were castigated by a leading Aboriginal activist, Michael Mansell, as indicative of racist triumphalism (*Mercury*, 23 November 2004). Conversely, there appeared in Mansell's remarks a touch of vituperation, further modifying the sentiments offered in the final paragraph of my chapter. Adding resonance is the fact that I was a judge of the prize won by Hill, and as an executive member of the Tasmanian Historical Research Association had an interest in the other.

16 TASMANIA'S BICENTENARY CELEBRATIONS

1 Keith Windschuttle, *The Fabrication of Aboriginal History*, Macleay Press, Sydney, 2002.

2 Copy of address in possession of author.

3 See chapters by Michael Roe and Marilyn Lake in this collection; see also Michael Roe, *The State of Tasmania: Identity at Federation Time*, Tasmanian Historical Research Association, Hobart, 2001, and Marilyn Lake, 'Monuments, Museums and Memory', in Alison Alexander (ed.), *The Companion to Tasmanian History*, Centre for Tasmanian Historical Studies, Hobart, 2005.

INDEX

Page numbers in **bold type** refer to illustrations.

Germany: Berlin Wall, 105; 'Museum
Island' (Berlin), 107; national soul-
searching in, 105; and the past,
104–5, 106; reunification of, 99,
107; 'The Topography of Terror'
(Berlin), 105
Gibson, William, 25
Glover, John, 10, 79, 200; and
Aborigines, 200–1; *A Corroboree ...*,
201
Goddard, Jean-Luc, 28
Godkin, E. L., 49
Great Fire of London, 85–6
Green, J. R.: *A Short History of the
English People*, 88
Grey, Lord, 87
Grey, Zane, 63–4
grief, 3
Grimstone, Mary Leman, 231–2
Gruffud, Pyrs, 9
Gunn, Tom, 270n. 5
Gunpowder Plot, 84

Haggard, H. Rider, 64–5, 68; *King
Solomon's Mines*, 65
Hamilton, Paula, 44
Hamlet: authorship of, 40
Harwood, Gwen, 15–16, 31
Havelock, A. E., 236
Hawke, Bob, 222–3
Hawthorne, Nathaniel, 53
Haygarth, Nic: *Baron Bischoff*,
204
Haynes, Roslynn, 10
Hector Peterson Museum, 103
Hein, Hilda: *The Museum in Transition*,
139–40
Hellyer, Henry, 156–7, 159, 163, 201,
202
Hemingway, Ernest, 71
Henderson, Carol, 131
Henderson, Ian, 190, 278n. 23
Henning, Rachel, 177–8
Herbert, Agnes, 67
Herbert, Cecily, 67

heritage: and identity, 9; and nostalgia,
74
Heroes of Modern Adventure (Bridges
and Tiltman), 70
Heyman, Michael, 95
Higgins, H. B., 44, 50, 54, 55–6
Hill, Barry: *Broken Song*, 242
Hirst, John, 45, 47; *The Sentimental
Nation*, 44, 47
historians: and the past, 30, 39; role of,
4–5, 34, 228, 229
Historian's Conscience, The (Macintyre),
120
historic sites: Gallipoli, 45, 52; Kokoda
Trail, 52; New England (US), 52–4;
Somme, the, 52
history, 102; and anniversaries, 83–7;
and change, 90; denial of, 229; and
education, 83; and forgetting, 29,
40; 'historic memories', 54; and
language, 118; and liberalism, 234;
and mass culture, 87–8; and
memory, 4, 6, 10, 29, 30, 43, 56–7,
89, 107–8; militarisation of, 5, 56;
and narrative closure, 4; and
nostalgia, 74, 75; as progress, 83,
122; and religion, 84; and truth,
36–7, 121–2; *see also* past, the
Hofer, Johannes, 72
Holmes, Katie, 9
Holmes, Oliver Wendell, 48
Holmes, Oliver Wendell snr, 50
Holocaust, the, 106, 107–8
Holocaust Museum (Jerusalem), 113
Home and Colonial Library (Murray),
262n. 44
homes, colonial, 166–7, 173, 176;
creation of, 179
Hood, Thomas, 32
Hopley, Edward: *A Primrose from
England*, **168**, 273n. 3
Horacek, Judy, 123
Howard, John, 73, 228; and the
National Museum of Australia,
93–4, 116

gardening, gardens; land
management practices ...
Lang, John Dunmore, 195–6
'languaging', 169–70
Lawson, Henry, 179–80
Lektsog, Venerable Tenzin, 149
Libeskind, Daniel, 6, 105, 106, 107,
266n. 31
libraries (public), 2, 5, 128–9; as
archives, 132; and copyright, 125–6,
130–1; and information technology,
8, 129, 131, 133; and knowledge
management, 128; and lending
rights, 130–1, 132–3; role of, 8, 128,
129, 132; and scientific journals,
135; see also information
literature: and colonial settlers, 184,
186–7; and commemoration, 231;
and empathy, 34; and gardening,
186–9; and horror, 209; and
landscape, 10, 203, 204–8; and
memory, 4, 15–17, 23–6, 29–30, 31,
33–4; and national identity, 186,
187, 277n. 12; and the past, 30, 34,
37–8, 39, 199, 206–9; and truth, 35
Locke, John: *Essay Concerning Human
Understanding*, 22–3, 24
Lone Hand (journal), 56
Longfellow, Henry Wadsworth, 50
Lopez, Barry, 34
loss, 3; of culture, 11; and memory, 28
Loudon, Mrs: *Flower Garden*, 170
Lovell, Samuel, 234, 235
Lovely, Louise, 204
Lowell, James Russell, 50
Lowenthal, David, 90
Lucas, Charles, 49
Lunan, David, 71
Luther, Martin, 84
Lycett, Joseph, 270n. 5; *Aborigines using
fire to hunt kangaroos*, **155**; *View from
near the top of Constitution Hill*, **156**

Mabo decision, 183, 276n. 3
MacArthur, Ann, 143

Macaulay, T. B: *History of England*, 88
Macmillan, W. N., 63
Malouf, David, 30
Malraux, André, 28
Manarlagenna, 216, 225
Mandela, Nelson, 101–2, 104
Mandler, Peter, 87, 88
manhood, 5; and national character,
47, 50, 51, 55, 56, 64; and railroad
workers, 50–1
Mann, Thomas, 31
Manne, Robert: *Whitewash*, 118
Mansell, Michael, 220–1, 282n. 11
Márquez, Gabriel García: *Living to Tell
the Tale*, 35–6
Marsden, Elizabeth, 79
Marti, José, 45
Martin, Susan, 9, 167, 181
Martineau, James, 234
Mauss, Marcel, 128
Maynard, Edgar Leopold, 216, 217,
225
Maynard, Maria, 216
McCalman, Alex, 69
McCalman, David, 69, 71–2, 74; and
game photography, **70**
McCalman, Iain, 3, 4, 5, 31, 49
McComas, J. F., 236
McKinley, William, 48
McPherson, Kaye, 248
Melbourne Museum, 114, 116
memorials, 44, 53–4; and Federation,
44, 45–6; see also monuments;
Tasmanian monuments and
memorials
memory, 19–25; classical
understandings of, 3, 15, 17–18, 22,
23, 26, 31; collective, 1, 2, 3, 5, 7, 8,
89, 109, 260n. 6; and creativity,
19–21; and empire, 59; and
forgetting, 33, 37; involuntary, 26,
29; national memory, 83–5; and
photography, 23, 25, 27; and pre-
existence, 27; and the Renaissance,
25; romantic, 3, 18, 31; and story, 29;

and truth, 24; *see also* archives; colonists; gardening, gardens; history; identity; literature

Menzies, Jackie, 143–5, 146, 147, 148

Mercer, J. E., 235

Mercury (Hobart), 233–4, 235, 238, 240, 241

Meredith, Louisa, 173–4

Meredith, Louisa Anne: *Our Island Home*, 197–8

metempsychosis, 20

Metropolitan Museum of Art (New York), 112

Mirror of Literature, Amusement and Instruction, The (journal), 88

Mitchel, John, 198

Miti (Maori man), 216

Mnemosyne, 3, 15–17, 23, 28, 31

Mogambo (Ford), 71

Mollison, Bill, 161–2

Molloy, Georgiana, 170

monuments, 5, 86, 89, 102, 262n. 32; and apartheid, 101; British Settler Monument (Grahamstown), 101, 102; and collective memory, 1–2, 25, 101–2; and colonial Australia, 87; and death, 16–17; London Monument, 89; and manhood, 45; and nation-building, 90; and political achievement, 44, 53–4, 101; and religion, 85–6; Voortrekker Monument (Pretoria), 101, 102, 104; *see also* Tasmanian monuments and memorials; war memorials

Morgan, Sally: *My Place*, 194

Morrison brothers, 204

Mulford, Clarence E., 69

multiculturalism, 97, 114, 139

Murdoch, Iris, 30

Murphy, John, 44

Museum Afrika (Johannesburg), 6, 102–3

Museum of Marxist-Leninism, 107

Museum of New Zealand: Te Papa, 97, 113, 114, 116

Museum of Scotland, 99, 100

museums (art): and aesthetic theory, 139, 150; architecture of, 139, 141; and Asia, 141; and community participation, 7–8, 140, 145, 150; and cultural diversity, 139, 140, 150; and elitism, 139, 140; as forums, 140; as monuments, 139, 150; *see also* Art Gallery of New South Wales

Museums Australia, 140

museums (history), 103; and nation-building, 98

museums (national), 2, 5, 113; and architecture, 106–7, 113; challenges, 112; and change, 113, 114–16, 117; and cultural values, 138; and diversity, 7, 117, 122; and funding, 112; and Indigenous peoples, 114; and knowledge, 94, 106; and national culture, 96, 98, 99; and national identity, 92–5, 97, 99, 108, 117; and national memory, 6, 90; and the past, 91, 104, 106–7, 117, 121–2; and public trust, 6, 91; role of, 6, 7–8, 89–90, 92, 94–7, 105–6, 108–9, 110–11, 114–16, 121; and tourism, 91, 113; and tradition and privilege, 138; *see also under individual museums*

myth, 15–17, 28; national myths, 83, 100, 101, 119–20, 277n. 12

Nabokov, Vladimir: *Speak, Memory*, 16, 29, 30–1

nationalism: and museums, 98; republican, 5; Scottish, 99

National Museum of American History, 95, 110

National Museum of Antiquities of Scotland, 99

National Museum of Australia, 5, 7, 114; and Aborigines, 107; and debate, 93, 108, 114, 116; funding, 122–3; and ideology, 116, 121;

mission, 111; and national identity, 93–4, 119; review of (2003), 92, 108, 116, 121; *see also* museums (national)
National Museum of Ireland, 96
National Museum of Scotland, 96, 99–101, 106
national selfhood, 104, 107; and national identity, 97
nationhood, 90; and collective memory, 89, 107
Natural History Museum (New York), 112
necromancer, the, 25
Newland, Victor, 60, 68
Newland and Tarlton ('N and T'), 60, 63, 68
Nora, Pierre, 2, 89
Norton, Charles Eliot, 51
nostalgia, 3, 4, 5, 9, 31, 59, 62, 73–5; and creativity, 74; and displacement, 72, 79, 90; and game hunting, 61, 66, 69; and gardening, 179–80, 182, 183; and photography, 69, **70**; and time, 73

Oliver, Miss, 179
Orwell, George, 69
Outram, George, 63

Painter, Kenyon, 63
Palawa, *see* Aborigines, Tasmanian
Parker, Florence, 235–6
past, the: acknowledgement of, 11; and archives, 125; commemoration of, 11, 86–7; and migration, 9; and politics, 108, 121; and present, 2, 74; reconstruction of, 40; reflecting on, 105; representations of, 1; and shame, 10, 118, 206; *see also* history
Paz, Octavio, 30
Pearce, Alexander, 208
Pearson, Charles Henry, 46–7, 49–51; *National Life and Character*, 50
Pearson, Christopher, 116

Peel, Sir Robert, 87
Pei, I. M., 107
Pelling, Freddie, 70
Penny Magazine (journal), 88
Peterson, Hector, 103
Petrarch, 20
Phillip, Arthur, 245
photography, **70**, 71, 206, 210
Pigott Report, 111–12
Piguenit, William Charles, 200, 210–11
Pitt, Marie, 204–5
place, place making, 172–3, 181, 194, 212, 274n. 16; *see also* gardening, gardens
Plangerperener, 215
Plato: and memory, 17, 22; *Theaetetus*, 17
pleasure: and memory, 27
Ploorernelle, 215
Plutarch: *Rerum memorandum libri*, 19
poetry, *see* literature
Poiner, Gretchen, 274n. 16
Pope, Sexton, 63
Porter, Hal, 10, 208
Prior, Nick, 150
Propsting, W. B., 233, 236
Proust, Marcel: and memory, 26–8, 29; *Remembrance of Things Past*, 26, 27–28
Prout, John Skinner, 200, 210
Public Library of Science, 135
publishing, 136; scholarly, 135; scientific, 134, 137

race, racism, 97, 217, 218, 219, 221
Rainey, Paul J., 68
Rainsford, W. S: *The Land of the Lion*, 63
Rait, Basil, 281–2n. 7
religion, 84, 85–6, 196; and colonisation, 188; and national identity, 101, 119–20
Revere, Paul, 54
Reynolds, Henry, 3, 11, 38, 241, 244, 249–50